Vegetarian Fast & Fancy

Renny Darling's

Vegetarian

Fast

and

Fancy

The New Garden of Eating

Leaner, Lighter & More Luscious

Simply Delicious Cookbooks
by Renny Darling

The Joy of Eating
The Love of Eating
The Joy of Entertaining
The Joy of Eating French Food
Great Beginnings & Happy Endings
With Love from Darling's Kitchen
Easiest & Best Coffee Cakes & Quick Breads
Entertaining! Fast & Fancy
The Moderation Diet
Cooking Great! Looking Great! Feeling Great!
The New Joy of Eating
Happy Holidays & Great Celebrations
Vegetarian Fast & Fancy

Cover art and borders by the distinguished artist
Christina Ladas

First Edition

Copyright © 1996 by Renny Darling

Published by Royal House Publishing Co., Inc.
433 No. Camden Drive, Suite 400
P.O. Box 5027 - Beverly Hills, CA 90210

Printed in the United States of America
Library of Congress Catalog Card Number: 94-66320
ISBN: 0-930440-35-8

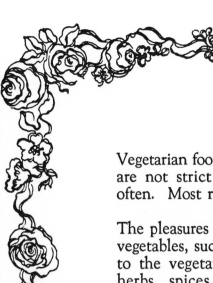

The Introduction

Vegetarian food is more popular today than it has ever been. Even those who are not strict vegetarians are enjoying vegetarian meals more and more often. Most restaurants feature vegetarian lunches and dinners.

The pleasures of the garden are a celebration of life. The richness of fresh vegetables, succulent fruits and aromatic herbs brings an exciting dimension to the vegetarian kitchen. Fine quality, fresh ingredients sparkled with herbs, spices, mustards, lemon, vinaigrettes add infinite variety and abundant diversity to the vegetarian palette and can produce a vegetarian feast at any time. Good food is one of life's great pleasures.

Americans are becoming more and more aware of the role of nutrition and exercise in good health. And while in the past, the siren call was just to be thin (and at any expense to our health), the emphasis now is a call to be healthy and fit. Slimness is achieved as a benefit and result of the healthier lifestyle. Americans are eating lighter and healthier foods, exercising regularly and enjoying the benefits of increased energy and vitality.

To attain nutritional balance, keep in mind that oils, sugar and salt should be limited, but not eliminated. Most foods can be enjoyed occasionally and in moderation, and that includes desserts.

Although much has yet to be scientifically proven about nutrition, the evidence today impels us to improve our eating habits, if, indeed, we want to be healthy and live longer. The relationship of diet and nutrition to good health is the subject of increasing interest and research. Americans are reminded constantly of how food relates to their good health and well-being.

In addition, there is a marked change in our life-style today. The pace is fast, the tension is high and commitments are more demanding of time and energy than it has been in the past. The need for quick and easy cooking reflects this change of life style.

I foresaw this as far back as 1968, when I first started to write food articles and it has been my underlying philosophy ever since. The basic premise of all my cookbooks has been to produce the most delicious dishes, with the minimum effort, and in the least amount of time. And I have never wavered from this dedication.

And that is at the heart of "Vegetarian Fast & Fancy." It addresses the vast numbers of those who follow moderate vegetarian principles with recipes that are quick, easy and marvelously delicious. My emphasis has always been "taste"...great tasting dishes that can be prepared in the minimum amount of time. The recipes reflect this basic philosophy. They are quick and easy to prepare and remarkably delicious.

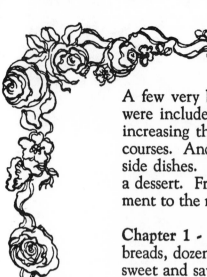

The Introduction, (Cont.)

A few very brief words about the arrangement of the recipes. The recipes were included in the chapter that was closest to their use. As a result, by increasing the portions, many vegetable side dishes can be considered main courses. And by decreasing the portions, many main courses can be served as side dishes. Many breakfast breads and pastries can certainly be included as a dessert. Fruits in the dessert section can easily be served as an accompaniment to the meal. So, keep in mind, that there is an overlap of categories.

Chapter 1 - Breads & Breakfast, is brimming with tender muffins and quick breads, dozens of dinner breads, popovers, biscuits and scones with a host of sweet and savory spreads. The blintzes, French toast, pancakes and breakfast pastries will enhance a breakfast or brunch buffet.

Chapter 2 - Hors d'Oeuvres & Small Entrees, includes dips and spreads with a lovely array of chips, breads and casings. Dozens of the small entrees, great for lunch or dinner. Torta de Polenta, Petite Soufflés, Quiches, Pies, Piroshkis, and the Royal Coulibiac are inventive and creative.

Chapter 3 - Salads & Dressings, features an exciting range of vegetable salads including artichokes, asparagus, carrots, eggplant, cabbage, peppers and more. Also included are the wonderful grain and legume salads, bulgur, cous cous, kasha, rice, taboulah, black and white beans and a whole lot more.

Chapter 4 - includes my beloved Soups & Garnitures. Many are so full of goodness, they can be considered main courses. The soups are varied and also include the gamut of vegetables, rice and grains. The garnitures that accompany the soups will add excitement and interest.

Chapter 5 - Casseroles & Main Courses, will truly amaze you. More than 50 recipes, for a year of Sundays, to please the most jaded palate. Frittatas, sautés, stuffed vegetables, chili, cous cous, gratins, stratas, puddings, to name a few.

Chapter 6 - Pastas & Pizzas, include the great Cannelloni, the Greek Pastitsio, a lesson on Ravioli. Pizzas, calzones, and quick pizzas made with puff pastry or tortilla shells. Fillings range from the basic Margherita to the more complex Eggplant, Mushrooms & Feta Cheese.

Chapter 7 - is a cornucopia of side dishes. Noodles, from the homey Velvet Pudding to the ultimate grand Royal Crown Ring with Apples. Rice...yellow, pink, golden, emerald, a blaze of colors and textures. Risotto, wild rice, brown rice...coupled with peppers, tomatoes, peas or apricots, pecans, raisins or almonds. This chapter is also a feast for the eyes.

Chapter 8 - Desserts...cakes, cookies, pies, ices, bread puddings...a buffet of indulgences rounding out the festive "Vegetarian Fast & Fancy."

As always, enjoy with love.

Renny Darling

The Contents

From my Notebook:

❦ Always READ A RECIPE over very carefully. Then, ASSEMBLE ALL YOUR INGREDIENTS before you start preparation.

❦ Always PREHEAT YOUR OVEN.

❦ COOKING TIMES are always approximate due to slight variations in oven temperatures, the kind of pan you are using, etc. Look for the description in the recipe to guide you, such as..."until a cake tester, inserted in center, comes out clean..." or "until top is lightly browned..."

❦ The number of SERVINGS is also approximate, depending on the number of courses and accompaniments.

❦ TO AVOID BREAKAGE, small delicate baked goods are much easier to cool on brown paper or parchment paper, rather than on a rack. These papers are inexpensive and can be purchased in rolls.

———

❦ Do not dilute BROTHS even if they are labeled "double strength".

❦ Unless noted otherwise, when BUTTER is called for, it is sweet or unsalted. When a recipe calls for "butter, softened", it is butter that is still slightly chilled but soft and pliable. "Butter, at room temperature" refers to butter that is soft, but not to the point where it is oily.

❦ The flavor of NUTS is greatly enhanced by toasting. Toast nuts in a single layer in a 350° oven for 8 minutes, or until just beginning to take on color. Do not overtoast or nuts will become bitter. Store nuts in the freezer for longer shelf life.

❦ When a recipe calls for **"ORANGE ZEST" OR "LEMON ZEST"** it refers only to the orange or yellow part of the peel. When "grated orange" or "grated lemon" is called for, this refers to grating the whole fruit. Of course, use thin-skinned oranges or lemons. If the skins are very thick, you will have to grate the zest and the fruit separately.

❦ LEMON JUICE is always freshly squeezed.

❦ Good OLIVE OIL, like wine, has a beautiful bouquet. I have tried many olive oils that were "cold pressed" "first pressed" "pure extra virgin", etc. that were less than satisfactory. You are going to have to experiment to find one with a wonderful fragrance and good flavor. Keep olive oil in the refrigerator for longer shelf life. It will firm up a little, but there is always some that remains liquid. In any case, it softens in seconds.

❦ Always sift POWDERED SUGAR to remove unsightly lumps.

❦ RICE is always long-grain, unless otherwise noted.

❦ To SEED TOMATOES, cut tomatoes in half and squeeze out the seeds. Or, use a small spoon and scoop out the seeds.

❦ As a general rule, "fresh" is better than "frozen", and "frozen" is better than "canned". Fresh herbs are better, but dried herbs are more readily available. Make certain dried herbs are fresh, as they lose their potency after 6 months.

Breads
&
Breakfast

Muffins, Quick Breads, Biscuits, Scones & Spreads

Dinner Breads & Spreads

Crepes & Blintzes

French Toast & Pancakes

Danish Pastries

Buttermilk Apple Muffins with Orange, Pecans & Lemon Orange Glaze

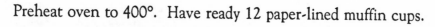

A delicious apple muffin, not too sweet and low in fat. The Lemon Orange Glaze adds the perfect tartness.

1	egg
1	cup buttermilk
1/4	cup vegetable oil
3/4	cup sugar
2	medium apples, peeled, cored and grated
3	tablespoons grated orange
1/2	cup chopped pecans
2 1/4	cups whole wheat flour
1	tablespoon baking powder
1	teaspoon cinnamon

Preheat oven to 400°. Have ready 12 paper-lined muffin cups.

In the large bowl of an electric mixer, beat first 7 ingredients until blended, about 30 seconds. Add the remaining ingredients and beat until dry ingredients are just moistened. (Do not overbeat!)

Divide batter between 12 paper-lined muffin cups and bake in a 400° oven for about 22 to 25 minutes or until muffins are lightly browned and a cake tester, inserted in center, comes out clean. Allow to cool in pan for 10 minutes, and then remove from pan, and continue cooling on a rack. Brush tops with Lemon Orange Glaze (optional). Yields 12 muffins.

Lemon Orange Glaze:
1	tablespoon orange juice
1	tablespoon lemon juice
1/3	cup sifted powdered sugar
2	teaspoons finely grated orange peel

Stir together all the ingredients until blended.

Jam-Filled Breakfast Muffins

This is a delicious little breakfast muffin that takes the place of toast with jam. Use apricot, seedless raspberry or any fruity jam. Top can be sparkled with a faint sprinkle of sifted brown sugar instead of the cinnamon sugar.

1/4	cup vegetable oil
1/2	cup sugar
1	egg, beaten
2/3	cup low-fat buttermilk
1	teaspoon vanilla

1 1/2	cups flour
2 1/2	teaspoons baking powder
1	teaspoon cinnamon

12	teaspoons strawberry jam
1	tablespoon cinnamon sugar

In a bowl, beat together first 5 ingredients until blended. Combine the next 3 ingredients and add, all at once, stirring until mixture is blended. Do not overmix.

Prepare 12 paper-lined muffin cups. Place 1 tablespoon batter into each cup and top with 1 teaspoon of jam. Divide remaining batter over the jam. Sprinkle tops with a little cinnamon sugar. Bake muffins at 400° for 20 minutes. Allow to cool for 10 minutes, and then remove muffins from the pan and continue cooling on a rack. Yields 12 muffins.

Cinnamon Cranberry & Orange Muffins

These muffins are really low in calories and one would never guess it. They are delicious and healthy, too, with whole wheat, bran, fruit and buttermilk.

2	tablespoons oil
3/4	cup buttermilk
1/2	cup sugar
1	egg
2	tablespoons grated orange peel

3/4	cup all-bran cereal
1	cup whole wheat flour
1	teaspoon cinnamon
2	teaspoons baking powder
1	teaspoon baking soda

1	cup fresh or frozen cranberries, sliced in half

More →

(Cinnamon Cranberry Muffins-Cont.)

In the large bowl of an electric mixer, beat together first group of ingredients until mixture is blended. Stir together next 5 ingredients and add, all at once, beating just until blended. Stir in the cranberries. Divide batter between 12 paper-lined muffin cups. Bake at 400-degrees for 20 minutes or until a cake tester, inserted in center, comes out clean. Yields 12 muffins.

To make into Peach or Apricot Muffins:
Substitute 1 cup chopped peaches or apricots for the cranberries.

Buttermilk Oat Bran Muffins with Orange & Bananas

These flavorful muffins are made with oat bran and whole wheat flour, sparkled with orange, banana and cinnamon and textured with raisins. They are really good...and good for you, too.

- 2 cups oat bran
- 1/2 cup water
- 1 cup buttermilk
- 4 tablespoons oil
- 1/4 cup honey
- 2 eggs

- 3 tablespoons grated orange (fruit, juice and peel)
- 1/4 cup yellow raisins

- 1 1/2 cups whole wheat flour
- 1 1/2 teaspoons cinnamon
- 1 teaspoon baking soda
- 1/2 teaspoon baking powder

- 1 medium banana, coarsely mashed

In a large bowl, beat together first 6 ingredients until blended. Stir in orange and raisins. Stir together next 4 ingredients, add to bran mixture and beat just until blended. Do not overmix. Stir in banana. Divide batter between 18 paper-lined muffin cups and bake at 350-degrees for 25 minutes. Yields 18 muffins.

Sour Cream Blueberry Muffins with Lemon & Walnuts

What could be nicer or more attractive to serve with brunch or lunch. The Lemon Glaze adds a little extra lemon flavor.

1	egg
1	cup low-fat sour cream
1/4	cup melted butter
3/4	cup sugar
2	tablespoons grated lemon, (use peel, juice and fruit)

2 1/4	cups flour
1	tablespoon baking powder
1	cup chopped walnuts

1 1/2   cups firm ripe blueberries, fresh or frozen

Preheat oven to 400°. Have ready 12 paper-lined muffin cups.

In the large bowl of an electric mixer, beat first 5 ingredients until blended. Add the flour, baking powder and walnuts and stir until dry ingredients are just moistened. (Do not overbeat!) Stir in the blueberries.

Divide batter between 12 paper-lined muffin cups and bake in a 400° oven for about 22 to 25 minutes or until muffins are lightly browned and a cake tester, inserted in center, comes out clean. Allow to cool in pan for 10 minutes and then remove from pan, and continue cooling on a rack. Brush tops with Lemon Glaze (optional). Yields 12 muffins.

Lemon Glaze:
1	tablespoon lemon juice
1/3	cup sifted powdered sugar
1	teaspoon finely grated lemon peel

Stir together all the ingredients until blended.

Apple & Orange Whole Wheat Muffins

These heavenly muffins are fragrant with cinnamon and orange and richly flavored with apples, currants and walnuts. They freeze beautifully and are nice to have on hand.

1	egg
1	cup buttermilk
1/4	cup honey
1	tablespoon oil
1/2	medium orange, grated
1	small apple, peeled, cored and grated
1/4	cup currants
1/4	cup chopped walnuts
1 1/2	cups whole wheat flour
1/2	cup Miller's bran flakes
2	teaspoons baking powder
1	teaspoon cinnamon
	pinch of ground nutmeg and ground cloves

Beat together first 4 ingredients until blended. Stir in the next 4 ingredients until blended. Stir together remaining ingredients and add, all at once, stirring just until blended. Do not overmix. Divide batter between 12 paper-lined muffin cups and bake at 350-degrees for 25 minutes, or until tops are browned. Yields 12 muffins.

Cajun Honey Corn Muffins with Currants

1	cup yellow cornmeal
1	cup milk
1/4	cup sour cream
1	egg
1/4	cup honey
1/3	cup butter, melted
1/3	cup sugar
1 1/4	cups flour
1	tablespoon baking powder
1	cup dried currants

Beat together first 7 ingredients until blended. Stir together next 3 ingredients and add, all at once, stirring until blended. Do not overmix. Divide batter between 12 paper-lined cups and bake in a 400° oven for 22 minutes, or until a cake tester, inserted in center comes out clean. Allow to cool for 10 minutes, and then remove from pan and continue cooling on a rack. Yields 12 muffins.

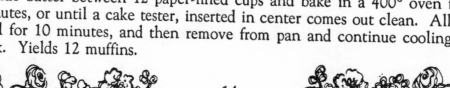
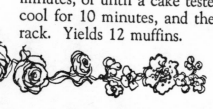

Sour Cream Orange Muffins with Orange Glaze

Tender, gossamer muffins, so full of flavor and goodness, these delicious muffins will be enjoyed by the most jaded appetites. The Orange Glaze is optional, but a lovely addition, for a brunch or luncheon buffet. 1/2 cup finely chopped walnuts is a nice optional.

1	egg
1	small orange, grated (about 6 tablespoons)
1/2	cup milk
1/2	cup sour cream
1/4	cup oil
3/4	cup sugar
2 1/4	cups flour
1	tablespoon baking powder

Preheat oven to 400°. Have ready 12 paper-lined muffin cups.

In the large bowl of an electric mixer, beat together first 6 ingredients until blended. Add the flour and baking powder and beat just until blended. (Do not overbeat.)

Divide batter between 12 paper-lined muffin cups and bake in a 400° oven for about 22 to 25 minutes or until muffins are golden brown and a cake tester, inserted in center, comes out clean. Allow to cool in pan for 10 minutes, and then remove from pan, and continue cooling on a rack. Brush tops with Orange Glaze (optional). Yields 12 muffins.

Orange Glaze:
1 1/2	tablespoons orange juice
1/3	cup sifted powdered sugar
1	tablespoon finely grated orange peel

Stir together all the ingredients until blended.

Moist Apple, Carrot, Cinnamon Bread

This is a delicious bread with deep, satisfying flavor. It is fruity and spicy, and nice around the holidays.

- 1 egg
- 1/2 cup buttermilk
- 1/3 cup oil

- 2 cups flour
- 1 cup brown sugar, sifted
- 1 tablespoon baking powder
- 2 teaspoons cinnamon

- 1 small apple, peeled, cored and grated
- 3/4 cup grated carrots
- 1/3 cup chopped walnuts

Preheat oven to 350°. Lightly grease a 9x5-inch loaf pan. Beat together first 3 ingredients until blended. Beat in next 4 ingredients until blended. Stir in remaining ingredients. Place batter into a greased 9x5-inch loaf pan.

Bake in a 350° oven for about 1 hour or until a cake tester, inserted in center, comes out clean. Allow to cool for 10 minutes and then remove from the pan and continue cooling on a rack. Drizzle top with Buttermilk Glaze when cool. Yields 1 loaf.

Buttermilk Glaze:
- 1 tablespoon buttermilk
- 1/2 teaspoon vanilla
- 1/2 cup sifted powdered sugar

Stir together all the ingredients until blended.

The Best Pumpkin Bread
with Apples, Raisins & Walnuts

1/2   cup melted butter
3/4   cup sugar
1   egg

2   cups flour
1   teaspoon baking powder
1   teaspoon baking soda
1   teaspoon pumpkin pie spice
1/8   teaspoon salt

1   cup canned pumpkin puree
1   apple, peeled and grated
1   cup chopped walnuts
1/2   cup yellow raisins

Preheat oven to 350°. Lightly grease a 9x5-inch loaf pan. In the large bowl of an electric mixer, beat together butter, sugar and egg until blended. Add the next 5 ingredients, all at once, and beat only until dry ingredients are moistened. Do not overbeat.

Place batter into a 9x5-inch greased loaf pan and bake in a 350° oven for 1 hour or until a cake tester, inserted in center, comes out clean. Allow bread to cool in pan for about 10 minutes and then remove from pan and continue cooling on a rack. When bread is cool, drizzle with Vanilla Cream Glaze. Yields 1 loaf.

Vanilla Cream Glaze:
1   tablespoon cream
1/2   teaspoon vanilla
1/2   cup sifted powdered sugar

Stir together all the ingredients until blended.

Apple Walnut Bread Ring
with Brown Sugar Cinnamon Topping

This delicious bread will grace a brunch table with taste and style. It is lovely to look at and delicious, too. It is also a treat at snack time.

1/2	cup butter
1	cup sugar
2	eggs
1	teaspoon vanilla
1 1/2	cups flour
1	teaspoon baking soda
1	teaspoon baking powder
1	teaspoon cinnamon
2	medium apples, peeled, cored and grated
1	cup chopped walnuts
2	tablespoons finely grated orange peel

Beat butter and sugar until light and creamy. Beat in eggs and vanilla until blended. Beat in flour, soda, baking powder and cinnamon until blended. Do not overbeat. Stir in apples, walnuts and orange peel.

Spoon batter into a 10-inch tube pan and sprinkle top with Brown Sugar Cinnamon Topping. Bake in a 350° oven for 55 to 60 minutes, or until a cake tester, inserted in center, comes out clean. Serves 12.

Brown Sugar Cinnamon Topping:

3	tablespoons brown sugar
3	tablespoons melted butter
1/2	teaspoon cinnamon

Combine all the ingredients until blended.

Sour Cream Banana Bread with Chocolate, Walnuts & Sour Cream Glaze

1/4   cup butter, softened
1/2   cup sugar
1   egg
1/2   cup sour cream
1/2   teaspoon vanilla

1   cup flour
1/2   teaspoon baking powder
1/2   teaspoon baking soda

1   banana, coarsely mashed
1/2   cup semi-sweet chocolate chips
1/2   cup chopped walnuts

Preheat oven to 350°. Grease 2 6x3-inch foil loaf pans. In the large bowl of an electric mixer, beat together first 5 ingredients until mixture is blended. Add the next 3 ingredients all at once. and beat until blended. Do not overbeat. Stir in the banana, chocolate and walnuts.

Divide mixture between 2 greased 6x3-inch loaf pans. Place pans on a cookie sheet and bake in a 350° oven for 35 to 40 minutes or until a cake tester, inserted in center, comes out clean. Allow to cool in pans for 10 minutes, and then remove loaves from pans and continue cooling on a rack. Brush tops lightly with Sour Cream Glaze. Yields 2 loaves.

Sour Cream Glaze:
1   tablespoon sour cream
1/4   cup sifted powdered sugar
1/4   teaspoon vanilla
2   teaspoons finely chopped walnuts

Stir together all the ingredients until blended.

Note: -Bread freezes beautifully. Wrap in double thicknesses of plastic wrap and then, foil. Remove wrappers while defrosting.

Farmhouse Buttermilk Date Nut Bread with Creamy Orange Glaze

1/2	cup sugar
1/4	cup butter (1/2 stick), softened
1	egg
1/2	cup buttermilk
1/2	teaspoon vanilla
1	cup flour
1/2	teaspoon baking soda
1/2	teaspoon baking powder
1/2	cup chopped dates
1/2	cup chopped walnuts
1	tablespoon grated orange peel

Preheat oven to 350°. Grease 2 6x3-inch foil loaf pans. Beat together first 5 ingredients until mixture is blended. Add the next 3 ingredients and beat until blended. Do not overbeat. Stir in the dates, walnuts and orange peel.

Divide batter between 2 greased 6x3-inch loaf pans. Place pans on a cookie sheet and bake in a 350° oven for 35 to 40 minutes or until a cake tester, inserted in center, comes out clean. Allow to cool in pans for 10 minutes, and then remove loaves from pans and continue cooling on a rack. Brush tops lightly with Creamy Orange Glaze. Yields 2 loaves.

Creamy Orange Glaze:
1	tablespoon cream
1/4	cup sifted powdered sugar
2	teaspoons grated orange peel
2	tablespoons finely chopped walnuts

Stir together all the ingredients until blended.

Note: -*Bread freezes beautifully. Wrap in double thicknesses of plastic wrap and then, foil. Remove wrappers while defrosting.*

Holiday Spiced Pumpkin Bread Ring
with Orange & Walnuts

2 cups sugar
2 eggs
2/3 cup oil
1/2 orange, grated (use fruit, juice and peel)
1 teaspoon vanilla
2 cups flour
1 teaspoon baking powder
1/2 teaspoon baking soda
3 teaspoons pumpkin pie spice
1 cup canned pumpkin
1 cup chopped walnuts
1/2 cup yellow raisins

Preheat oven to 350°. Grease and lightly flour a 10-inch tube pan with a removable bottom.

In the large bowl of an electric mixer, combine all the ingredients and beat until blended. Do not overbeat. Place batter into a 10-inch tube pan with a removable bottom, that has been greased and lightly floured. Bake in a 350° oven for 1 hour 10 minutes or until cake tester, inserted in center, comes out clean. Allow to cool in pan. Remove from pan and drizzle top with Orange Glaze. Serves 12.

Orange Glaze:
1 tablespoon orange juice
1 tablespoon grated orange peel
2 tablespoons finely chopped walnuts
1/2 cup sifted powdered sugar (about)

Combine all the ingredients and stir until blended.

Note: -Do not glaze this bread before freezing . Glaze it after defrosting.

Sweet Biscuit Bread with Currants

Try serving this moist, tender and delicious bread with cheese and a glass of wine. It is equally good with cream cheese, sliced strawberries and a sprinkling of pecans. It is far more interesting than a cracker and whenever I have served it, there are always a few people who will not leave until I give them the recipe.

4	cups flour
2	teaspoons baking powder
1/4	teaspoon salt
1/2	cup sugar
1/2	cup cold butter or margarine, cut into 4 pieces
1/2	cup dried currants
3	eggs
1 1/8	cups cream

In the large bowl of an electric mixer, beat together first 5 ingredients until butter is finely dispersed. Beat in currants. Thoroughly beat together eggs and cream and, with the motor running, slowly add to the flour mixture just until blended. Do not overbeat. Spread dough evenly into a greased 10-inch springform pan. Bake at 350° for 35 to 40 minutes or until top is golden brown.   To serve, cut into thin wedges. Yields 16 slices.

Whole Wheat Buttermilk Biscuits with Poppy Seeds & Onions

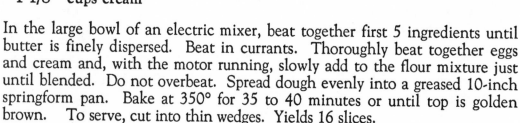

1 1/2	cups whole wheat pastry flour
1/2	cup unsweetened wheat germ
1	tablespoon baking powder
6	tablespoons cold margarine, cut into 6 pieces
1	cup buttermilk
1	tablespoon dried onion flakes
1	teaspoon poppy seeds

In the bowl of a food processor, mix first 3 ingredients. Add margarine, and blend, with quick on/off pulses, until margarine is the size of small peas. Add the buttermilk, and pulse again, until mixture is blended. Pulse in the onion and poppy seeds. Do not overmix.

Drop biscuits by rounded tablespoonful on a lightly greased cookie sheet and bake at 450-degrees for 15 minutes, or until tops are flecked with brown. Yields 20 biscuits.

Note: -As these are made with whole wheat flour and wheat germ, biscuits are dark and appear browned. Bake for the full amount of time.

Buttery Scones with Apricots

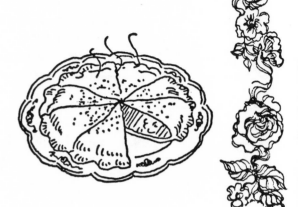

2 cups flour
2 1/2 teaspoons baking powder
2/3 cup sugar
1/3 cup butter

1/2 cup finely chopped dried apricots

2 eggs
1/2 cup sour cream
1 teaspoon vanilla

1 teaspoon sugar

Beat together first 4 ingredients until mixture resembles coarse meal. Stir in dried apricots. Beat together eggs, sour cream and vanilla until blended, and add, all at once, to the flour mixture. Beat only until blended and do not overbeat.

Spread batter, (it will be very thick,) into a greased 10-inch springform pan and sprinkle top with 1 teaspoon sugar. Bake at 350° for 25 to 30 minutes, or until top is nicely browned. Allow to cool in pan. When cool, remove from pan and cut into wedges to serve. Serve with Devonshire-Style Cream and fresh strawberries. Serves 10.

Cream Scones with Currants

This is a variation of my Victorian Cream Scones. Serve it with Devonshire Cream and Strawberries for an English breakfast treat. This recipe is a little more moist and tender than the traditional scone. Chopped dried apricots can be substituted for the currants. As a variation, add 2 tablespoons of toasted chopped almonds.

3 cups flour
2 teaspoons baking powder
1/4 teaspoon salt
1/2 cup sugar
1/2 cup cold butter or margarine, cut into 4 pieces

1/3 cup dried currants

2 eggs
1 cup cream

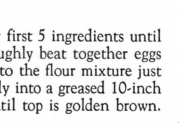

In the large bowl of an electric mixer, beat together first 5 ingredients until butter is finely dispersed. Beat in currants. Thoroughly beat together eggs and cream and, with the motor running, slowly add to the flour mixture just until blended. Do not overbeat. Spread dough evenly into a greased 10-inch springform pan. Bake at 350° for 30 minutes or until top is golden brown. To serve, cut into thin wedges. Yields 12 slices.

Devonshire-Style Cream

8 ounces low-fat cream cheese, softened
1/4 cup half and half
1/4 cup low-fat sour cream
2 tablespoons sifted powdered sugar
1/2 teaspoon vanilla

Beat cream cheese until light and fluffy. Beat in remaining ingredients until blended. Place mixture in a bowl, cover securely with plastic wrap and refrigerate for 4 to 6 hours. Overnight is good, too. Yields 1 1/2 cups.

Low-Cal Fresh Strawberry Jam

This little gem is very much like the expensive fruit spreads that are so popular. Be certain that the strawberries are well cooked through, or the jam will not last more than 2 to 3 days.

1 envelope unflavored gelatin
1/4 cup water
1/4 cup orange juice

2 tablespoons sugar or honey
2 tablespoons lemon juice
1 very thin slice lemon (about 1/8-inch)
2 cups (1 pint) strawberries, sliced

In a 1-cup metal measuring cup, soften gelatin in water and orange juice. Place cup in a larger pan with simmering water and stir until gelatin is dissolved.

Meanwhile, in a saucepan, place the remaining ingredients and simmer mixture, stirring now and again, for about 10 minutes, or until strawberries are cooked through. Discard lemon slice. Stir in gelatin mixture until thoroughly blended and simmer for 30 seconds, stirring. Allow to cool slightly and place jam in a jar with a tight-fitting lid. Store in the refrigerator. Yields about 2 cups.

Fresh Apple & Cinnamon Sauce

One could never guess that this sauce is so low in calories. It is flavored with fresh fruit and juice and sparkled with spices. Serve over frozen yogurt, pancakes, French toast or sponge cake.

1	apple, peeled, cored and grated
1	teaspoon butter or margarine
1	cup apple juice
1	cup orange juice
2	tablespoons cornstarch
1	tablespoon sugar or honey
1/2	teaspoon cinnamon
1/8	teaspoon powdered cloves
1/8	teaspoon ground nutmeg

In a saucepan, saute apple in butter until softened. Stir together juices and cornstarch until blended. Add to apple mixture with the remaining ingredients and simmer mixture, stirring, until sauce is slightly thickened and clear, about 10 minutes. Place in a jar with a tight-fitting lid and store in the refrigerator. Yields about 2 1/4 cups sauce.

Fresh Strawberry Sauce

This sauce is tart and fruity and very good on pancakes, French toast, sponge cake or frozen yogurt. It is the essence of simplicity to prepare and can be prepared 3 days before using.

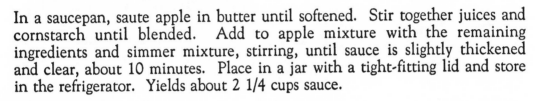

1/2	cup orange juice
2	tablespoons sugar or honey
1	tablespoon cornstarch
1	very thin slice lemon (about 1/8-inch)
1	pint strawberries, hulled and sliced

In a saucepan, stir together first 4 ingredients until blended. Simmer mixture, stirring, for about 5 minutes, or until slightly thickened. Stir in strawberries and simmer for an additional 5 minutes, stirring now and again, until syrup is clear. Discard lemon slice. Refrigerate until ready to use. Yields about 2 cups sauce.

Italian Country Raisin & Walnut Bread

This is a dinner bread. While this bread is filled with raisins and walnuts, it is not sweet. It can be prepared with only raisins or walnuts...I prefer using both. It is a very simple bread to prepare, quite rustic, but truly a taste treat. By substituting the raisins and walnuts, the basic bread can be made into dozens of different loaves. Some suggestions appear below.

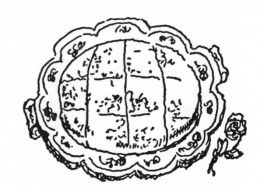

2	cups warm water (105°)
1	package dry yeast
4	cups bread flour
1	tablespoon sugar
1 1/2	teaspoons salt
1	cup bread flour
3/4	cup chopped walnuts
3/4	cup yellow raisins
2	tablespoons olive oil

In the large bowl of an electric mixer, dissolve yeast in warm water and allow to stand for 10 minutes. Add the 4 cups flour, sugar and salt and with the paddle beater, beat for 5 minutes. Using a dough hook, beat in the remaining 1 cup flour and beat for 3 minutes. Beat in the walnuts and raisins until blended.

Place 1 tablespoon oil on the bottom of a 12-inch round baking pan. Spread dough evenly in pan and drizzle top with remaining oil. Cover pan with a towel and allow dough to rise in a warm place until almost doubled in volume, about 1 hour. Place pan in a preheated 350° oven and bake for 50 to 55 minutes, or until top is golden brown. Serves 12.

To Make Apricot & Pine Nut Bread:
Delete raisins and walnuts and add 1 cup chopped apricots and 1 cup toasted pine nuts.

To Make Olive & Rosemary Bread:
Delete raisins and walnuts and add 1/2 cup sliced black olives, 1/2 cup sliced green olives and 2 tablespoons crumbled rosemary.

To Make Onion & Cheese Bread:
Delete raisins and walnuts and add 1 cup chopped green onions. Before baking, sprinkle top with 2 tablespoons grated Parmesan cheese.

Spicy Mexican Cornbread

Cheese, chiles and pimientos decorate the top of this spicy flatbread. It is good to serve with soup or salad, and quite lovely to serve with Savory Mexican Cheesecake Spread.

1	cup flour
1	cup yellow cornmeal
2	teaspoons baking powder
1	teaspoon oregano
1/2	teaspoon ground cumin
1/4	teaspoon salt
1 1/4	cups buttermilk
1/4	cup vegetable oil
2	tablespoons honey
2	eggs, beaten

Topping:

1	cup (4 ounces) grated Cheddar cheese
1	can (4 ounces) diced green chiles
1/2	cup chopped marinated red pepper

In the large bowl of an electric mixer, stir together first group of ingredients until well mixed. Beat in the next 4 ingredients until just blended. Do not overmix. Spread batter evenly into an oiled 9x9-inch baking pan. Sprinkle top evenly with cheese, chiles and red pepper and press it lightly into the batter.

Bake at 350° for about 25 to 30 minutes or until top is lightly browned and a cake tester, inserted in center comes out clean. Allow to cool in pan. Cut into squares to serve. Yields 16 2-inch squares.

Giant Popovers with Garlic & Rosemary

1	cup flour
1/4	teaspoon salt
3	eggs
1	cup milk
1/4	cup melted butter
1 1/2	teaspoons crushed rosemary
1/4	teaspoon garlic powder

In the large bowl of an electric mixer, beat together all the ingredients until nicely blended, about 1 minute. Divide batter between 6-oiled popover tins and bake at 350° for 40 to 45 minutes, or until tops are a deep golden brown. Yields 6 popovers.

Onion & Sun-Dried Tomato Bread

This is the easiest bread that can be prepared in literally minutes. It is a variation of the famous Beer Bread. It is impossible for me to recount the number of versions and styles I have made of this very simple bread. It lends itself to almost any nation or cuisine. Although, above all, I prefer the 12-inch round bread, this does produce a beautiful large loaf, or 2 mini-loaves or 12 muffin-sized rolls.

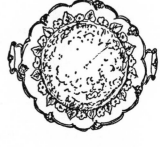

- 3 cups self-rising flour
- 3 tablespoons sugar
- 1 can (12 ounces) beer

- 1/2 cup chopped green onions
- 1/2 cup chopped sun-dried tomatoes

- 2 tablespoons oil

In the large bowl of an electric mixer, beat together flour, sugar and beer until blended (about 30 seconds). Do not overbeat. Beat in the onions and sun-dried tomatoes.

Place 1 tablespoon oil on the bottom of a 12-inch round baking pan. Spread batter evenly in pan and drizzle remaining oil on top. Bake at 350° for 45 minutes, or until top is golden brown. Cut into wedges to serve. Serves 12.

Irish Soda Bread with Raisins & Walnuts

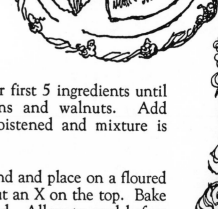

- 2 cups flour
- 1/2 cup quick-cooking (not instant) oats
- 1 1/2 teaspoons baking soda
- 1/4 teaspoon salt
- 1/3 cup cold butter, cut into small pieces

- 1 cup yellow raisins
- 1/2 cup chopped walnuts

- 1 cup buttermilk

In the large bowl of an electric mixer, beat together first 5 ingredients until mixture resembles coarse meal. Toss in raisins and walnuts. Add buttermilk and beat until dry ingredients are moistened and mixture is blended.

With floured hands, shape dough into an 8-inch round and place on a floured 8x3-inch round baking sheet. With a sharp knife, cut an X on the top. Bake at 400° for 35 to 40 minutes or until top is browned. Allow to cool before slicing.

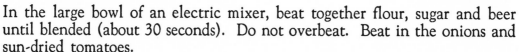

Old-Fashioned Buttermilk Corn Bread

1 cup cornmeal
1 cup flour
1/4 cup sugar
1 tablespoon baking powder
1/2 teaspoon salt

3/4 cup buttermilk
1/2 cup low-fat sour cream
2 eggs, beaten
6 tablespoons melted butter (3/4 stick)

Mix together dry ingredients. Mix together remaining ingredients. In a large bowl, stir together all the ingredients until mixture is blended. Pour batter into a 9x9-inch buttered pan and spread evenly.

Bake in a 350° oven for 25 to 30 minutes or until top is golden brown and a cake tester, inserted in center, comes out clean. Remove from the oven, cut into squares and serve warm. Serves 8.

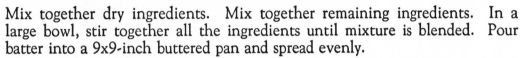

Parmesan, Herb & Onion Cheese Bread

This is a nice "conversation" bread that puts everyone in a good mood. It is very attractive served on a large platter. Cut it into serving pieces or let everyone tear off a piece or two.

3 cups self-rising flour
1 teaspoon baking powder
1/3 cup grated Parmesan cheese
2 tablespoons sugar
1 teaspoon Italian Herb Seasoning
1/2 cup chopped green onions
pinch of salt

3/4 cup milk
1 cup sour cream
1/2 cup butter, melted

Beat together first group of ingredients until blended. Beat in remaining ingredients until blended, about 1 minute. Do not overbeat. Spread batter evenly into an oiled 12-inch round baking pan. Brush top with a little oil and sprinkle with additional grated Parmesan cheese.

Bake in a 350° oven for about 40 to 45 minutes, or until top is golden brown. Cut into wedges (squares or diamonds) to serve. Excellent with soups or salads. Yields about 12 servings.

Best Butter & Egg Bread with Poppy Seeds

This is a great loaf. Making it is so satisfying and, enjoying it freshly baked, is sheer poetry. It is a little more work to prepare, but worth every bit of it, I promise you.

1	package dry yeast
1	cup warm water (105°)
2	heaping tablespoons sugar
2	cups flour
3/4	teaspoon salt
3/4	cup butter, softened
4	eggs
3	cups flour
1	egg yolk mixed with 1 teaspoon water for egg wash
	poppy seeds

1. In the large bowl of an electric mixer, place yeast, water and sugar. Allow to rest for 10 minutes or until yeast is dissolved and starts bubbling. Add the 2 cups of flour and salt and beat for 30 seconds. Add the butter and the eggs, beating well after each addition. Beat for 3 minutes using the paddle beater.

2. Beat in 2 cups of the remaining flour and beat another 3 minutes. Add the remaining 1 cup of flour and beat another 3 minutes. Place dough in an oiled bowl and then turn, so that it is oiled on top. Cover with a towel and allow to rest in a warm place until it is doubled in bulk, about 1 hour. Punch dough down and break off 1/4 of it. Now, separate each piece into 3 sections. Roll each piece into a rope, 12-inches long.

3. Braid the 3 larger pieces, tuck in the ends and place on a greased cookie sheet. Braid the 3 smaller pieces and place on top of the larger braid. Allow to rest again, for 1 hour or until doubled in bulk.* Baste the top and sides with the egg wash and sprinkle generously with poppy seeds. Bake in a 400° oven for 35 minutes or until top is a deep golden brown. If bread is browning too quickly, tent loosely with foil. Allow to cool in pan and cut into slices with a serrated knife. Yields 1 large 12-inch loaf.

Note: -*During the second rising, place 3 long sandwich-type toothpicks in the dough, and tent it with plastic wrap. If the plastic wrap touches the dough, it will stick and be a little tricky to remove. You must use a paddle beater, or a dough hook. The rotary beaters will not work for this method.

Stir-&-Bake Italian Garlic Bread Sticks
(Grissinis)

This is another favorite that is delicious and satisfying and a great accompaniment to soup, salad or dinner in general. It is an adaptation of my chewy dough and very simple to prepare, as dough does not have to be kneaded nor does it have to rise...just stir and bake.

1	package dry yeast
1/2	cup lukewarm water (110°)
1	teaspoon sugar
1	cup lukewarm water (110°)
3	cups flour
1	tablespoon sugar
3/4	teaspoon salt
1	cup flour
1	egg, beaten
	coarse-grind garlic powder, grated Parmesan cheese and/or sesame seeds for sprinkling on top

Soften yeast in 1/2 cup water and sugar until yeast starts to foam. If yeast does not foam, it is inactive and should be discarded.

To the bowl, add the next 4 ingredients and beat, for about 3 minutes, or until dough is very smooth. (This takes the place of kneading.) Now, slowly beat in the remaining 1 cup flour until blended. Turn dough out onto a lightly floured board and shape into a smooth ball.

Divide dough into 24 pieces. Roll each piece of dough, between your palms, into a 1/4-inch thick rope and place on a lightly greased cookie sheet. Brush top with beaten egg and sprinkle with coarse-grind garlic powder, and/or grated Parmesan and/or sesame seeds.

Bake in a 400° oven for about 15 to 18 minutes, or until tops are lightly browned. Yields 24 bread sticks.

New Orleans Red Hot Chile & Cheese Bread

This is a nice bread to serve with hot and spicy New Orleans dishes, soups or stews. It has quite a bite, for me. But red pepper (cayenne) can be increased to taste.

1/2	cup butter, cut into 8 pieces
2	cups flour
2	teaspoons baking powder
1	cup grated Swiss cheese
2	tablespoons grated Parmesan cheese
1	can (4 ounces) diced green chiles
1/4	teaspoon cayenne pepper
2	eggs
1/2	cup sour cream
1	tablespoon oil (for bottom)
1	tablespoon oil (for top)
2	tablespoons grated Parmesan cheese
2	tablespoons sesame seeds

In the large bowl of an electric mixer, beat together butter, flour and baking powder until butter particles are like coarse meal. Stir in the next 4 ingredients until nicely combined.

Beat eggs with sour cream and add to flour mixture, beating until a soft dough forms. Spread 1 tablespoon oil in a 12-inch round baking pan. Scrape batter into pan and spread to even. Drizzle top with 1 tablespoon oil. Sprinkle with grated Parmesan and sesame seeds.

Bake in a 350° oven for 35 to 40 minutes or until top is golden brown. Allow to cool in pan. Can be served warm or at room temperature. Cut into wedges or squares to serve. Serves 10.

Note: -*Can be prepared earlier in the day and heated before serving.*

Chewy French Bread Sticks

Try these chewy delicious bread sticks some evening soon. They are exceedingly easy to prepare, the dough is easily handled and does not need to rise.

1 1/2	cups lukewarm water (105°)
2	teaspoons sugar
1	envelope dry yeast
4	cups flour
3/4	teaspoon salt

Topping:
1	egg, beaten

Choice of onion or garlic powder, coarse salt, sesame seeds, poppy seeds, grated Parmesan cheese, or combination

In a large bowl of an electric mixer, place water, sugar and yeast and allow mixture to rest for 5 minutes or until yeast is softened. Add flour and salt and beat until blended. Use a dough hook, or knead by hand until dough is smooth and soft, about 5 minutes. Do not let dough rise.

Divide dough into 16 pieces. Roll each piece of dough into 1/4-inch thick rope and place on a greased cookie sheet. Brush tops with beaten egg and sprinkle top with garlic powder and grated Parmesan (or other choice).

Bake in a 400° oven for about 15 minutes or until bread sticks are lightly browned. Yields 16 bread sticks.

Hot Pepper Bread with Onions & Cheese

This bread is a good choice to serve with Moroccan or Mexican food. Let me say, at the outset, that I do not relish food that is overly hot because the flavor of the dish is overpowered. Not so with this delightful bread. It has only a light bite, and is delicately flavored with the onions and cheese.

3	cups self-rising flour
3	tablespoons sugar
1	can (12 ounces) beer
1/3	cup grated Parmesan cheese
2	tablespoons instant minced onion flakes
3/4	teaspoon crushed red pepper flakes
3	teaspoons grated Parmesan cheese

More →

(Hot Pepper Bread, Cont.)

Preheat oven to 350°. Oil 3 foil 6x3-inch mini-loaf pans. In the large bowl of an electric mixer, combine first 6 ingredients and beat for 2 minutes, or until mixture is nicely blended and smooth. Do not overbeat.

Spoon batter evenly into 3 foil mini-loaf pans, (6x3-inches), that have been oiled, (about 2 teaspoons oil). Sprinkle top with additional cheese.

Bake in a 350° oven for 30 to 35 minutes, or until tops are golden brown. Allow breads to cool about 10 minutes, then remove from pans and continue cooling on a rack. Yields 3 mini-loaves.

Burgundian Cheese & Onion Bread
(French Gougere)

Whenever I serve this bread, it creates a great deal of spirit and excitement. Serve it with an herbed cheese or a delicate spread, add a glass of wine and it will feel like a party. This is also a great accompaniment to soup or salad.

- 1 cup milk
- 4 tablespoons butter (1/2 stick)

- 1 cup flour
- 1 tablespoon dried onion flakes

- 4 eggs, at room temperature

- 1/2 teaspoon salt
- 2 tablespoons grated Parmesan cheese

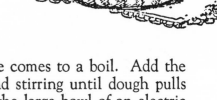

In a saucepan, heat milk and butter until mixture comes to a boil. Add the flour and onion flakes, and continue cooking and stirring until dough pulls away from the sides of the pan. Place dough in the large bowl of an electric mixer and beat in the eggs, one at a time, beating well after each addition. Beat in the remaining ingredients until blended.

Grease a 10-inch porcelain quiche baker. Spoon dough along the edge of the pan to form a 1 1/2-inch ring. Bake in a 400° oven for 15 minutes. Lower heat to 350° and continue baking for about 30 minutes or until pastry is puffed and golden brown. Serve warm with soup, salad or simply with a glass of wine. Serves 8.

Note: -Batter can be made earlier in the day, spooned into the porcelain baker and refrigerated until ready to bake. Add a few minutes to baking time.
-This pastry can be baked earlier in the day and heated before serving. But, it is best baked at serving time.

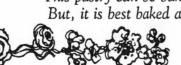

Special Spreads for Bread

In restaurants, pestos are being served more and more often with bread. Maybe because they are made with olive oil. Many are the times that butter has to be requested. These pestos are quite delicious spread on flat breads, foccaccias or slices of crusty Italian bread.

Basically made with olive oil, basil and garlic, there are a host of ingredients you could add that would lend sparkle and excitement to dinner. Black or green olives, sun-dried tomatoes, shallots, chives, green onions, Parmesan cheese...the list is abundant. You could add different herbs, cheeses, and pine nuts, walnuts or pistachios.

You will notice that I recommend coarsely grated Parmesan cheese. It adds quite a different flavor than the finely ground. Here are a few special recipes.

Black Olive & Garlic Spread

1/2	cup pitted black olives
2	cloves garlic, sliced
1	shallot, minced (about 2 tablespoons)
3	tablespoons parsley leaves
3	tablespoons fresh basil leaves
2	tablespoons olive oil
2	tablespoons coarsely grated Parmesan cheese

In a food processor, blend together first 5 ingredients ingredients until mixture is finely chopped. (Some texture should remain.) Stir in the oil and cheese until blended. Serve with flatbreads or crusty sliced Italian bread. Yields about 3/4 cup.

Basil & Pine Nut Spread

1/2	cup fresh basil leaves
1/4	cup chopped chives
1	clove garlic, sliced
1/4	cup pine nuts
2	tablespoons olive oil
2	tablespoons coarsely grated Parmesan cheese

In a food processor, finely chop first 4 ingredients. Stir in the oil and cheese until blended. Serve with flatbreads or crusty sliced Italian bread. Yields about 3/4 cup.

Sun-Dried Tomato & Parmesan Spread

1/2	cup sun-dried tomatoes, packed in olive oil
2	tablespoons Italian parsley leaves
2	tablespoons fresh basil leaves
2	tablespoons pine nuts
3	tablespoons chopped chives
1	tablespoon red wine vinegar
2	tablespoons olive oil
2	tablespoons coarsely grated Parmesan cheese

In a food processor, finely chop first 6 ingredients. Stir in the oil and cheese until blended. Serve with flatbreads or crusty sliced Italian bread. Yields about 3/4 cup.

Roasted Garlic Spread

2	whole heads garlic
2	teaspoons olive oil
2	tablespoons olive oil

Cut 1/2-inch off the heads of garlic, rub them with olive oil and wrap them in foil. (If you own a garlic baker, use it, of course.) Place the garlic in a small baking pan, and bake at 325° for 40 minutes or until garlic is soft. Allow to cool. Squeeze out the soft garlic from its skin and place into a bowl. Stir in olive oil. Serve with flatbreads or crusty sliced Italian bread. Yields 1/2 cup.

Fresh Tomato & Green Onion Spread

4	tomatoes (about 1 pound), seeded and finely chopped
1/3	cup chopped green onions
2	tablespoons olive oil
1	tablespoon red wine vinegar
2	tablespoons grated Parmesan cheese

In a bowl, stir together all the ingredients, cover bowl and store in the refrigerator for several hours. Serve with Cheese Toast. Yields 2 cups.

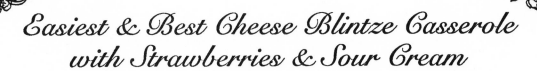

Easiest & Best Cheese Blintze Casserole with Strawberries & Sour Cream

Nothing could be easier to prepare than this delicious casserole. It has all the character and flavor of cheese blintzes with none of the work. This is a good choice for a breakfast or brunch, as it can be prepared in advance and heated before serving. The original of this recipe appeared in my newsletter in 1968. To this day, it is still enjoyed by everyone. This version is a little lighter.

Batter:

1/2	cup (1 stick) butter or margarine, melted
1/2	cup sugar
2	eggs
1	cup flour
1/2	cup milk
3	teaspoons baking powder
1	teaspoon vanilla
1	tablespoon cinnamon sugar

In the small bowl of an electric mixer, beat together all the ingredients (except the cinnamon sugar), until the mixture is nicely blended. Spread 1/2 the batter in a buttered 9x13-inch baking pan. Spoon the Lemon Cream Cheese Filling evenly on the top and cover it with the remaining batter. Sprinkle top with cinnamon sugar.

Bake at 350° for 45 minutes, or until top is browned. Cut into squares and serve warm with a dollop of low-fat sour cream and a spoonful of crushed strawberries or raspberries. A teaspoon of frozen strawberries or raspberries is very good, too. Serves 10.

Lemon Cream Cheese Filling:

1	package (8 ounces) light cream cheese, at room temperature
1	cup small curd low-fat cottage cheese
1	egg
1/3	cup sugar
3	tablespoons lemon juice

Beat cream cheese until lightened, about 1 minute. Beat in remaining ingredients until blended.

Delicate Cheese Blintzes

These are like little cheesecakes and loved by everyone. They can be prepared 2 days earlier and stored in the refrigerator. By adding a little margarine to the batter, you will eliminate greasing the pan after each crepe.

Basic Crepes:

3	eggs
1	cup flour
1	cup milk
1/4	cup water
4	tablespoons melted butter or margarine

Beat together all the ingredients until blended. Cover and refrigerate batter for 30 minutes. In a 7-inch skillet or frying pan with rounded sides, heat 1 teaspoon butter and spread it with a paper towel. Pan should be very hot, but butter should not brown.

Pour in about 1/8 cup batter and quickly tilt and turn pan so that the bottom is covered with a thin layer of batter. Cook the crepe for 45 seconds, or until the top appears dry; then turn and cook the other side for 15 seconds. Remove crepe onto a large platter. Repeat with remaining batter.

Place 1 tablespoon filling on one side of the crepe and, starting with that side, roll it up jelly-roll fashion. (Alternatively, fold in the sides and roll up the blintze.) Place filled crepes on a platter, cover with plastic wrap and store in the refrigerator.

Just before serving, cook blintzes in a buttered skillet until browned on both sides. Serve with a dollop of sour cream and sliced strawberries or simply with a spoonful of fruit-sweetened jam. Yields about 16 to 18 blintzes.

Lemon Cheese Filling:

12	ounces cream cheese
1/3	cup sugar
4	tablespoons lemon juice

Stir together all the ingredients until blended.

Strawberry Sauce:

1/2	cup strawberry jam
1	pint fresh strawberries, stemmed and chopped
1	tablespoon lemon juice

Heat strawberry jam. Add strawberries and lemon juice and simmer for 5 minutes.

Old World Cheese Blintzes with Strawberries

1 cup small curd non-fat cottage cheese
1 package (8 ounces) low-fat cream cheese
2 tablespoons low-fat sour cream
1/2 cup sugar
1 tablespoon grated lemon peel
1/2 cup yellow raisins

Beat together cottage cheese and cream cheese until blended. Add the remaining ingredients and beat until blended.

Divide mixture between 16 crepes. Roll crepes up, jelly roll fashion, and place in one layer, seam side down, in a greased baking pan. (If you do not own a 12x16-inch pan, you will have to use 2 smaller ones.)

Bake in a 350° oven for about 15 minutes or until heated through. Serve with a dollop of sour cream and a tablespoon of strawberries in syrup. Yields 16 crepes.

Basic Crepes:
1 cup flour
1 cup milk
3 eggs
4 tablespoons melted butter
1/4 cup water
pinch of salt

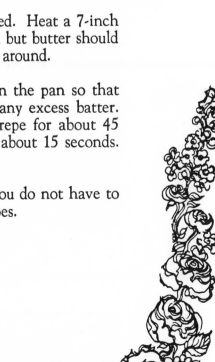

Combine all the ingredients in a bowl and beat until blended. Heat a 7-inch skillet and butter it with a paper towel. Pan should be hot, but butter should not brown. A drop of water, splashed in pan, should skitter around.

Pour about 1/8 cup batter into pan. Quickly tilt and turn the pan so that the bottom is completely covered with batter. Pour out any excess batter. Place pan back on the heat and continue cooking the crepe for about 45 seconds or until top is dry. Turn and cook other side for about 15 seconds. Remove crepe onto a platter.

Heat pan and start again. As the batter contains butter, you do not have to butter the pan after each crepe. Yields about 16 7-inch crepes.

French Orange Toast
with Country Orange Marmalade

8   slices French bread, cut into 1/2-inch slices

3   eggs
1   cup milk
2   tablespoons finely grated orange zest (orange part of the peel)
2   tablespoons cinnamon sugar

Country Orange Marmalade

In a 9x13-inch pan, place bread slices in one layer. Beat together eggs, milk, zest and cinnamon sugar until blended. Pour egg mixture evenly over the bread. Allow bread to soak up egg, turning now and again until evenly moistened.

In a buttered skillet, saute bread slices until golden brown on both sides. (French toast can be baked in the oven for a slightly different effect. After the eggs are nicely soaked up, place pan in a 350° oven and bake until bread is golden and puffed.)

Serve with Orange Country Marmalade or your favorite syrup. Serves 4.

Country Orange Marmalade:
   1   cup orange marmalade
   2   tablespoons lemon juice
   4   tablespoons chopped walnuts
   3   tablespoons yellow raisins
   2   tablespoons chopped Maraschino cherries

In a glass jar with a tight-fitting lid, combine all the ingredients and stir until blended. Store in the refrigerator until ready to use. Yields 1 1/2 cups.

Blintze-Style French Toast with Cheese Cake Filling

This is a beautiful casserole to serve on a buffet. Decorate it with fresh fruit and a sprinkling of sifted powdered sugar. It can be prepared earlier in the day and heated at time of serving.

12 slices cinnamon-raisin bread, crusts removed

Cheese Cake Filling:
1 package (8-ounces) low-fat cream cheese
1/4 cup non-fat milk
1 egg, beaten
3 tablespoons sugar
1 tablespoon grated lemon

Custard Mixture:
3 eggs
1 cup non-fat milk
1 cup low-fat sour cream
1/4 cup sugar
1/2 teaspoon vanilla

In a buttered 9x13-inch baking pan, lay 6 slices of bread. Beat together Cheese Cake ingredients and spread evenly over the bread. Place remaining bread slices on top. Beat together Custard ingredients and pour evenly over all. Allow to stand in the refrigerator for 1 hour, or until bread is evenly moistened.

Bake at 350°, loosely tented with foil, for about 1 hour or until top is golden brown. Cut into 6 servings as a main course or into 12 servings as an accompaniment. Serve with a dusting of sifted powdered sugar and fresh strawberries, raspberries or sliced peaches.

French Toast Layered with Strawberry Jam

8   thin slices good quality white bread, about 1/4-inch thick and
    4x4-inches

4   tablespoons strawberry jam (or peach or apricot jam), heated

2   eggs
1/2 cup milk

Spread 4 slices of bread with strawberry jam and cover each with another bread slice. Pat it down gently to seal. Beat together eggs with milk until blended and pour into an 8x8-inch baking pan. Set the stuffed bread into the pan, turning from time to time, until egg mixture is completely absorbed.

In a buttered skillet, saute bread "sandwiches" until golden brown on both sides. Serve with maple syrup or fresh strawberries and a dollop of sour cream. Serves 4.

German Apple Pancake with Sour Cream & Lingonberries

2   apples, peeled and grated and tossed with
        2 tablespoons lemon juice
1/2 cup yellow raisins
1/2 cup chopped walnuts
2   tablespoons sugar
1/4 teaspoon cinnamon

3   eggs
1   cup flour
1   cup milk
2   tablespoons melted butter
2   tablespoons sugar
1/2 teaspoon vanilla

In an oiled 10-inch, round baking pan (or skillet that can go into the oven), saute together the first 6 ingredients, until apples are softened.

Meanwhile, beat together the remaining ingredients until nicely blended. Pour batter evenly over the apple mixture and bake in a 350° oven until omelet is puffed and golden, about 30 minutes.

Cut into wedges and serve with a spoonful of low-fat sour cream and lingonberries. Strawberries are good, too. Serves 4.

Vanilla Raisin Toast with Cinnamon & Orange Honey

3	eggs
1/2	cup milk
3	tablespoons cinnamon sugar
1/2	teaspoon vanilla
8	slices raisin bread

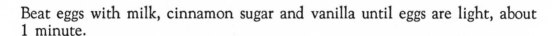

Beat eggs with milk, cinnamon sugar and vanilla until eggs are light, about 1 minute.

Dip bread into egg mixture and let it soak up the egg. In a buttered skillet or griddle, cook the bread until golden brown. Turn and brown the other side. Keep warm in a low oven, until all the bread is sauteed. Serve warm with Orange Honey. Serves 4.

Orange Honey:
1	cup honey
2	teaspoons grated orange peel
1/4	cup orange juice concentrate

In a saucepan, heat together all the ingredients until they are well blended.

Royal French Toast

3	eggs
1/2	cup non-fat milk
1/2	cup low-fat sour cream
3	tablespoons cinnamon sugar
8	slices cinnamon bread

Beat eggs with milk, sour cream and cinnamon sugar. Dip bread slices in egg and saute them in a buttered skillet until they are golden brown. Turn and brown the other side. Serve warm with syrup, honey or cinnamon sugar. Serves 4.

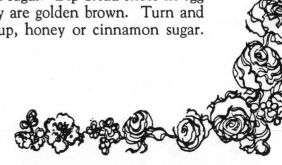

Cornmeal Pancakes with Hot Maple Syrup

This is a delicious dense pancake, flavored with cornmeal. It is basically simple to prepare. Be certain you get pure maple syrup and heat it before serving.

1	egg
2/3	cup milk
1/3	cup low-fat sour cream
3/4	cup flour
1/3	cup cornmeal
2	teaspoons baking powder
1	tablespoon sugar
1/2	teaspoon vanilla
2	tablespoons melted butter

In a bowl, whisk together all the ingredients until blended. Do not overmix. On a lightly greased, preheated griddle, pour about 1/8-cup batter, for small pancakes. When bottom of pancake is golden brown and top is bubbly, turn and brown other side. Serve warm with hot maple syrup. Makes about 16 pancakes and serves 4.

Oven-Baked French Toast

Baking the French toast in the oven eliminates the use of any fat or oil. However, these can be prepared in a skillet, with just a wiping of oil and the toast will be a little more tender. Cook until browned on both sides.

1	egg
1/2	cup non-fat milk
4	slices whole wheat bread, cut in half

Beat together egg and milk until blended. Place bread in a 7x11-inch non-stick shallow pan and pour egg mixture over all. Allow to stand for about 5 minutes, or until egg is absorbed, turning once. Place pan in a 350-degree oven and bake for 10 minutes, turn and bake for another 3 or 4 minutes, or until puffed and golden. Serve each slice with 1 tablespoon Fresh Apple & Cinnamon Sauce or a sprinkle of cinnamon sugar. Serves 4.

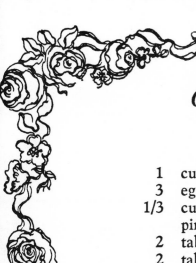

Cottage Cheese Pancakes with Honey Butter Syrup

    1   cup cottage cheese
    3   eggs
    1/3 cup flour
        pinch of salt
    2   tablespoons sugar
    2   tablespoons melted butter
    1   teaspoon baking powder
    1/2 teaspoon vanilla

Place all the ingredients in a mixing bowl and beat with a fork until they are blended. Do not overmix.

Pour 1/4 cup batter on a lightly greased, preheated Teflon griddle. When bottom of pancake is golden brown and top is bubbly, turn and brown other side.

Serve warm with sliced strawberries and a sprinkling of toasted pecans. It is also very good with applesauce sprinkled with cinnamon. If you like syrup with your pancakes, you will enjoy the unusual Honey Butter Syrup. Makes 12 pancakes.

Honey Butter Syrup:
    1   cup honey
    2   tablespoons butter
    2   tablespoons undiluted frozen orange juice concentrate
    1   tablespoon lemon juice
    1/8 teaspoon cinnamon

Combine all the ingredients in a saucepan and simmer mixture for 2 minutes. Yields about 1 1/3 cups syrup.

Dutch Babies-Popover Pancakes

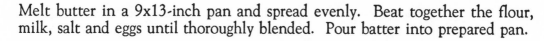

Try this delightful dish some Sunday morning for an exciting and fun breakfast. This beautiful puffy pancake looks and serves so well and it really is easy to prepare.

3   tablespoons butter

1   cup flour
1   cup milk
1/4   teaspoon salt
4   eggs

Melt butter in a 9x13-inch pan and spread evenly. Beat together the flour, milk, salt and eggs until thoroughly blended. Pour batter into prepared pan.

Bake in a 400° oven for about 30 minutes or until pancake is puffed and golden. Sprinkle generously with sifted powdered sugar and serve with one of the following toppings. Serves 6.

Honey Orange:
Heat together 1 cup honey and 3 ounces concentrated orange juice until blended. Spoon over pancake to taste. Unused honey can be stored in the refrigerator.

Yogurt and Strawberries:
Serve pancake with a dollop of non-fat yogurt and sliced strawberries.

Cinnamon Sugar:
Sprinkle top with cinnamon sugar to taste and serve with a dollop of low-fat sour cream and strawberry jam.

Apples and Raisins:
Cook together 3 cups sliced apples, 1/2 cup yellow raisins, 1/4 cup sugar, 1/3 cup orange juice, 1 thin slice lemon and 1 teaspoon vanilla until apples are soft. Sprinkle top of pancake with cinnamon sugar and serve with cooked apples.

Strawberry Orange Topping:
In a bowl, combine 1 package (10 ounces) frozen sliced strawberries with 3 ounces concentrated frozen orange juice. Serve pancake with a dollop of sour cream and a few tablespoons of Strawberry Orange Topping.

Cinnamon Brown Sugar:
In a bowl, stir together 1 cup low-fat sour cream with 2 tablespoons brown sugar and cinnamon to taste. Allow to stand until sugar is dissolved.

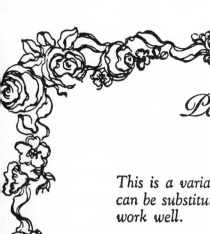

Petite Breakfast Crescents with Walnuts & Apricots

This is a variation of crescents made with a cottage cheese dough. The apricots can be substituted with any manner of dried fruits. Raisins, dates, prunes, etc. all work well.

1 cup cottage cheese
3 ounces butter (3/4 stick)
1 cup flour

Filling Ingredients:
1/2 cup finely chopped walnuts
1/2 cup finely chopped dried apricots
1/2 cup sugar
1 teaspoon cinnamon

cinnamon sugar

Beat together cottage cheese and butter until blended. Beat in flour until blended, about 1 minute. Shape dough into a ball and sprinkle with a little flour to ease handling. Cut dough into thirds. In a bowl stir together filling ingredients until blended.

Roll each third out on a floured pastry cloth to measure a 10-inch circle. Sprinkle 1/3 the filling ingredients over the dough, and cut dough into 8 triangular wedges. Roll each triangle from the wide end toward the center and curve into a crescent. Sprinkle with cinnamon sugar and place on a lightly buttered cookie sheet. Repeat with remaining dough.

Bake at 350° for about 30 to 35 minutes, or until tops are golden brown. Remove from the pan and allow to cool on brown paper. Yields 24 crescents.

To make Cinnamon Sugar:
In a glass jar with a tight-fitting lid, shake together 1/2 cup sugar with 2 teaspoons cinnamon until blended. Unused Cinnamon Sugar can be stored indefinitely.

Miniature Hungarian Strudels

This is my Mother-in-Law's favorite dough. She filled these lovely pastries with prunes or apricots or cinnamon and raisins. These freeze beautifully, wrapped in double thicknesses of wax paper and then foil. Do not sprinkle with powdered sugar before freezing. Sprinkle with sugar after defrosted.

Cream Cheese Pastry:
- 1 package (8 ounces) cream cheese
- 1 cup butter (2 sticks)
- 1 egg yolk
- 2 cups flour
- 1/8 teaspoon salt

In the large bowl of an electric mixer, beat together the butter and cream cheese until the mixture is blended. Beat in the egg yolk. Add the flour and salt and beat until blended. Do not overbeat. Turn dough out on a floured wax paper. Form dough into a circle, wrap it in the wax paper and refrigerate it for several hours or overnight.

Divide dough in fourths. Roll out one part at a time to measure a 10-inch square. Spread 1/4 of the Chocolate Quik over the dough. Sprinkle with 1/4 of the chocolate chips and optional walnuts. Roll it up, jelly-roll fashion to measure a 10x3-inch roll. Place seam side down on a 12x16-inch teflon-coated baking pan. Repeat with the remaining 3 parts dough.

Bake in a preheated 350° oven for 30 minutes or until the top is lightly browned. Cool in pan. Cut into slices and sprinkle tops generously with sifted powdered sugar. Yields 24 to 28 slices.

Chocolate Chip Filling for 4 rolls:
- 12 tablespoons Nestle's Chocolate Quik
- 6 ounces semi-sweet chocolate chips
- 1/2 cup chopped walnuts (optional)

Cinnamon Raisin Nut Filling for 4 rolls:
- 4 tablespoons cinnamon sugar
- 3/4 cup yellow raisins (or other chopped dried fruits such as dates, prunes, apricots)
- 3/4 cup chopped walnuts

Apricot Jam & Walnut Filling for 4 rolls:
- 1 cup apricot jam
- 1 cup chopped walnuts

Divide filling ingredients between the 4 rolls.

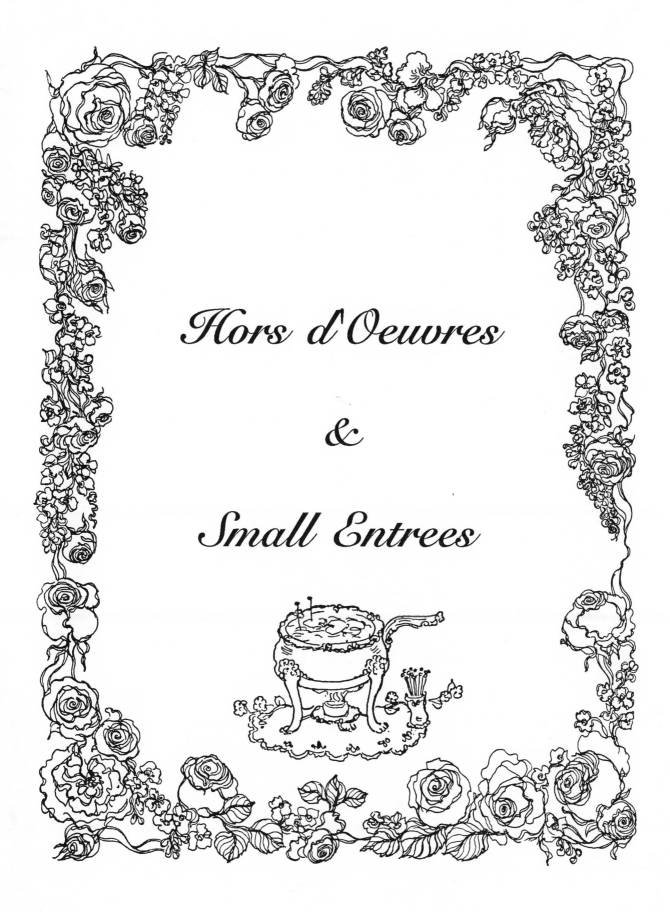

Hors d'Oeuvres

&

Small Entrees

Red Pepper & Chili Salsa with Toasted Olive Pita Chips

4 marinated red peppers, finely chopped
1 can (7 ounces) diced green chiles
2 large tomatoes, seeded and finely chopped
1 tablespoon olive oil
2 tablespoons lemon juice
1 tablespoon cider vinegar
1/2 teaspoon ground cumin
2 tablespoons minced cilantro
   pinch of red pepper flakes

In a glass bowl, stir together all the ingredients. Cover bowl and refrigerate for several hours. Serve with Toasted Pita Chips for dipping. Toasted Olive Pita Chips are a little more work, but well worth the effort. Yields about 2 cups salsa and serves 6.

Toasted Pita Chips:
With kitchen shears, cut around the edge and separate pitas into 2 circles. Cut each circle into 6 wedges and toast in a 350° oven for 6 minutes, or until pitas are crisped. Watch carefully, as there are only a few seconds between toasted and burnt. Each pita bread yields 12 chips.

Toasted Olive Pita Chips:
3 pitas
12 pitted black olives
2 tablespoons olive oil

With kitchen shears, cut around the edge and separate pitas into 2 circles. In a food processor, puree olives with oil and spread mixture thinly on the 12 pita halves. Cut each half into 6 wedges. Place on a cookie sheet, in one layer and bake at 350° for 6 minutes or until pitas are crisped. Watch carefully so pitas do not burn. Yields 36 chips.

Note: -2 cloves minced garlic can be added to the mixture. It is a nice addition.

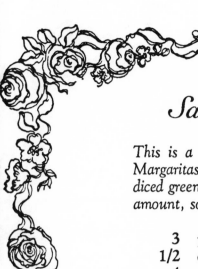

Savory Mexican Cheesecake Spread

This is a great starter for a dinner in a Mexican mood. Serve it with frosty Margaritas or Mexican beer and surround with large corn chips for spreading. The diced green chiles are mild. Don't use any of the "hot" chiles. This produces a large amount, so it is a good choice when you are expecting a large crowd.

3	packages (8 ounces, each) low-fat cream cheese, softened
1/2	cup low-fat sour cream
4	tablespoons lemon juice
2	cups (8 ounces) grated Cheddar cheese
1	can (4 ounces) diced green chiles
1/2	cup finely chopped green onions

Topping:

3/4	cup low-fat sour cream
1/3	cup thinly sliced black pitted olives
1/3	cup finely chopped green onions
2	tomatoes, seeded and finely chopped
1/4	cup mild taco sauce

In an electric mixer, beat together cream cheese, sour cream and lemon juice until mixture is light and fluffy, about 2 minutes. Stir in the next 3 ingredients until blended. Do not overmix as you do not want to break up the chiles and cheese.

Spread mixture evenly into a 12x1-inch round pan lined with plastic wrap. Cover pan and refrigerate. A few hours before serving, invert pan onto a 14-inch serving platter, remove plastic wrap and spread top with sour cream.

Decorate the top with a border of olives. Leave 1-inch sour cream exposed and then make another circle with green onions. Mix the tomatoes with the taco sauce and spread this in the center, leaving another little circle of sour cream exposed. This will produce a pretty decorative top. Serve with Spicy Mexican Cornbread or firm corn chips. Will yield 24 servings.

Guacamole Mold
with Tomatoes, Onions & Chiles

1	package unflavored gelatin
1/2	cup water

4	avocados, mashed
1	cup low-fat sour cream
1	can (4 ounces) chopped green chiles
4	tablespoons lemon juice, or more to taste
1	small onion, grated
1	tomato, peeled, seeded and chopped
2	tabasco peppers, finely minced (or to taste)

In a metal measuring cup, soften gelatin in water. Place cup in a pan of simmering water and stir until gelatin is dissolved.

In a large bowl, stir together the remaining ingredients until well mixed. Stir in the dissolved gelatin. Spoon mixture into a 6-cup mold and refrigerate until firm.

Unmold onto a lovely platter and decorate with green leaves and scored lemon slices. Serve with toasted flour tortillas as an accompaniment.

Note: - *To toast flour tortillas, place in a toaster oven (not a pop-up toaster) and toast for about 1 or 2 minutes or until tortillas are crispened. Bubbles will form (this is normal).*

Marinated Olives

2	cups black pitted olives
2	tablespoons olive oil
2	cloves minced garlic
	red wine vinegar to cover

In a glass jar, with a tight-fitting lid, shake together all the ingredients. Refrigerate for several days to allow flavors to blend. Will keep for weeks in the refrigerator and improves with time. Use on salads or where olives are called for.

Eggplant, Red Pepper & Onion Dip

1   eggplant (about 1 pound) peeled and thinly sliced
1   red pepper, seeded and chopped
1   onion, chopped
1   tablespoon olive oil

1/3   cup lemon juice
2   tablespoons olive oil
1/3   cup finely chopped parsley leaves
1   teaspoon dried sweet basil leaves or 1 tablespoon fresh
1   tablespoon minced cilantro
     salt and pepper to taste

Place vegetables in a 9x13-inch baking pan and drizzle with oil. Cover pan tightly with foil and bake at 350° for 30 minutes, or until vegetables are soft. Place mixture in a bowl and cut up the eggplant into fine dice.

Stir together the remaining ingredients until blended and pour over the vegetables. Cover bowl and refrigerate until serving time. To serve place eggplant in a serving bowl and surround with Pita Chips with Black Olive Spread.

Pita Chips with Black Olive Spread

6   Pita breads, separated into halves

1/2   cup pitted black olives
3   tablespoons chopped green onions
1   clove garlic, sliced
1 1/2   tablespoons lemon juice
1   tablespoon olive oil
     salt and pepper to taste

Place pita halves on a 12x16-inch baking pan. Finely grind next 6 ingredients in a food processor. Spread a thin layer of olive mixture on each pita, cut each pita into 6 wedges and bake at 350° for 5 minutes, or until pitas are crisped. Great to serve with eggplant dip or with soups or salads.

Mushrooms Stuffed with Goat Cheese & Garlic Crumbs

1   pound medium mushrooms, cleaned and stems removed

Filling:
- 1/4   pound low-fat cream cheese
- 1/4   pound goat cheese
- 1/2   cup garlic croutons, finely crushed
- 3   tablespoons chopped chives

Parmesan cheese, grated
paprika

Prepare mushrooms and place on a cookie sheet. Beat together Filling ingredients until blended. Mound mixture into mushroom caps. Sprinkle tops generously with grated Parmesan and lightly with paprika. Broil until piping hot. Yields about 24 bite-size appetizers.

Mushrooms with Dill & Yogurt Stuffing

1   pound mushrooms, cleaned and stems removed (about 24). Chop stems finely.

- 1   onion, minced
- 2   shallots, minced
- 1   garlic clove, minced
- 1/2   teaspoon dried dill weed
- 1   teaspoon oil

- 1/2   cup finely crushed garlic croutons,
- 1/2   cup unflavored non-fat yogurt or low-fat sour cream

- 4   tablespoons grated Parmesan cheese
  paprika

Prepare mushrooms and place them on a non-stick baking pan. In a skillet, saute together mushroom stems and next 5 ingredients until onion and shallots are soft and liquid rendered is evaporated.

In a bowl, mix together onion mixture, garlic croutons and yogurt until blended. Fill mushrooms with about 1 tablespoon filling and sprinkle tops with grated Parmesan and paprika. Bake at 350-degrees about 20 minutes. Broil for a few seconds to brown tops. Serves 8.

Piroshkis with Herbed Mushroom Filling

Using the prepared puff pastry cuts preparation time to a minimum. And preparing these in 8-inch logs, that you will later cut into small squares, is another timesaver.

Herbed Mushroom Filling:

1	tablespoon butter or margarine
1	large onion, minced
4	shallots, minced
2	cloves garlic, minced
1/2	pound mushrooms, minced
2	teaspoons lemon juice
1/4	teaspoon ground poultry seasoning
1/8	teaspoon thyme flakes
	salt and pepper to taste
2	tablespoons flour
1/2	cup low-fat sour cream

Saute together first 4 ingredients until onion is transparent. Add the next 2 ingredients and continue sauteing until mushrooms are tender and all the liquid is absorbed. Add seasonings and flour and cook and stir for 2 minutes. Add sour cream and cook and stir for 2 minutes or until mixture is very thick. Allow mixture to cool.

Using Prepared Puff Pastry:

1	package Pepperidge Farms Puff Pastry (2 large sheets)
1	egg, beaten
12	tablespoons grated Parmesan cheese

Cut pastry sheets in thirds on the fold. Cut each third in half crosswise. You will have 12 pieces. On a floured pastry cloth, roll out each piece to measure 4x8-inches. Place a few tablespoons mushroom mixture along the 8-inch side, fold dough over and press edges down firmly with the tines of a fork to seal tightly. Scallop the edges.

Place piroshkis on a greased cookie sheet, brush tops with beaten egg and sprinkle with cheese. Pierce tops with the tines of a fork. Bake at 400° for 25 to 30 minutes, or until tops are nicely browned. Allow to cool on brown paper.

To reheat, place piroshkis on a cookie sheet, cut each into 4 pieces and heat in a 350° oven for 15 minutes, or until heated through. Yields 48 piroshkis.

Royal Coulibiac of Mushrooms with Cheese & Chives

Prepare this recipe when you are preparing a dinner fit for a king. There are few small entrees that are more beautiful or more delicious than this one. Spiced apricots, served warm, is a grand accompaniment. This can be prepared earlier in the day and reheated at serving time

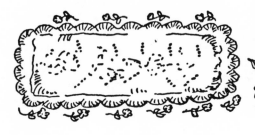

1 1/2	pounds mushrooms, thinly sliced
4	shallots, minced
4	cloves garlic, minced
	salt and pepper to taste
2	tablespoons butter
3	tablespoons flour
1/2	cup light sour cream
1/2	cup light cream
1/2	teaspoon, each, thyme flakes and sage flakes
1	teaspoon Dijon mustard
1/4	cup grated Parmesan cheese
1/4	cup chopped chives
1/2	pound puff pastry (1 sheet Pepperidge Farms)
1	egg, beaten (to brush on top)
2	tablespoons grated Parmesan cheese

In a large skillet, saute together first 5 ingredients until shallots are tender and liquid rendered is evaporated. Add the flour and cook and stir for 2 minutes. Stir together creams, seasonings and mustard and add, all at once, cooking and stirring until mixture thickens. Allow mixture to cool. Stir in the cheese and chives.

Roll out the pastry to measure a 12x14-inch rectangle and cut it in half on the 12-inch side, producing 2 halves 14x7-inches. Place one half on a lightly greased 10x15-inch jelly roll pan. Spread filling on top, leaving a 1-inch border. Cover filling with second half and seal the edges with the tines of a fork. Scallop the edges and pierce the top in several places with the tines of a fork.

Brush top with beaten egg and sprinkle with additional grated Parmesan. Bake in a 350° oven for about 30 minutes or until top is golden brown and pastry is puffed and beautiful. To serve, cut into slices with a serrated knife. Serves 12 as a small entree or 6 as a main course.

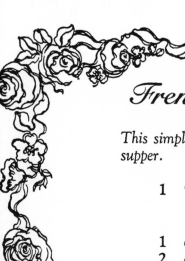

French Potato Pie with Cheese & Chives

This simple little homey dish is wholesome and very satisfying for a light lunch or supper.

1   9-inch deep dish frozen pie shell, baked in a 400° oven for
    about 10 minutes or until very lightly browned

1   cup mashed potatoes (can use instant mashed potatoes)
2   cups non-fat cottage cheese
1/4   cup low-fat cream cheese (2 ounces)
2   eggs
1/2   cup low-fat sour cream
1/3   cup grated Parmesan cheese
1/3   cup chopped chives
1   tablespoon chopped parsley
    salt and pepper to taste

Prepare pie shell. Combine the remaining ingredients and beat until thoroughly blended. Pour mixture into prepared pie shell and place on a cookie sheet. Sprinkle top with a little additional grated Parmesan cheese.

Bake in a 350° oven for about 40 to 45 minutes or until top is golden brown. Serves 6.

Quiche with Spinach Souffle & Cheese

1   9-inch deep dish frozen pie shell, baked in a 400° oven for
    about 10 minutes or until very lightly browned

1   package (10 ounces) frozen chopped spinach, defrosted
1/2   cup low-fat cream cheese (4 ounces), at room temperature
1/2   cup milk
2   eggs
1/3   cup fresh bread crumbs
1/2   cup grated Parmesan cheese
1/3   cup finely chopped green onions
    pinch nutmeg
    salt and pepper to taste

Prepare pie shell. Combine the remaining ingredients and beat until thoroughly blended.

Pour mixture into the prepared pie shell and place pan on a cookie sheet. Bake in a 350° oven for 45 minutes or until filling is set and top is golden. Serves 6.

Crustless Tart with Tomatoes & Goat Cheese

Goat cheese (Chevre) is somewhat like Feta cheese (made from sheep's milk). It is intensely flavorful and very popular. Here it is paired with tomatoes, onions and herbs for a delicious tart that serves well for lunch or brunch.

1	can (1 pound) stewed tomatoes, chopped. Do not drain.
1	onion, minced
2	shallots, minced
1	clove garlic, minced
1	tablespoon lemon juice
1/2	teaspoon sweet basil flakes
	pepper to taste
4	eggs, beaten with
1	tablespoon chopped parsley leaves
1/4	cup crumbled goat cheese (2 ounces)

In an uncovered saucepan, simmer together first group of ingredients for 20 minutes, or until onion is soft. If most of the juice has not evaporated, cook over high heat until very little liquid remains. Of course, watch carefully not to scorch. Allow to cool for about 5 minutes.

Stir in the beaten eggs and place mixture into a lightly oiled 9-inch quiche pan. Sprinkle top with cheese. Bake at 350-degrees for about 20 minutes, or until eggs are set. Serve with a vegetable salad. Serves 6.

Artichoke, Tomato & Chevre Cheese Pie

1	deep dish 9-inch frozen pie shell
1	jar (6 ounces) marinated artichoke hearts, drained and cut into small pieces. Reserve the marinade for another use.
1/3	cup chopped chives
4	ounces Chevre cheese, diced
2	eggs
1	cup milk
2	tablespoons grated Parmesan
6	thin tomato slices to lay on top
1	tablespoon grated Parmesan

Place pie shell on a cookie sheet. Place artichokes, chives and cheese evenly into pie shell. Beat together eggs, milk and Parmesan until blended and pour evenly into the pie shell. Lay the tomatoes slices on the top and sprinkle with the Parmesan. Bake at 350° for 45 minutes, or until custard is set. Serves 6.

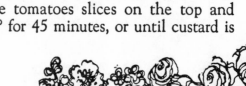

Puff Pastry Pie with Feta, Sun-Dried Tomatoes & Olives

This extravagantly attractive and delicious pie will earn you a reputation as an inventive cook. It should be assembled in advance and baked before serving. To scallop the edge, simply place one index finger on the rim and with the other finger, push dough toward center, about 1/2-inch down. Continue around the edge. This will create an attractive scalloped border.

1	package (6) frozen patty shells, defrosted in refrigerator

1	package (8 ounces) low-fat cream cheese
1	cup (4 ounces) Feta cheese, mashed
1/4	cup packed-in-oil sun-dried tomatoes, chopped and drained
1/4	cup chopped chives
3	tablespoons sliced black olive rings
1/3	cup fresh bread crumbs

Topping:
1	tablespoon grated Parmesan cheese
1	tablespoon sesame seeds

Stack 3 patty shells together and roll them out to measure 8-inches. Place pastry on a lightly greased cookie sheet. Stir together next 6 ingredients until thoroughly blended and place in center of the pastry, leaving a 1-inch border along the edge.

Roll out the remaining shells in the same fashion and place over the filling. Press and seal the edges with the tines of a fork. Scallop the edges in a decorative fashion. Pierce the top in several places with the tines of a fork, brush top with a little water and sprinkle top with Parmesan and sesame seeds. (Can be held at this point in the refrigerator.)

Bake at 400° for about 25 minutes, or until top is a deep golden brown. Place on a platter and cut into wedges to serve. Serves 6.

French Tomato & Cheese Pie

This is a pizza, made into a real pie. Nice to serve and fun to eat.

1   9-inch deep dish frozen pie shell, defrosted. Carefully lift pie shell and place it into a 10-inch quiche pan. Pat it down to fit.

1   can (1 pound) stewed tomatoes, drained and finely chopped
1/4 pound mushrooms, thinly sliced
1   cup grated Swiss cheese (3 ounces)
1   tablespoon chopped parsley
1/4 teaspoon each basil and thyme flakes
1/2 cup grated Parmesan cheese

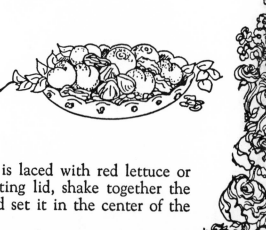

Toppings:
    sliced olives, thinnest onion ring slices or capers to taste

Bake pie shell in a 400° oven for about 10 minutes or until lightly browned. Combine the next group of ingredients and toss to mix well. Spread these evenly into the prepared shell. Place olives, onion rings or capers to taste on top. Bake in a 350° oven until cheeses are melted and top is lightly browned, about 15 to 20 minutes. Serves 6.

Steamed Vegetables with Honey Mustard Sauce

Steamed vegetables take on a totally different character when dipped in this very pleasant sauce. Carrots, broccoli, and cauliflower are good choices.

2   bags (1 pound, each) Del Sol Vegetables, a combination of carrots, broccoli and cauliflower. These are excellent as the carrots are cut into sticks and the broccoli and cauliflower are trimmed right down to the florets. Plunge vegetables in boiling water for 3 minutes, and drain.

Honey Mustard Sauce:
  2   tablespoons Dijon mustard
  2   tablespoons oil
1/4 cup seasoned rice vinegar
1/4 cup honey
1/4 cup chopped chives
  3   tablespoons water

Encircle the vegetables on a large platter that is laced with red lettuce or butter lettuce leaves. In a jar with a tight-fitting lid, shake together the sauce ingredients, place it in a lovely bowl, and set it in the center of the platter. Serves 12 as an hors d'oeuvre.

Bread & Cheese Dumplings with Fresh Tomato Sauce

This is a rather unusual small entree or first course. Plump little cheese dumplings, with a hint of tomato sauce, is a first cousin to Mozzarella Marinara, but better to my taste. Normally deep-fried, these are baked, eliminating excessive oil. Dumpling can be shaped earlier in the day and baked before serving. Sauce can be prepared earlier in the day and stored in the refrigerator.

8 slices stale white bread, soaked in cold water and squeezed dry
2 eggs, beaten
1/4 pound Swiss cheese, grated
1/3 cup grated Parmesan cheese
1/4 cup minced green onions
1 teaspoon minced parsley

Stir together all the ingredients until nicely blended. Shape mixture into 3/4-inch balls and flatten to form patties. Place on an oiled non-stick baking sheet, brush dumplings very lightly with oil and bake at 350-degrees until firm and browned. Serve with a spoonful of Fresh Tomato Sauce on top. Yields 16 dumplings.

Fresh Tomato Sauce:
2 tomatoes, peeled, seeded and very finely chopped
2 green onions, minced
1 tablespoon minced parsley
1 teaspoon red wine vinegar
1 teaspoon minced fresh basil
faint sprinkle of cayenne pepper

In a glass bowl, stir together all the ingredients until blended. Refrigerate. Bring to room temperature before serving. Yields about 2/3 cup sauce.

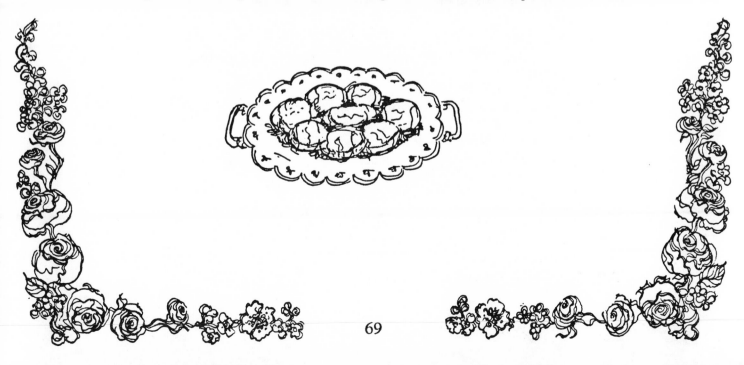

Mozzarella Puffs with Marinara Sauce

This savory hors d'oeuvre, sparkled with cheese, is just delicious with the Marinara Sauce. It has a little "bite" with the addition of cayenne pepper.

1	cup milk
1/4	cup butter (1/2 stick)
1	cup flour
4	eggs
1/2	cup grated Parmesan cheese
1/4	cup chopped chives
1	tablespoon chopped parsley
	pinch of salt

Filling:
   8   ounces grated Mozzarella cheese

In a saucepan, bring milk and butter to a boil. Add the flour, all at once, and cook, stirring, until dough forms a ball, and leaves the side of the pan, about 2 minutes. Place dough in the large bowl of an electric mixer and beat in eggs, one at a time, beating well after each addition. Beat in the remaining ingredients until blended.

Drop batter, by the tablespoonful, onto a greased non-stick baker, and bake at 350° until puffed and golden brown. Time will depend on the size of the puffs. Can be held at this point.

Before serving, place puffs on a cookie sheet and split in half. Place a little of the Mozzarella cheese in the center and reset the tops. Heat in a 350° oven until heated through and cheese is melted. Serve warm with Marinara Sauce, on the side, for dipping.

Marinara Sauce:

1	can (1 pound 12 ounces) crushed tomatoes in tomato puree
1	teaspoon sugar
1	tablespoon oil
2	tablespoons instant onion flakes
1 1/2	teaspoons Italian Herb Seasoning
1/4	teaspoon garlic powder
	small pinch of cayenne pepper
	salt and pepper to taste

Combine all the ingredients and simmer sauce for 10 minutes.

Spinach & Ricotta Dumplings with Yogurt, Lemon & Chive Sauce

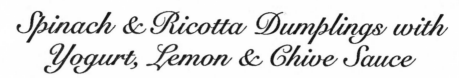

1   package (10 ounces) frozen chopped spinach, defrosted. Place
      spinach in a strainer and press out excess liquid.
1/2 cup low-fat Ricotta cheese
1   egg, beaten
1/3 cup grated Parmesan cheese
1/4 cup Ritz cracker crumbs (4 crackers)

In a large bowl, stir together all the ingredients until nicely blended. Divide mixture into 16 balls and flatten them slightly to form patties about 1/2-inch thick. Heat a lightly oiled non-stick skillet and cook dumplings until they are firm and browned on both sides. This will take about 15 minutes. (Important to use a non-stick skillet or dumpling will stick to the pan and you will wish you never started the whole thing.)

Serve warm with a spoonful of Yogurt Lemon & Chive Sauce (optional). Yields 16 dumplings and will serve 4 as a first course or 2 as a main course.

Yogurt, Lemon & Chive Sauce:
1/2 cup unflavored non-fat yogurt
1   tablespoon lemon juice
2   tablespoons chopped chives
1/4 teaspoon dried dill weed

Stir together all the ingredients until blended. Yields 1/3 cup.

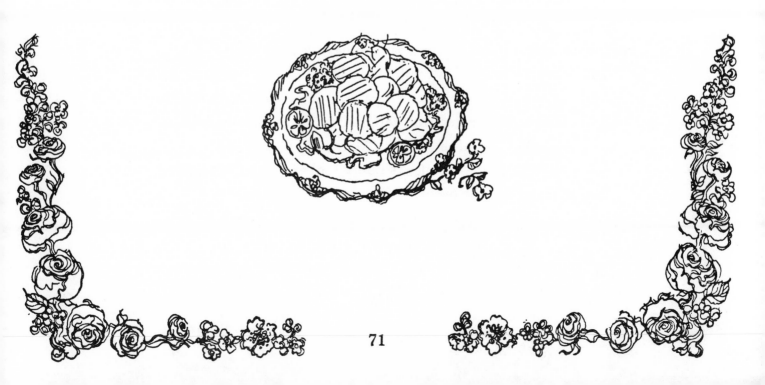

Petite Sandwiches with Brie & Berries

These are nice for brunch or tea. They can be adapted to accompany soups or salads. Use a good quality, dense, thinly sliced white bread. Using the large 12x16-inch Teflon-coated electric griddle is especially helpful as it can prepare 30 or more little sandwiches at the same time. There are an infinite number of combinations you can use. Listed below are just a few of them. Make certain the cheese and the fruits are very thinly sliced and the nuts are finely ground. Several of these can also be served cold, in which case, they can be prepared earlier in the day, place on a platter and tightly wrapped with double-thicknesses of plastic wrap.

> 1   package (1 pound) thinly sliced white bread (about 30 slices). Remove the crusts and cut each slice into hearts, rounds, squares or triangles. Or use any shape cutter that enhances the season or occasion.

> 1   pound firm brie, rind removed and cut into very thin slices
> 1   basket strawberries, hulled and cut into thin slices
> 1/2   cup finely chopped toasted pecans

1. Place a little brie, a slice or two of strawberries and a faint sprinkle of pecans on bread cut-outs.

2. Cover with another similar cut of bread. Place sandwiches on a large buttered griddle and cook until bottoms are lightly browned. Turn and brown the other sides. Serve immediately.

Variations:

1. St. André with Raspberries (hot or cold)
2. Camembert with Chopped Raisins, Apricots or other dried fruit (hot or cold)
3. Blue cheese with thinly-sliced Figs, dried Cranberries or other dried fruit (hot or cold)
4. Cream Cheese and Papaya Chutney (cold)
5. Cream Cheese with Fresh Herbs (cold)
6. Cream Cheese flavored with a little sugar and lemon (cold)
7. Gorgonzola Cheese with thinly-sliced Pears (hot or cold)
8. Caponata (4-ounce can) and Mozzarella Cheese (hot)
9. Mild diced Green Chiles (4 ounce can) and Jack Cheese (hot)
10. Caramelized Onions with Gruyere Cheese (hot)

To Caramelize Onions:
In a skillet, over low heat, sauté together 1 finely chopped large onion, 1 teaspoon sugar, 1 tablespoon butter and salt to taste. Stir every now and again, until onion is very soft and darkened, but not fried, about 30 minutes.

American Blinis with Golden Caviar & Creme Fraiche

I call these "American" because they are made with white flour instead of the usual buckwheat. These are interesting little rounds of dough and deeply flavorful and aromatic. Serve them with a dollop of Creme Fraiche and a dot of caviar on top. A faint sprinkle of chopped chives or dill is very nice, also. Serve these warm. They can be prepared in advance and heated before serving.

1	package (1/4 ounce) dry yeast
1/2	teaspoon sugar
1/3	cup warm water (105°)
2 1/4	cups flour
1 3/4	cups warm milk (105°)
1	egg, beaten
1	teaspoon sugar
1/4	teaspoon salt
4	tablespoons butter, melted and cooled
1/4	cup water

Toppings:
2/3	cup Creme Fraiche
3	ounces golden caviar
	finely minced chives and/or dill weed

In a small bowl, stir together yeast, sugar and water and set aside for 10 minutes. Yeast should start to bubble and foam, and if it does not, yeast is not active and should be discarded. This is called "proofing" the yeast.

In the large bowl of an electric mixer, beat together next 6 ingredients until blended. Add the proofed yeast and beat for 1 minute. Cover bowl with plastic wrap and refrigerate for several hours or overnight. When ready to cook blini, stir in the remaining 1/4 cup water.

On a hot and buttered griddle, for each blini, spoon 1 tablespoon of batter. (This will produce a 2-inch blini.) Cook until bottoms are browned, about 1 minute. Turn and brown other side about 1/2 minute. Place blinis in a 9x13-inch baking pan while you continue with the rest of the batter. Cover pan tightly with foil and refrigerate until serving time.

To serve, heat blinis in a 350° oven until warm, not hot, about 5 minutes. Serve with a dollop of Creme Fraiche, a bit of caviar and an optional sprinkle of chives or dill. Yields 48 blinis.

To make Creme Fraiche:
Stir together 1/3 cup half and half and 1/3 cup low-fat sour cream until blended. Cover bowl with plastic wrap and refrigerate until serving time. Yields 2/3 cup.

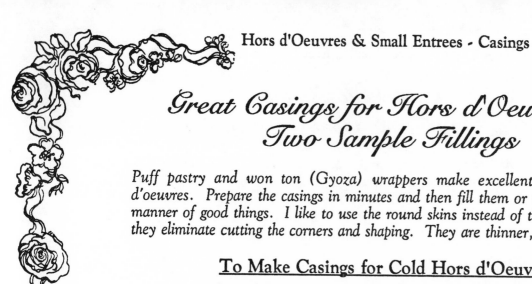

Great Casings for Hors d'Oeuvres & Two Sample Fillings

Puff pastry and won ton (Gyoza) wrappers make excellent casings for hors d'oeuvres. Prepare the casings in minutes and then fill them or top them with any manner of good things. I like to use the round skins instead of the square ones, as they eliminate cutting the corners and shaping. They are thinner, so handle gently.

To Make Casings for Cold Hors d'Oeuvres

1   package (10 ounces) round (Gyoza) skins, about 60 skins

Lightly grease a mini-muffin tin (with 12 or 24 molds) with butter or margarine. Gently separate the skins and ease them into each mold, spreading the sides to form a cup. Bake at 350° for 5 to 6 minutes, or until lightly browned and crisp. Continue with remaining skins. Can be held at this point at room temperature. Fill with desired filling and serve.

Sample Filling:
4   ounces feta cheese or goat cheese, at room temperature
4   ounces low-fat cream cheese, at room temperature
1   tablespoon lemon juice

3   tablespoons minced chives
3   tablespoons minced sun-dried tomatoes or minced olives or
       minced fresh tomatoes

Beat together first 3 ingredients until blended. Stir in chives and optional filling. Place a teaspoon of filling into each casing and sprinkle tops with a few minced chives. Will fill 36 casings.

To Make Pastry Bases for Hot Hors d'Oeuvres

1   frozen puff pastry sheet (about 8 ounces) defrosted
       in the refrigerator

Lightly grease a 10x15-inch jelly-roll pan with butter or margarine. On a floured board, roll out the puff pastry to measure about 12x12-inches. Cut rounds, hearts, triangles with a biscuit cutter and place them on the prepared baking pan. Place a little topping in the center of each and bake at 400° for about 20 minutes, or until nicely browned. Yields 16 pastry bases.

Sample Topping, Baby Pizzas:
16   teaspoons grated Mozzarella cheese
16   teaspoons pizza sauce

Sprinkle tops of rounds with a little Mozzarella cheese and a teaspoon of Pizza Sauce over the cheese.

Salads

&

Dressings

Antipasto Salad with Herbs & Cheese Dressing

Salad:
Depending on the number of people you are serving, use lettuce, tomatoes, sliced mushrooms, black pitted olives, sliced Mozzarella cheese, garbanzos, artichoke hearts, or any blanched (not raw) vegetable, in any combination or quantity.

Place the salad on a large platter in a decorative fashion. Do not toss, but set the ingredients individually, varying the colors and textures. Drizzle with a little dressing and pass the remaining dressing at the table.

Herb & Cheese Dressing:
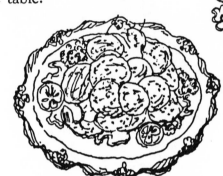

    1   cup tomato juice
    1/4   cup grated Parmesan cheese
    1/4   cup oil
    1/4   cup lemon juice
    1/8   teaspoon garlic powder
    1   teaspoon oregano flakes
    1   teaspoon sweet basil flakes
            salt and pepper to taste

Combine all the dressing ingredients in a glass jar with a tight-fitting lid and shake until blended. Store in the refrigerator for several hours before using. Dressing will last for 2 weeks in the refrigerator. Yields about 2 cups.

Black Bean Tomato Salad & Dip

    1   can (1 pound) black beans, rinsed and drained
    2   large tomatoes, seeded and finely chopped
    1/2   medium red onion, minced (about 6 tablespoons)
    2   cloves garlic, put through a press
    2   tablespoons olive oil
    4   tablespoons lemon juice
    4   tablespoons minced parsley leaves
            pinch of cayenne pepper

In a glass bowl, stir together all the ingredients. Cover bowl and refrigerate for several hours. Serve with Pita Pockets to scoop up the dip. Serves 6.

Pita Pockets:
Do not separate pita halves. With kitchen shears, cut each pita into 6 wedges. Each wedge will open to form a scoop, making dipping easy. Pitas should be served fresh and soft...and should not be toasted.

Antipasto Salad with Artichokes & Peppers

1   jar (7 ounces) marinated artichoke hearts, cut into fourths. Do not drain.
2   marinated red peppers, cut into thin strips
1/4   pound Provolone cheese, sliced and cut into thin strips
1/4   cup black olives, pitted and sliced
1   tomato, chopped
1/2   small red onion, very thinly sliced
1/2   cup garbanzos, drained
1/2   cup kidney beans, drained

In a large bowl, place all the ingredients. Add Lemon Vinaigrette Dressing to taste and toss to blend. Allow to marinate in the refrigerator for 2 to 3 hours. Serve on a bed of shredded lettuce with Cheese Toast. Serves 6 to 8.

Lemon Vinaigrette Dressing:
1/3   cup olive oil
1/3   cup lemon juice
2   tablespoons red wine vinegar
1/4   teaspoon oregano flakes
1/4   teaspoon sweet basil flakes
1   clove garlic, minced
1/4   cup minced green onions
1   tablespoon minced parsley leaves
   salt and freshly ground pepper to taste

Combine all the ingredients in a jar with a tight-fitting lid and shake to blend. Store unused dressing in the refrigerator. Yields about 1 cup.

Cheese Toast:
On the diagonal, cut Italian baguette into 1/4-inch slices. Spread a thin coat of butter on each slice and sprinkle generously with grated Parmesan cheese. Place bread on a cookie sheet and cover securely with foil. Before serving, remove foil and broil for about a minute to brown the cheese. Allow at least 2 slices per serving.

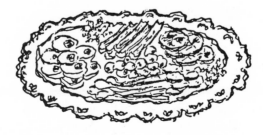

Oven-Roasted Tomato Salad with Garlic & Parmesan

This is one of the most beautiful and delicious salads. It can be served with diagonals of toasted Italian bread as a salad, or it adds a wonderful flavor when served in sandwiches.

6   Italian plum tomatoes, cut into 1/2-inch slices sprinkled
      with garlic powder to taste

1/3   cup chopped chives
  2   tablespoons grated Parmesan cheese
1/2   teaspoon, each, sweet basil flakes and oregano
  2   tablespoons oil
  2   tablespoons red wine vinegar

Place the tomato slices in one layer in an 8x12-inch roasting pan and bake at 325° for 45 minutes, or until tomatoes are still intact but beginning to shrink. Place tomatoes in a rimmed serving platter. Sprinkle with chives, cheese and herbs. Drizzle with oil and vinegar. Refrigerate for several hours. Serve as part of an antipasto, with toasted diagonals of Italian bread or as a topping for sandwiches. Yields 24 slices.

Roasted Red & Yellow Peppers with Red Onions

2   red peppers, cored and cut into 1-inch slices
2   yellow peppers, cored and cut into 1-inch slices
1   small red onion, peeled and cut into 1/4-inch rings
1   tablespoon olive oil

1   tablespoon vinegar
1   tablespoon lemon juice
1/4   cup minced chives
1/2   teaspoon, each, sweet basil flakes and oregano flakes
      salt and pepper to taste

In a 9x13-inch baking pan, place peppers and onion and drizzle them with oil. Cover pan with foil and bake at 350° for 20 minutes. Remove foil and continue baking for 15 or 20 minutes, or until vegetables are tender. Broil for a few seconds so that vegetables are flecked with brown.

Place vegetables in a rimmed serving platter and sprinkle with the remaining ingredients. Refrigerate until serving time. Serves 4 to 6.

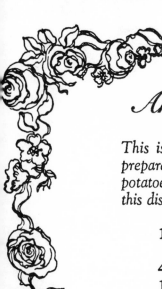

Artichoke, Red Pepper & Potato Salad

This is one of the most beautiful salads. It is equally delicious. This can be prepared from scratch by steaming frozen artichokes, fresh red peppers and baby potatoes. It is certainly much easier using the prepared ingredients, so remember this dish on a night when you are running late.

1 jar (6 ounces) marinated artichokes, cut into fourths. Do not drain.
4 marinated red peppers, cut into strips
1 can (1 pound) sliced potatoes, rinsed and drained
1/3 cup chopped green onions
1 tablespoon reserved artichoke marinade
4 tablespoons lemon juice

In a bowl, toss together first 4 ingredients until nicely mixed. Add the remaining ingredients and toss to blend. Cover bowl with plastic wrap and refrigerate until about 20 minutes before serving. Serve mildly chilled, but not straight from the refrigerator. Serves 6.

Provençal Salad with Marinated Tomatoes, Onions & Olives

1 pound tomatoes, cut into 1/4-inch slices
1/2 medium red onion, very thinly sliced and separated into rings
1 can (2 ounces) sliced black olives
2 tablespoons chopped parsley leaves
4 ounces crumbled feta or goat cheese

Dressing:
1/4 cup olive oil
1/4 cup white wine vinegar
1/4 cup grated Parmesan cheese
1 clove garlic, minced
    salt and pepper to taste

1/2 cup garlic croutons. (Use the croutons that resemble pennies.)

In a bowl, toss together salad ingredients. In a glass jar with a tight-fitting lid, shake together dressing ingredients and pour over the salad. Cover bowl and refrigerate for several hours. Just before serving, toss garlic croutons into the salad. Serves 6.

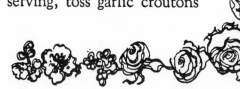

Florentine Bread
& Herbed Tomato Salad
(Bruschetta)

This is one of the easiest salads to prepare and one of the best, too. It is an excellent first course to an Italian feast. Prepare the salad earlier in the day and toss in the bread before serving. A good quality garlic crouton can be substituted for the bread, but it is better, made with fresh Italian bread.

3	large tomatoes, seeded and chopped
3	cloves garlic, mashed
3	tablespoons lemon juice
1	tablespoon olive oil
1	tablespoon chopped fresh basil leaves
	salt and pepper to taste

6   1/2-inch thick slices lightly toasted Italian bread,
    cut into 1/2-inch cubes (about 4 cups). Bread should
    still be a little soft in the center.

In a bowl, stir together first group of ingredients until blended. Cover bowl and refrigerate for several hours. Just before serving, toss in the bread. Serves 6.

Red Cabbage with Apples, Raisins
& Honey Dressing

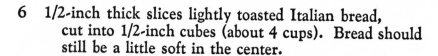

This delicious salad is excellent served either hot or cold. If served warm, Potato Onion & Apple Pancakes is a nice accompaniment.

1	medium head red cabbage (about 1 to 1 1/4 pounds), shredded
3/4	cup apple juice
	salt to taste
2	apples, peeled, cored and thinly sliced
1/2	cup yellow raisins
3	tablespoons cider vinegar
4	tablespoons honey
1	tablespoon oil

In a Dutch oven casserole, place cabbage, apple juice and salt and simmer mixture for 15 minutes. Add the remaining ingredients and continue simmering for 30 minutes, or until cabbage and apples are tender and most of the liquid is absorbed. Refrigerate until serving time and heat before serving. Serves 6.

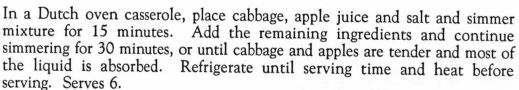

Bean Salad with Italian Herb Dressing

This is a nice salad to serve for a backyard picnic or barbecue. It is an easy salad to prepare, and may be prepared the day before serving. Unused dressing can be stored for 1 week in the refrigerator.

Bean Salad:
- 1   can (15 ounces) garbanzo beans, rinsed and drained
- 1   can (15 ounces) red kidney beans, rinsed and drained
- 1/2   cup finely chopped green onions
- 1/4   cup chopped red onions

Italian Herb Dressing:
- 1/4   cup oil
- 1/4   cup red wine vinegar
- 1   shallot, minced
- 1   teaspoon oregano flakes
- 1   teaspoon sweet basil flakes
- 1/4   teaspoon thyme flakes
- 2   cloves garlic, put through a press
  - salt and freshly ground pepper to taste

In a bowl, toss beans and onions. Combine dressing ingredients in a glass jar with a tight-fitting lid and shake vigorously until blended. Pour dressing to taste over the beans and toss to combine. Cover bowl and refrigerate until ready to serve. Serves 8.

White Bean Salad with Tomatoes & Scallions

- 1   can (15 ounces) Great Northern beans, rinsed and drained
- 1/2   cup sliced cherry tomatoes, seeded
- 1/4   cup minced red onions
- 1/3   cup minced green onions (scallions)
- 1   clove garlic, minced
- 1/4   cup seasoned rice vinegar
- 1   teaspoon olive oil
- 1   teaspoon Italian Herb Seasoning flakes
  - pepper to taste

In a bowl, stir together all the ingredients, cover bowl and refrigerate for several hours, stirring from time to time. Nice salad to serve on a buffet or part of an antipasto. Serves 6.

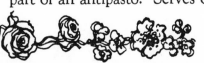

Confetti Cole Slaw in Horseradish Vinaigrette

1   small head cabbage, a little under 1 pound, (cored and grated)
2   carrots, peeled and grated
1/3 chopped green onions
1/2 red bell pepper, chopped
1   teaspoon sugar
3   tablespoons vinegar

2   tablespoons prepared horseradish
1/4 cup buttermilk
1/4 cup low-fat mayonnaise
     salt and pepper to taste

In a large bowl, stir together first 6 ingredients and allow mixture to stand for 10 minutes. Stir together the remaining ingredients until blended and pour over cabbage mixture, tossing until everything is nicely combined. Cover bowl and refrigerate until ready to serve. Serves 8.

Note: -Can be prepared up to 4 hours earlier. Do not prepare 1 day earlier, as cabbage renders a good deal of liquid.

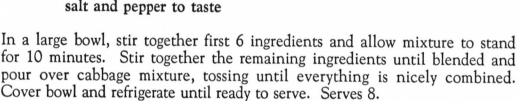

Cole Slaw with Pineapple & Raisins

This is a lovely salad to serve on a buffet, for the colors are so inviting. Basically, it is a subtle sweet and sour dressing. Toss this shortly before serving, as cabbage can render a good deal of liquid.

1   small head cabbage, grated, about 6 cups
6   medium carrots, grated, about 3 cups
1   red bell pepper, cored, seeded and finely chopped
1   cup chopped green onions
1/2 cup yellow raisins

1   cup drained unsweetened crushed pineapple
1/4 cup lemon juice
1/2 cup low-calorie mayonnaise

In a bowl, toss together first 5 ingredients. Stir together the remaining ingredients in a jar, with a tight-fitting lid. Shortly before serving, pour dressing over the vegetables and toss until salad is nicely coated. Refrigerate until serving time. Serves 12.

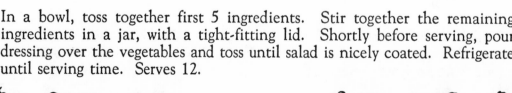

Asparagus Vinaigrette with Cheese & Chives

1   pound asparagus. Trim off the tough bottoms and if the
      asparagus is thick-skinned, peel it with a vegetable peeler.
3   tablespoons vegetable broth
3   tablespoons white wine vinegar

3   tablespoons chopped chives
2   tablespoons grated Parmesan cheese

In a large covered skillet, cook asparagus in broth and vinegar until
asparagus is tender, about 4 to 5 minutes. Sprinkle with chives and cheese
and refrigerate until serving time. Before serving sprinkle with a little
parsley. A few toasted pine nuts are excellent but optional. Serves 4 to 6.

Baby Carrot Salad with Honey Dill Vinaigrette

*Now that fresh baby carrots can be found in most supermarkets, it isn't necessary
anymore, to purchase the frozen ones. This is a beautiful light salad, bright orange
flecked with green, and contains no oil. Of course, using fresh dill is better, but, in
its absence, dried dill weed is very acceptable.*

1   pound fresh baby carrots, cooked in boiling water
      for 6 minutes and thoroughly drained

Honey Dill Vinaigrette:
   1/4   cup honey
   1/4   cup seasoned rice vinegar
   1/4   cup water
     1   tablespoon sugar
   1/2   cup finely chopped green onions
     3   tablespoons chopped parsley leaves
   1/2   teaspoon dried dill weed (or 1 tablespoon fresh dill)

Place carrots in a plastic bowl with a tight-fitting lid. Stir together the
vinaigrette ingredients and pour over the carrots. Toss to combine carrots
with the dressing. Cover bowl and refrigerate for several hours or overnight.
Every so often, give the bowl a shake or two to distribute the dressing. Drain
to serve. Serves 6.

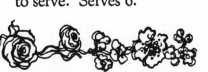

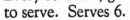

Corn Salad with Red Peppers & Cilantro

Corn salads are becoming more and more popular lately. This colorful salad is lovely to serve on a buffet.

- 3 packages (10 ounces, each) frozen corn
- 1 marinated red pepper, cut into small dice
- 1/4 cup chopped chives
- 2 tablespoons finely chopped cilantro
- 1 tablespoon chopped parsely leaves
- 3 tablespoons seasoned rice vinegar
- 1 tablespoon lemon juice
  pepper to taste

Cook the corn for 2 minutes in a saucepan and drain. In a large bowl, place the corn with the remaining ingredients and toss to blend. Refrigerate until serving time. Serves 6.

Wilted Cucumber Salad with Chives & Dill

- 2 long hot-house cucumbers, peeled. Scrape out the seeds with a spoon and cut into 1/4-inch slices.
- 1 cup dry white wine
  salt to taste

Dressing:
- 1/4 cup white vinegar
- 1/4 cup water
- 2 tablespoons sugar
- 1 teaspoon dried dill weed
- 1/4 cup chopped chives

In a saucepan, simmer together first 3 ingredients for 20 minutes, or until cucumber slices are wilted. Thoroughly drain the cucumbers and place into a bowl. Allow to cool and then refrigerate.

In a glass jar, stir together the Dressing ingredients until sugar is dissolved and then refrigerate. Two hours before serving, pour dressing over the cucumbers and refrigerate until serving time. Serves 6.

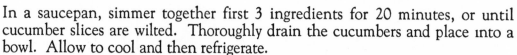

Hungarian Cucumber Salad

I like to add the vinaigrette just before serving, as the cucumbers have a tendency to render a great deal of liquid which dilutes the dressing. Drain the cucumbers before serving and add dressing to taste.

Vinaigrette Dressing:
- 1/3 cup white vinegar
- 3 tablespoons water
- 2 tablespoons sugar

Cucumber Salad:
- 6 large cucumbers, peeled and sliced very thin
- 1/2 cup minced green onions
- 2 teaspoons dried dill weed
- salt to taste

In a glass jar with a tight-fitting lid, stir together vinegar, water and sugar until sugar is dissolved. In a large bowl, place the salad ingredients. Before serving, drain thoroughly and add Vinaigrette to taste. Serves 12.

Cucumber Salad with Currants & Peanuts

- 2 large cucumbers, peeled and thinly sliced

Vinaigrette:
- 2 tablespoons water
- 2 tablespoons vinegar
- 2 teaspoons sugar
- salt and pepper to taste

- 1/4 cup dried currants
- 1/4 cup chopped roasted peanuts

Place cucumbers in a covered bowl and refrigerate for several hours. In a glass jar shake together next 5 ingredients until sugar is dissolved. Before serving, remove cucumbers from the refrigerator and drain thoroughly. Toss with the Vinaigrette and sprinkle with currants and peanuts. Serves 6.

Tomato, Eggplant & Pepper Salad with Tomato Vinaigrette Dressing

1 eggplant, (about 1 pound), sliced. Do not peel.
1 yellow bell pepper, seeded and cut into strips
1 red bell pepper, seeded and cut into strips
1 tablespoon oil

1 small red onion, cut into the thinnest slices
1/3 cup chopped parsley leaves
4 tomatoes, peeled and sliced

Tomato Vinaigrette Dressing

In a 9x13-inch pan, drizzle eggplant and peppers with the oil. Cover the pan tightly with foil and bake in a 400° oven for about 20 to 30 minutes or until vegetables are tender.

In a large bowl, layer eggplant and pepper slices with onion, parsley and tomatoes. Pour Tomato Vinaigrette Dressing to taste over the top and refrigerate salad for several hours to allow flavors to blend. Serves 8.

Tomato Vinaigrette Dressing:
    1/2 cup tomato juice
    1/3 cup oil
    1/2 cup red wine vinegar
    2 cloves garlic, minced
    1 teaspoon dried oregano leaves
    1/4 cup chopped green onions
    1 teaspoon Dijon mustard

Combine all the ingredients in a jar with a tight-fitting lid and shake until blended.

Note: -Salad can be prepared 1 day earlier and stored in the refrigerator.
       -Dressing can be prepared 3 days earlier and stored in the refrigerator

Eggplant & Mozzarella Salad
with Peppers & Tomatoes

1   can (1 pound) stewed tomatoes, finely chopped. Do not drain.
1   eggplant, peeled and sliced
1   yellow bell pepper, cut into strips
1   red bell pepper, cut into strips

1   package (6 ounces) Mozzarella cheese, grated
6   green onions, finely chopped

Dressing:
   1/4   cup oil
     3   tablespoons red wine vinegar
     3   tablespoons lemon juice
   1/4   cup grated Parmesan cheese
     1   teaspoon sweet basil flakes
        salt and pepper to taste

In a 9x13-inch pan, place first 4 ingredients. Cover pan tightly with foil and bake in a 400° oven for 30 minutes or until vegetables are soft. Allow to cool.

In a large bowl, toss vegetables with cheese and green onions. In a jar with a tight-fitting lid, shake together Dressing ingredients and pour it over the salad. Refrigerate for several hours to allow flavors to blend. Serves 8.

Honey Sesame Points:
     8   slices egg bread, crusts removed. Roll flat with a rolling pin
            and cut diagonally into 2 triangles.
     8   teaspoons butter, melted
     8   teaspoons honey
     4   teaspoons sesame seeds

Place prepared bread triangles on a buttered cookie sheet. Spread each bread slice with butter and honey and sprinkle with sesame seeds. Bake in a 350° oven until bread is crisped, about 3 minutes. Serves 8.

Herbed Eggplant with Tomatoes & Onions & Lemon Vinaigrette

This is excellent served hot as an accompaniment to dinner, or served cold as an antipasto or salad. It can be prepared several days earlier and stores well in the refrigerator.

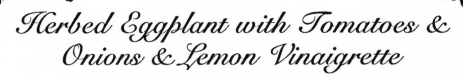

1 eggplant (about 1 pound). Remove peel, cut in half, lengthwise, and cut into 1/4-inch thick slices.
1 tablespoon oil
2 tablespoons lemon juice
4 cloves garlic, finely minced

1 can (1 pound) stewed tomatoes, drained and chopped
1 tablespoon sweet basil flakes
2 tablespoons chopped parsley leaves
1 onion, grated
3 tablespoons lemon juice
1 tablespoon oil
salt and pepper to taste

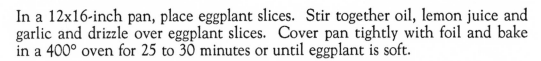

In a 12x16-inch pan, place eggplant slices. Stir together oil, lemon juice and garlic and drizzle over eggplant slices. Cover pan tightly with foil and bake in a 400° oven for 25 to 30 minutes or until eggplant is soft.

Meanwhile in a Dutch oven casserole, place the remaining ingredients and simmer mixture for 10 minutes. Add the eggplant and the juices in the pan, stir to combine and simmer mixture for another 10 minutes, uncovered. Can be served cold as a first course or part of an antipasto platter. Serves 6.

Green Pea, Pimiento & Green Onion Salad

2 packages (10 ounces, each) frozen petite sweet peas, cooked in boiling water for 2 minutes and drained.
1/3 cup finely chopped green onions
1 jar (2 ounces) slivered pimiento or marinated red peppers

Dressing:
1 tablespoon oil
4 tablespoons Seasoned Rice Vinegar
1 tablespoon grated Parmesan cheese
salt and pepper to taste

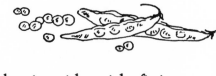

In a bowl, toss together first 3 ingredients. In a glass jar with a tight-fitting lid, shake together dressing ingredients until blended. Pour dressing over pea mixture, cover and refrigerate until serving time. This is delicious served warm or cold. Serves 8 to 10.

Mushroom Salad with Lemon & Garlic Dressing

Mushroom salads are always a delight to serve. This is a simple salad, delicate and delicious and mildly flavored with lemon juice. Unused dressing can be stored for 1 week in the refrigerator.

The Salad:

1	pound mushrooms, cleaned and thinly sliced
1/2	cup chopped chives

Lemon & Garlic Dressing:

1/4	cup olive oil
1/4	cup lemon juice
2	tablespoons chopped chives
2	cloves garlic, minced
1	teaspoon Dijon-style mustard
2	tablespoons grated Parmesan cheese
	salt and pepper to taste

In a bowl, place mushrooms and chives. Combine dressing ingredients in a glass jar with a tight-fitting lid and shake vigorously until blended. Pour dressing to taste over the mushrooms, cover bowl and refrigerate until ready to use. Serves 6.

Tomato, Mushroom & Mozzarella Salad

2	medium tomatoes, coarsely chopped
1/4	pound part-skim Mozzarella cheese, grated
1/2	pound mushrooms, sliced
1/4	cup chopped green onions
2	tablespoons chopped red onions
2	tablespoons grated Parmesan cheese
1	teaspoon oil
1/4	cup rice vinegar
	pepper to taste

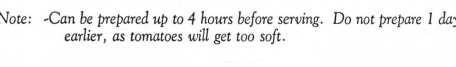

In a large bowl, toss together all the ingredients until nicely mixed. Cover bowl and refrigerate until ready to serve. Serves 8.

Note: -Can be prepared up to 4 hours before serving. Do not prepare 1 day earlier, as tomatoes will get too soft.

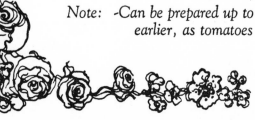

Mushrooms a la Grecque
with Garlic Lemon Dressing

1   pound mushrooms, cleaned and sliced

2   tablespoons oil
6   tablespoons lemon juice
2   cloves garlic, minced
2   green onions, finely chopped
1/2 teaspoon oregano flakes
1/4 teaspoon sweet basil flakes
    salt and pepper to taste

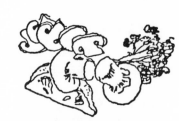

Place mushrooms in a bowl. Combine the remaining ingredients in a jar with a tight-fitting lid and shake until blended. Pour dressing to taste over the mushrooms. Unused dressing can be stored in the refrigerator. Yields about 1/2 cup dressing. Serves 6.

Mushroom, Artichoke & Tomato Salad
with Lemon Dijon Dressing

1   pound mushrooms, cleaned and sliced
4   tomatoes, peeled, seeded and cut into chunks
1   jar (7 ounces) marinated artichoke hearts, cut into fourths.
    Do not drain.
1/2 cup finely chopped green onions
2   tablespoons finely chopped parsley

6   tablespoons lemon juice
1   clove garlic, minced
1   teaspoon Dijon mustard
    salt and pepper to taste

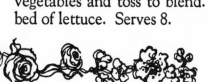

In a bowl toss together the first 5 ingredients until mixture is blended. Stir together the remaining ingredients until blended. Pour dressing over the vegetables and toss to blend. Refrigerate salad for several hours. Serve on a bed of lettuce. Serves 8.

Spanish Red Pepper Salad with Tomatoes & Raisins

If you are looking for a colorful and interesting salad, this is a good one to try. It is exceedingly simple to assemble when you use prepared marinated red peppers. Marinated red peppers usually come halved...sometimes quartered. You will need 4 whole peppers.

4	marinated red peppers, cut into thin strips
1	can (1 pound) stewed tomatoes, drained, seeded and chopped. Reserve juice for another use.
1/2	cup dark raisins
1/3	cup finely chopped green onions
1/3	cup seasoned rice vinegar
1	tablespoon oil
1	teaspoon sugar
	salt and pepper to taste

In a large bowl, toss together all the ingredients until thoroughly mixed. Cover bowl and refrigerate for several hours before serving. Serves 6.

Red & Yellow Pepper, Artichoke & Green Onion Salad

This is a beautiful salad, just bursting with color and excitement. Salad can be prepared earlier in the day and stored in the refrigerator. It can be served warm or chilled.

2	red bell peppers, cut into thin 1-inch strips
2	yellow bell peppers, cut into thin 1-inch strips
1	tablespoon olive oil
1	cup chopped green onions
2	jars (6 ounces, each) marinated artichoke hearts, cut into fourths. Do not drain.
3	tablespoons lemon juice
	salt and pepper to taste

In a skillet, saute together peppers in oil until peppers are tender. In a large bowl, toss together peppers and all the ingredients until nicely mixed. Cover bowl and refrigerate until serving time. Serves 8.

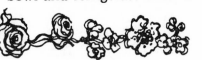

Baby Red Potato Salad

There is something so attractive when potato salad is made with baby red potatoes. The dressing is an old favorite.

2 1/2   pounds baby red potatoes, scrubbed and cooked, unpeeled, in boiling water until tender. Do not overcook. Drain potatoes and refrigerate until chilled.

   3   carrots, peeled and grated
1/3   cup finely minced red onion
   1   tablespoon sugar
   3   tablespoons lemon juice
   1   teaspoon dried dill weed
      salt and pepper to taste

3/4   cup low-fat mayonnaise

Cut potatoes into 1/4-inch wedges and place in a large bowl. Add the next 7 ingredients and toss potatoes to coat evenly. Allow mixture to rest for 10 minutes. Stir in mayonnaise until blended. Cover bowl and refrigerate. To serve, decorate platter with green onion frills and carrot curls. Serves 8.

Spinach, Mushroom & Red Onion Salad

   1   pound fresh spinach, stems removed. Wash spinach three times in a sinkful of water until every trace of sand is removed. Drain on paper towelling and tear into bite-size pieces.
1/2   pound mushrooms, stems removed, cleaned and thinly sliced
1/2   medium red onion, cut into very thin slices
   1   tomato, peeled, seeded and chopped
   2   shallots, minced
1/4   cup chopped chives

   2   tablespoons red wine vinegar
   2   tablespoons lemon juice
   2   tablespoons water
1 1/2   teaspoons olive oil
   2   teaspoons Dijon mustard

In a large bowl, toss together first 6 ingredients. Stir together remaining ingredients and toss into salad just before serving. Serves 4.

Tomatoes with Garlic Croutons & Parmesan

This is one of the most delicious and attractive salads. Use the best tomatoes you can find.

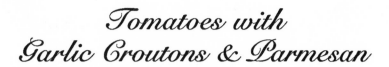

4	medium tomatoes, seeded and cut into 1/4-inch slices
1/4	cup garlic croutons crushed
1/4	cup chopped chives
2	tablespoons grated Parmesan cheese
2	tablespoons red wine vinegar
1	tablespoon water
1	teaspoon Italian Herb Seasoning flakes
1	teaspoon olive oil
	freshly ground black pepper

In a 10-inch round porcelain serving dish, lay tomato slices, overlapping, in a decorative fashion. Sprinkle with croutons, chives and Parmesan cheese. Stir together next 5 ingredients and drizzle evenly over all. Cover and refrigerate for several hours. Serves 6.

Salad of Tomatoes, Onions & Feta Cheese

1/2	large red onion, cut into very thin slices
2	tablespoons chopped parsley leaves
1	tablespoon grated Parmesan cheese
4	tablespoons rice vinegar
1	tablespoon water
3	large tomatoes, cut into 1/4-inch slices
4	ounces feta cheese, crumbled

In a large bowl, toss together first 5 ingredients, cover bowl and refrigerate for several hours or overnight. Place tomatoes on a platter, top with onions and vinegar mixture and sprinkle top with feta cheese. Serves 6.

Tabouleh-Bulgur Salad with Tomatoes, Onions & Lemon Vinaigrette

1 cup Bulgur, cracked wheat
2 cups water

1 cup chopped green onions (use the whole onion)
1 tomato, peeled, seeded and chopped
3 tablespoons chopped parsley
   salt and pepper to taste

1/4 cup olive oil
1/3 cup lemon juice
1 clove garlic, minced

In a saucepan, bring water to boil and slowly add the bulgur, while water continues boiling. Stir, lower heat and cover saucepan, and cook bulgur at a simmer, until liquid is absorbed, about 10 to 15 minutes. Continue cooking bulgur, stirring, for several minutes, so that grains become dry and fluff up.

Place bulgur into a deep bowl and allow to cool. Toss with the onions, tomato, parsley and seasonings. Shake together oil, lemon juice and garlic and pour dressing over salad. Serve on a bed of lettuce or in small bowls. Serves 6.

Oven Roasted Vegetable Salad with Garlic & Rosemary

2 onions, cut into 1/2 inch slices
1 sweet red bell pepper, seeded and cut into 1-inch wedges
1 green bell pepper, seeded and cut into 1-inch wedges
3 carrots, peeled and cut on the diagonal into 1/2-inch slices
6 small baby potatoes, scrubbed and cut into halves
2 teaspoons dried rosemary, crushed
   salt and pepper to taste
2 tablespoons olive oil
2 tablespoons lemon juice

In a 9x13-inch baking pan, toss together all the ingredients until nicely mixed. Cover pan with foil and bake in a 350° oven for 30 to 40 minutes or until vegetables are tender. Remove foil, toss vegetables and broil, 4-inches from the heat, turning now and again, until vegetables are nicely flecked with brown. Sprinkle with additional lemon juice to taste. Serve with lemon wedges on the side and garnish with chopped parsley leaves and chives. Serves 6.

Kasha Salad with Tomatoes, Cucumbers & Lemon Vinaigrette
(Cracked Wheat Salad)

Looking for a healthy salad, that is also delicious? Well, here's one to consider. This can also be prepared with cooked vegetables. You can use any number of cooked vegetables, carrots, peas, broccoli florets, cauliflower florets, etc.. Kasha has a way of soaking up the dressing, so, add dressing to taste.

1 1/2	cups kasha (cracked wheat)
3	cups boiling water
2	cucumbers, peeled and chopped
2	tomatoes, peeled, seeded and chopped
1/2	cup chopped green onions
1/4	cup chopped parsley leaves (no stems)
1/2	cup lemon juice
2	tablespoons olive oil
	salt and pepper to taste

In a large bowl, soak cracked wheat in boiling water for about 1 1/2 hours. Line a collander with double thicknesses of cheese cloth and thoroughly drain cracked wheat. In a large bowl, combine the cracked wheat with the remaining ingredients and toss until mixture is nicely blended. Cover bowl and refrigerate until ready to serve. Adjust seasonings. Serves 6.

Leeks & Tomatoes in Lemon Dressing

This is another of my Mom's specialties. She loved leeks and used them as salads, vegetables and even made leek patties for dinner.

4	leeks. Cut off roots and remove tough outer leaves. Trim off tops, leaving soft green leaves. Cut each leek in half lengthwise wash thoroughly, and remove every trace of sand. Now, cut into 1-inch pieces.
1	can (1 pound) stewed tomatoes, chopped. Do not drain.
3	tablespoons lemon juice
1	teaspoon oil
	pepper to taste
1/4	cup chopped green onions

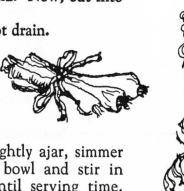

In a saucepan, place first 2 ingredients. With cover slightly ajar, simmer mixture until leeks are tender and soft. Place in a bowl and stir in remaining ingredients. Cover bowl and refrigerate until serving time. Serve as a first course on a bed of lettuce. Serves 6.

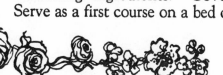

Curried Cous Cous Salad with Pineapple, Raisins & Almonds

3   cups boiling water
2   cups pre-cooked cous cous

1   can (1 pound 4 ounces) crushed pineapple, drained.
       Reserve juice for another use.
3/4   cup yellow raisins
1   cup toasted slivered almonds
2   tablespoons chopped parsley

4   tablespoons oil
4   tablespoons lemon juice
2   tablespoons honey
1   teaspoon curry powder

In a saucepan, bring water to a boil. Slowly sprinkle in the cous cous, cover pan and cook for 1 minute. Remove pan from the heat and after 1 minute, with a fork, fluff up cous cous to separate grains. Allow to cool and transfer to a large bowl. Toss in next 4 ingredients.

Heat together next 4 ingredients until just blended. Toss salad with dressing to taste. Store unused dressing in the refrigerator. Serve on a bed of lettuce. Serves 10.

Note: -If you are preparing this earlier in the day, so that they don't get soggy, add almonds before serving.

Pea Pod Salad with Water Chestnuts

2   packages (10 ounces, each) frozen pea pods. Blanch in boiling
       water for 2 minutes or until firm tender.
1/4   cup chopped green onions
1/4   cup sliced water chestnuts

4   tablespoons seasoned rice vinegar
1   tablespoon soy sauce
1   teaspoon honey
     salt to taste

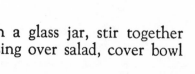

In a bowl, stir together first 3 ingredients. In a glass jar, stir together remaining ingredients until blended. Pour dressing over salad, cover bowl and refrigerate until serving time. Serves 6.

Cous Cous Salad with Artichokes, Red Peppers, Garbanzos & Raisins

This salad is gorgeous and so easy to prepare. It is a great dish to serve a large group, as it can be prepared a day before serving and stored in the refrigerator. As an added touch, before serving, sprinkle top with whole cashews and a few additional raisins. Do not add the cashew nuts earlier as they can become soggy.

3	cups water
2	cups pre-cooked cous cous
2	jars (7 ounces) marinated artichoke hearts. Do not drain.
4	marinated red peppers, cut into 1/4-inch strips
1	can (1 pound) garbanzos, rinsed and drained
1/2	cup dark raisins, (plumped in orange juice and drained)
1/2	cup chopped green onions
1/4	cup lemon juice

Sprinkle on Top:
    cashew nuts
    additional plumped raisins

In a saucepan, bring water to a boil. Sprinkle in the cous cous, cover pan and cook for 1 minute. Remove pan from the heat. After another minute, fluff the cous cous several times, to separate the grains. Allow to cool. In a large bowl, toss the cous cous with the remaining ingredients, cover bowl and refrigerate. Before serving decorate top with cashews and extra raisins. Serve with spiced peaches or apricots. Pita with Honey & Sesame Seeds is lovely. Serves 6 to 8.

Pita with Honey & Sesame Seeds:
6	pita breads, split in half. You will have 12 halves.
12	teaspoons butter
12	teaspoons honey
6	teaspoons sesame seeds

Spread each pita half with butter, honey and sprinkle with sesame seeds. Place pitas in a 12x16-inch baking pan and bake at 350° for 5 minutes, or until pitas are crisped (not browned). Yields 12 halves.

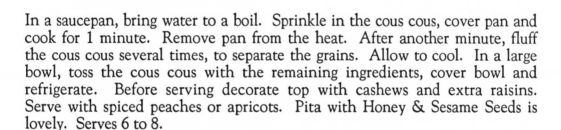

Rice Salad with Tomatoes & Green Onions

This is an especially attractive salad to serve on a buffet. It is a blaze of colors and textures. It can be prepared a day earlier and stored in the refrigerator.

To make Brown Rice:
In a covered saucepan, simmer together 1 1/2 cups long-grain brown rice, 3 1/4 cups water, 1 tablespoon oil and salt to taste, for 35 minutes, or until rice is tender and liquid is absorbed.

Salad Ingredients:
- 3 medium tomatoes, seeded and coarsely chopped
- 1/2 cup diced red peppers
- 1/2 cup diced yellow peppers
- 1/2 cup chopped green onions
- 1/4 cup sliced black olives

Dressing Ingredients:
- 1/4 cup red wine vinegar
- 2 tablespoons lemon juice
- 2 tablespoons olive oil
- 1/2 teaspoon garlic powder
- 1/2 teaspoon dried dill weed
- salt and pepper to taste

In a large bowl, toss together cooked rice and Salad Ingredients. In a jar with a tight-fitting lid, shake together Dressing Ingredients until blended. Toss dressing with the salad until nicely blended. Place salad on a rimmed serving platter, cover securely and refrigerate until serving time. Overnight is good, too. Decorate with green onion frills and thin tomato slices. Yields 8 servings.

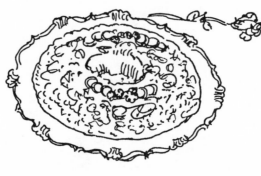

Soups

&

Garnitures

Homemade Vegetable Broth

When preparing any broths, bring the mixture to a boil, immediately lower heat and allow soup to simmer gently. Also, leave the cover slightly ajar. Boiling broths, with lids tightly on, will make the broth bitter. Allow the vegetables to simmer until they are soft and have released their nutrients into the broth. Using 2 cups less water will intensify the flavor of the broth. The tomato will add a little color to the broth and just a hint of flavor. If serving this as a soup, then simmer for 45 minutes and serve in deep bowls with a sprinkle of grated Parmesan.

- 2 large onions, peeled and sliced, about 2 cups
- 4 shallots, peeled and sliced
- 3 cloves garlic, peeled and sliced
- 1 stalk celery, sliced
- 3 medium carrots, peeled and sliced
- 1 large apple, peeled and sliced
- 1 tomato, sliced and seeded
- 1 large potato, peeled and diced
  pepper to taste
- 8 cups water

Optionals:
- 1 large sweet potato
- 1 parsnip, peeled and sliced
- 1/4 cup parsley leaves

In a stock pot with cover slightly ajar, bring all the ingredients to a boil. Lower heat, and simmer mixture for 1 hour or until vegetables are soft. Pour the soup through a strainer into a clean saucepan and press on the solids to extract as much flavor as possible. Store broth in pint containers in the freezer. This will yield about 7 to 8 cups broth.

To Make Extra-Rich Vegetable Broth:
Instead of using 8 cups of water, use 4 cups of water and 4 cups of canned vegetable broth.

Golden Beet Soup with Shallots

This is one of the most gorgeous soups. If you are not lucky enough to find these beautiful golden beets in your market, then substitute red beets which are always available. Soup can be served hot or chilled.

1	pound golden beets, tops removed
1	large onion minced
6	shallots finely minced
3	cloves garlic, minced
1	tablespoon butter
3	cups rich vegetable broth
	salt and pepper to taste
3/4	cup half and half
	sour cream and chives for garnish

Steam beets in a steamer for 30 minutes and allow to cool. When cool, peel beets and puree them in a food processor. Place beets in a Dutch oven casserole. In a skillet, saute onion, shallots and garlic in butter until shallots are soft. Add to the casserole with the vegetable broth and seasonings and simmer mixture for 20 minutes. Add the cream and simmer for 10 minutes longer. Refrigerate until serving time. Serve hot or chilled with a dollop of sour cream and a generous sprinkle of chives on top. Crostinis of Cheese are a lovely accompaniment. Serves 6.

Crostinis of Cheese:
Remove the crusts from 6 slices of good quality white bread and flatten them slightly with a rolling pin. Brush each slice with a little butter and sprinkle with a little grated Parmesan cheese. Cut slices in half on the diagonal and place on a cookie sheet. Cover pan with foil until ready to serve. When ready to serve, broil Crostinis about 4-inches from the heat until cheese is melted and tops are just beginning to color. Watch carefully, as there are only a few seconds between golden and burnt.

Greek Spinach & Rice Soup with Lemon & Dill & Croustades of Cheese & Chives

This yummy soup can be prepared in literally minutes when using the frozen spinach. If you have the time, 2 pounds of spinach, stemmed, rinsed of every trace of sand and chopped, can be substituted. Do not overcook.

1	onion, chopped
3	cloves garlic, minced
4	shallots, minced
2	tablespoons butter or margarine
5	cups vegetable broth
2	packages (10 ounces, each) frozen chopped spinach
1	cup cooked rice (or 1 1/2 cups if you like a thick soup)
4	tablespoons lemon juice
	salt and pepper to taste
6	tablespoons non-fat unflavored yogurt
6	tablespoons chopped chives

In a Dutch oven casserole, saute together first 4 ingredients until onion is soft. Stir in the next 6 ingredients and simmer mixture for 10 minutes. Serve soup in deep bowls with a tablespoon of yogurt and chopped chives. Serves 6.

Croustades of Cheese & Chives:

6	slices sourdough bread
6	teaspoons melted butter or margarine
6	teaspoons grated Parmesan
3	tablespoons chopped chives
1/2	teaspoon dill weed

Place bread on a 9x13-inch baking pan. Stir together the remaining ingredients and spread evenly on the bread. Broil for a minute or so until cheese is bubbly. Serves 6.

Grand Split Pea Soup with Sesame Crisps with Chives & Cheese

Here, a homey, country soup is elevated with the accompaniment of Sesame Crisps. The soup is thick and full of flavor and goodness.

1	pound dried split peas, rinsed and picked over for foreign particles
2	onions, minced
6	shallots, minced
2	cloves garlic, minced
4	carrots, grated
1	can (1 pound) stewed tomatoes, chopped. Do not drain.
6	cups vegetable broth
	salt and pepper to taste

In a Dutch oven casserole, place all the ingredients and bring mixture to a boil. Lower heat and, with cover just barely ajar, gently simmer soup for 1 1/2 hours or until split peas are very soft. Serve with Sesame Crisps with Chives & Cheese. Serves 8.

Sesame Crisps with Chives & Cheese:

16	thin slices French bread (1/2 ounce, each)
8	teaspoons light mayonnaise
1/2	cup grated Parmesan cheese
1/2	cup minced chives
16	sprinkles sesame seeds

Spread each slice of bread with 1/2 teaspoon mayonnaise and place on a cookie sheet. Sprinkle each slice evenly with 1 teaspoon cheese, 1 teaspoon chives and a sprinkle of sesame seeds. Broil for a few minutes to brown tops. Careful not to burn. Serves 8.

Company Cabbage & Tomato Soup

This soup is a delicious choice for a dinner with family and friends. The Honey & Sesame Crisps are a nice accompaniment. The crisps can be prepared earlier in the day and stored in a plastic bag. Serve crisps at room temperature as they do not need to be heated before serving. Soup can be prepared earlier in the day, or 1 day earlier, and stored in the refrigerator.

2	onions, chopped
6	shallots, minced
6	cloves garlic, minced
1	tablespoon butter
1	small head cabbage, (about 1 pound), coarsely chopped
1	can (1 pound) stewed tomatoes, chopped. Do not drain.
4	cups vegetable broth
2	cups tomato juice
2	tablespoons lemon juice
1	tablespoon honey
1	teaspoon sweet basil flakes
1	teaspoon Italian Herb Seasoning (flakes)
	salt and pepper to taste
1	sprinkle cayenne pepper

In a Dutch oven casserole, saute together first 4 ingredients until onions are transparent. Add the remaining ingredients and simmer soup, with cover slightly ajar, for about 1 hour or until cabbage is soft. Serve in deep bowls with Honey & Sesame Crisps. Serves 8.

Honey & Sesame Crisps:

4	pita breads, split into halves
8	teaspoons butter
8	teaspoons honey
8	sprinkles sesame seeds

On a 12x16-inch baking pan, spread each pita half with butter and honey Sprinkle with sesame seeds. Bake at 350° for 10 minutes, or until pitas are crisped and just beginning to take on color. Serves 8.

Caramelized Onion & Mushroom Soup & Croustades of Cheese & Chives

4	medium onions, chopped
4	cloves garlic, minced
4	shallots, chopped
1	teaspoon honey
3	tablespoons butter
1	pound mushrooms, cleaned and very thinly sliced
2	tablespoons butter
1/4	cup dry white wine
	salt and pepper to taste
2	tablespoons flour
5	cups vegetable broth
1/2	cup cream

In a Dutch oven casserole, over very low heat, cook together first 5 ingredients, stirring now and again, until onions are soft and golden (not fried), about 30 minutes.

Meanwhile, in a skillet, saute mushrooms in butter until mushrooms are tender. Add the wine and seasonings and cook until wine has evaporated. Add the flour and cook for 2 minutes, stirring.

Add the mushroom mixture to the onions in the casserole, and stir in the broth. Simmer soup for 5 minutes and then add the cream. Simmer soup for another 2 minutes. Serve with Croustades of Cheese & Chives. Serves 8.

Croustades of Cheese & Chives:

8	thin slices good quality white bread, crusts removed. Brush with a little melted butter and bake for a few minutes in a 350° oven until slightly crisped, but not browned.
8	teaspoons low-fat sour cream
8	teaspoons grated Parmesan cheese
8	teaspoons finely chopped chives

Spread each slice of bread with a little sour cream, sprinkle with cheese and chives and cut each slice on the diagonal. Place on a cookie sheet and just before serving, place under the broiler for 1 minute to brown tops. Be careful as there are only a few seconds between brown and burned. Serves 8.

Potage of Tomato & Rice with Croustades of Cheese & Dill

This is a delicious soup, in the French mood, to serve family or friends. It is relatively simple to prepare, can be prepared 1 day earlier and is made with cupboard ingredients. The Croustades can be assembled earlier in the day. Cover the pan tightly with foil. Remove foil and broil before serving.

2   onions, chopped
2   shallots, chopped
2   cloves garlic, minced
1   teaspoon sugar
1   tablespoon olive oil

2   cans (1 pound, each) stewed tomatoes, very finely chopped.
    (This can be done in a food processor.) Do not drain.
2   tablespoons tomato paste
4   cups vegetable broth, home-made or canned
1/4   teaspoon, each, dried thyme, basil and dill weed
      salt and pepper to taste
1/2   cup rice

In a Dutch oven casserole, saute together first 5 ingredients until onions are transparent. Add the remaining ingredients and simmer soup for 30 minutes or until rice is tender. Serve with Croustades of Cheese & Dill Serves 8.

Croustades of Cheese & Dill:
8   thin slices of sourdough bread
8   teaspoons low-fat sour cream
8   tablespoons grated Swiss cheese
8   teaspoons chopped chives
1/2   teaspoon dill weed

Brush bread with sour cream and sprinkle with Swiss cheese, chives and dill weed. Broil for a minute or so, or until cheese is melted.

Leek & Vegetable Soup with Potatoes & Herbed Crispettes & Chives

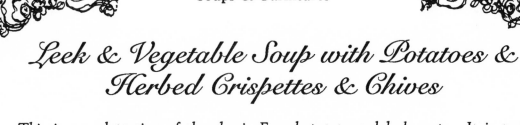

This is an adaptation of the classic French potato and leek soup. It is truly wonderful and I do hope you enjoy it as much as our friends did.

1   pound leeks, thinly sliced. (Use the white part and a little of the tender green tops and thoroughly rinse.)
2   medium onions, chopped
4   shallots, finely chopped
6   cloves garlic, thinly sliced
4   medium carrots, thinly sliced
3   medium potatoes, diced
1   can (1 pound) stewed tomatoes, chopped. Do not drain.
4   cups vegetable broth
1   teaspoon thyme flakes
     salt and pepper to taste

In a Dutch oven casserole, place all the ingredients and bring mixture to a boil. Lower heat and with cover slightly ajar, simmer soup for 45 minutes, or until vegetables are tender. Serve in bowls with a dollop of yogurt and a sprinkling of chives. Serves 6.

Herbed Crispettes with Chives:
6   slices egg bread, crusts removed and rolled flat with a rolling pin
6   teaspoons melted butter
6   teaspoons minced chives
6   sprinkles minced thyme leaves
6   sprinkles minced parsley leaves
6   teaspoons grated Parmesan cheese

Brush each bread slice with butter and sprinkle evenly with the remaining ingredients. Bake in a 350° oven for 5 minutes and then broil for a few minutes to brown tops. Serves 6.

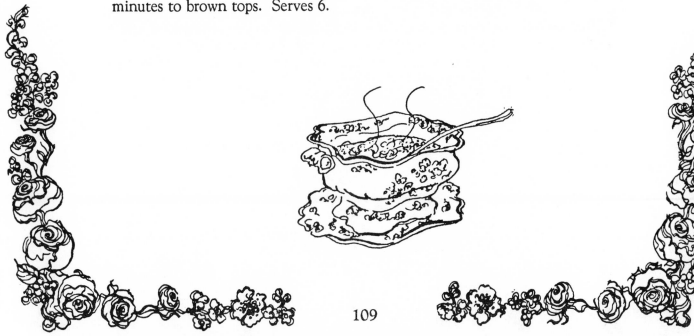

Leek & Tomato Soup with Orzo and Cici Peas with Pita Cheese Crisps

Orzo and cici peas (garbanzos) add solid character to this soup. It is flavored with all manner of good things...tomatoes, leeks, garlic, onions. Orzo comes in 3 sizes...small, medium and large. The large size is a little harder to find. But it can be found in most continental markets. Serve this hearty country soup with Pita Cheese Crisps.

2	onions, chopped
2	leeks, white and tender green part only, thoroughly rinsed and finely chopped
3	carrots, peeled and grated
3	cloves garlic, minced
1	can (1 pound) stewed tomatoes, finely chopped. Do not drain.
1	can (1 pound) cici peas, rinsed and drained
1/4	cup large-size orzo
4	cups vegetable broth
1	tablespoon chopped parsley
1	teaspoon dried sweet basil flakes
	salt and pepper to taste

In a Dutch oven casserole, stir together all the ingredients and bring mixture to a boil. Lower heat, cover pan and simmer soup for 30 to 35 minutes or until orzo is tender. (Smaller-sized orzo will cook faster.) To serve, ladle soup in bowls, sprinkle with a little grated Parmesan and serve 6.

Pita Cheese Crisps:
3	pita breads, split in half
6	teaspoons butter
6	teaspoons grated Parmesan cheese
3	teaspoons sesame seeds

In a 12x16-inch baking pan, place pita breads in 1 layer. Spread 1 teaspoon butter and cheese on each pita half. Sprinkle each with 1/2 teaspoon sesame seeds. Bake at 350° for about 10 minutes, or until edges are just beginning to brown. Careful! as there are only seconds between brown and burnt. Serves 6.

Royal Zucchini, Mushroom & Onion Soup with Feather Cream Biscuits

This is an impressive soup that is great for a dinner party or to serve informally to family and friends.. It is a beautiful blend of flavors. The Feather Biscuits are delicate and light and a lovely accompaniment. Soup can be prepared 1 day earlier and stored in the refrigerator.

6	medium zucchini, unpeeled and thinly sliced
3/4	pound mushrooms, cleaned and thinly sliced
5	small shallots, finely chopped
2	large onions, finely chopped
4	cloves garlic, minced
3	tablespoons butter
1/4	cup dry white wine
3	tablespoons flour
4	cups vegetable broth
1/2	teaspoon dried dill weed
1/4	teaspoon ground poultry seasoning
	salt to taste

In a Dutch oven casserole, over medium-low heat, place first 6 ingredients and saute mixture until vegetables are soft and all the liquid rendered is evaporated.

Add the wine and cook until it has evaporated. Stir in flour and cook and stir for about 2 minutes, turning all the while. Add broth and seasonings and stir until blended. Simmer soup, uncovered for about 15 minutes, stirring now and again. Serve hot, with a dollop of low-fat sour cream on top and a faint sprinkle of dill. Serves 8 to 10.

Feather Cream Biscuits:

1 1/4	cups flour
1	tablespoon baking powder
1/3	teaspoon salt
1/4	cup cold butter (1/2 stick,) cut into 4 pieces
1 1/8	cups cream

Place flour, baking powder and salt in large bowl of an electric mixer. Beat for a few seconds to blend. Add the butter and beat until mixture resembles coarse meal. By hand, stir in the cream until blended. Drop batter by the heaping tablespoon on an ungreased cookie sheet and bake in a 425° oven for 20 minutes. Yields 12 to 14 biscuits.

Elegant Dilled Zucchini Soup with Cheese & Chive Toast Points

There are few soups you can make that are more delicious or more elegant than this one. It is a beautiful harmony of flavors...very delicate and yet, rich and satisfying. The Cheese & Chive Toast Points are a delicate accompaniment. Not the least of its virtues, this lovely soup can be served hot or cold.

6	medium zucchini, peeled and sliced
2	large onions, finely chopped
6	shallots, minced
6	cloves garlic, minced
4	cups vegetable broth
	salt to taste

1/4	cup buttermilk
3/4	cup low-fat sour cream
1/2	teaspoon dried dill weed

In a Dutch oven casserole, with cover slightly ajar, simmer together first 6 ingredients for 40 minutes, or until vegetables are very soft. Meanwhile, in a bowl, stir together last three ingredients and allow to stand at room temperature.

With a slotted spoon, remove vegetables to a food processor or blender, and blend until the vegetables are pureed. Return the pureed vegetables to the broth, stir in the sour cream mixture until blended and heat through. Do not boil. Serve with Cheese & Chive Toast Points. Serves 6.

Cheese & Chive Toast Points:

6	slices white bread, crusts removed. Roll slices flat with a rolling pin and cut on the diagonal into triangles.
6	teaspoons melted butter or margarine
6	teaspoons grated Parmesan
6	teaspoons chopped chives

Place bread in a 9x13-inch baking pan. Brush bread on both sides with melted butter and toast in a 350° oven for 10 to 12 minutes or until bread is crisped and just beginning to take on color. Do not brown. (Bread can be toasted earlier in the day.) Divide the remaining ingredients over the bread and broil for a few seconds to brown the cheese. Serves 6.

The Best Vegetable Soup with Basil Garlic Pesto & Chive & Cheese Points

This hearty vegetable soup has deep solid character and is full of flavor and goodness. The Chive & Cheese Points are a lovely accompaniment.

- 5 cups vegetable broth, home-made or canned
- 1 can (1 pound) stewed tomatoes, chopped. Do not drain.
- 2 large onions, finely chopped
- 3 carrots, sliced
- 1 stalk celery, thinly sliced
- 1/4 pound green beans, cut into 1-inch lengths
- 2 potatoes, peeled and cubed
- 1 cup, each, canned garbanzos and red kidney beans, rinsed and drained
- 1 cup shredded cabbage
- 1 teaspoon oregano flakes
  salt and pepper to taste

Basil Garlic Pesto:
- 3 cloves garlic, mashed
- 3 tablespoons chopped fresh basil
- 2 tablespoons olive oil

In a Dutch oven casserole combine first group of ingredients and bring soup to a boil. Lower heat and simmer soup, with cover slightly ajar, for 40 minutes or until vegetables are soft.

Meanwhile, mash together the garlic, basil and olive oil and pound it until it is nicely blended. When vegetables are soft, add it to the soup and simmer an additional 10 minutes. Serve with a sprinkle of grated Parmesan. Chive & Cheese Points are a nice accompaniment. Serves 6.

Chive & Cheese Points:
- 6 slices white bread, crusts removed. Roll slices flat with a rolling pin and cut on the diagonal into triangles.
- 6 teaspoons melted butter
- 6 teaspoons grated Parmesan cheese
- 6 tablespoons finely chopped chives

Bake bread in 350° oven for about 5 minutes or until bread is lightly crisped. Brush bread with melted butter and sprinkle with cheese and chives. When ready to serve, broil bread for about 1 to 2 minutes or until cheese is melted. Serve at once. Serves 6.

Potage of Zucchini & Tomatoes with Batonettes of Cheese

What a nice thick soup, marvelously flavored with onions and garlic and herbs. The Batonettes are incredibly good, and exceptionally easy, starting, as they do with frozen puff pastry.

1 1/2	pounds Italian zucchini, scrubbed. Do not peel. Cut into thin slices.
2	large onions, chopped
4	cloves garlic, minced
2	shallots, chopped
2	tablespoons butter

1	can (1 pound) stewed tomatoes, chopped. Do not drain.
4	cups vegetable broth
2	teaspoons lemon juice
1	tablespoon chopped parsley leaves
1/2	teaspoon dried dill weed
	salt to taste

In a Dutch oven casserole, saute together first 5 ingredients, until vegetables are soft and liquids rendered are evaporated. Do this over medium heat, stirring from time to time. Place mixture in a food processor and blend until vegetables are coarsely chopped.

Spoon vegetables back into Dutch oven and add the next 6 ingredients. Simmer soup for 30 minutes, uncovered. Serve with a dollop of low-fat sour cream, a sprinkling of dill and with Batonettes of Cheese as a lovely accompaniment. Serves 8.

Batonettes of Cheese:

1	sheet frozen puff pastry, about 12x12-inches
1	egg, beaten
1/2	cup grated Parmesan cheese
1/4	teaspoon dill weed

Cut puff pastry into thirds, yielding 3 strips 4x12-inches. Cut each strip into 1-inch batonettes (little batons), yielding 36 slices, measuring 4x1-inches. Place on a cookie sheet and brush with beaten egg. Sprinkle with combination of cheese and dill. Bake in a 350° oven until puffed and brown. Store unused batonettes in an air-tight container. Yields 36 batonettes.

Cucumber & Chive Soup with Lemon & Dill

3   medium cucumbers, peeled and cut in half lengthwise. With a spoon, scrape out the seeds. Cut cucumbers into 1-inch chunks.

1/3   cup chopped chives
1   cup unflavored non-fat yogurt
1   cup buttermilk
2   tablespoons lemon juice
1   teaspoon dried dill weed
    pinch of salt

1   tablespoon, each chopped chives and minced parsley for garnish

Finely chop cucumbers in food processor and drain. In a large bowl, stir together cucumbers with the next 6 ingredients until blended. Refrigerate until serving time. Serve in glass bowls with a dollop of yogurt and a sprinkle of chopped chives and parsley. Serves 4 to 6.

Cold & Creamy Dilled Zucchini Soup

Delicious served cold or hot. If serving hot, do not allow to boil after adding the buttermilk.

6   Italian zucchini, stemmed and partially peeled. (This means that you will leave a few strips of green for color.)
2   onions, chopped
4   shallots, chopped
6   cloves garlic, sliced
4   cups vegetable broth
1/2   teaspoon dried dill weed or 1 tablespoon fresh dill weed

1   cup buttermilk

In a Dutch oven casserole, simmer together first 6 ingredients until vegetables are soft, about 30 minutes. Puree mixture in batches in a food processor. Return soup to pan, add the buttermilk and heat through. Do not boil after adding the buttermilk. Add a little dill to taste. Refrigerate soup until serving time. Serve with a dollop of yogurt and float a few chopped chives on top. Beautiful and delicious. Serves 6.

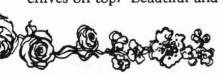

German-Style Sauerkraut Soup with Black Raisin Pumpernickel

    3   onions, finely chopped
    3   cloves garlic, minced
    3   carrots, peeled and grated
    1   can (1 pound) stewed tomatoes, chopped. Do not drain.
    1   cup sauerkraut, drained
    1   head cabbage (about 1 pound) shredded or coarsely chopped
    3   tablespoons lemon juice
    3   tablespoons honey
    3   cups tomato juice
    2   cups vegetable broth
  1/2   cup raisins
        salt and freshly ground pepper to taste

In a Dutch oven casserole, place all the ingredients and bring mixture to a boil. Lower heat, and simmer mixture for about 1 hour, or until cabbage is soft. Serve in deep bowls with a sprinkling of grated Parmesan cheese. Serve with Black Raisin Pumpernickel Bread or Black Pumpernickel Bread & Cheese, both delicious accompaniments. Serves 8.

Black Raisin Pumpernickel Bread:
    8   thin slices raisin pumpernickel bread
    8   teaspoons butter
    8   teaspoons honey

Spread each slice of bread with butter and honey. Broil for a few seconds until honey bubbles. Serves 8.

Black Pumpernickel Bread & Cheese:
    8   very thin slices pumpernickel bread (from the refrigerated
            section of the market)
    8   teaspoons butter
    8   teaspoons grated Parmesan cheese

Spread each slice of bread with butter and sprinkle with cheese. Broil for a few seconds until cheese just begins to take on color. Serves 8.

Old-Fashioned Vegetable Chowder with Red Hot French Cheese Bread

2 tablespoons oil
2 onions, finely chopped
3 cloves garlic, minced
1 can (1 pound) stewed tomatoes, chopped. Do not drain.
2 cups vegetable broth
2 cups tomato juice
2 tablespoons tomato paste
2 potatoes, peeled and diced
2 carrots, grated
1 stalk celery, thinly sliced
1 tablespoon chopped parsley leaves
1 teaspoon dried thyme flakes
1/2 teaspoon turmeric
1/4 teaspoon red pepper flakes

Combine all the ingredients in a Dutch oven casserole and simmer mixture for 45 minutes or until vegetables are tender. Serve with Red Hot French Cheese Bread as a wonderful accompaniment. Serves 6.

Red Hot French Cheese Bread:
12 slices French bread, cut about 1/4-inch thick

12 teaspoons butter, at room temperature
   garlic powder
   paprika
12 teaspoons grated Parmesan cheese

Place French bread slices on a cookie sheet. Spread 1 teaspoon butter on each slice of bread. Sprinkle lightly with garlic powder and paprika. Sprinkle with grated Parmesan. Cover pan tightly with foil. Just before serving, remove foil and broil for about 1 minute, or until tops are just beginning to brown. Watch carefully or bread will burn. Serve 6.

Royal Vegetable Chowder
with Lemon Garlic Crisps with Herbs

The beauty of this soup is to finely mince (and not puree) the vegetables Vegetables can be finely chopped in the food processor.

- 2   onions, minced
- 4   cloves garlic, minced
- 4   shallots, minced
- 2   potatoes, peeled and grated
- 4   carrots, peeled and grated
- 1   stalk celery, peeled and very thinly sliced
- 1   can (1 pound) stewed tomatoes, chopped. Do not drain.
- 2   tablespoons tomato paste
- 2   cups tomato juice
- 2   cups vegetable broth
- 1   tablespoon chopped parsley

Seasonings:
- 1   teaspoon sugar
- 1   teaspoon oregano flakes
- 1   teaspoon ground turmeric
- 1/2   teaspoon ground cumin
- 1/8   teaspoon red pepper flakes
-     salt and pepper to taste

In a partly covered Dutch oven casserole, simmer together all the ingredients for 45 minutes, or until vegetables are soft. Serve with a sprinkle of grated Parmesan on top. Lemon Garlic Crisps with Herbs is a nice accompaniment. Serves 6.

Lemon Garlic Crisps with Herbs:
- 6   slices egg bread, crusts removed. Roll bread flat with a rolling pin and cut into decorative shapes...triangles, fingers, circles, rectangles. Decorative cookie cutters are nice around the holidays.

- 3   tablespoons butter
- 2   tablespoons lemon juice

- 1/4   teaspoon Italian Herb Seasoning
- 6   sprinkles garlic powder
- 2   tablespoons minced chives
- 6   teaspoons grated Parmesan cheese

Prepare bread slices and toast lightly in a 350° oven for about 10 minutes. Melt butter with lemon juice and spread on each piece of bread. Toss together the remaining ingredients and sprinkle evenly over the bread. Before serving, broil for a minute or two to lightly brown the tops. Serves 6.

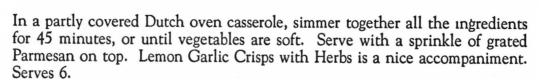

Minestrone di la Piazza Navonna Roma

During our stay in Rome, we enjoyed many versions of the classic Italian Minestrone. The variations were many, but the following includes most of the basics. It is a thick and hearty soup and just right for sipping by the fire. Add an antipasto salad and it is a complete meal.

- 2 large onions, chopped
- 4 cloves garlic, minced
- 1 tablespoon olive oil

- 4 carrots, thinly sliced
- 1 stalk celery, thinly sliced
- 1 can (1 pound) stewed tomatoes, undrained and chopped
- 1 cup chopped cabbage
- 6 cups vegetable broth
- 1 bay leaf
- 1 teaspoon oregano flakes
- salt and pepper to taste

- 3/4 cup canned garbanzos, rinsed and drained
- 3/4 cup canned red kidney beans rinsed and drained
- 1 package (10 ounces) frozen cut green beans
- 1 package (10 ounces) frozen peas
- 1 cup spaghetti broken into small pieces

In a Dutch oven casserole, place onions, garlic and oil and cook and stir for 10 minutes. Add the next group of ingredients, cover pan and simmer for about 30 minutes or until vegetables are tender. Add the remaining ingredients and simmer soup for an additional 30 minutes or until spaghetti is tender. Serve with crusty Italian bread. Instead of butter, try garlic-flavored olive oil. Serves 10 to 12.

Note: -This soup freezes nicely. As it is a bit heavy on ingredients, I thought it best to prepare a double batch and freeze leftovers.

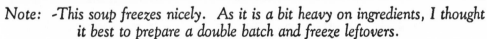

Leek & Potato Soup with Chives

2   leeks, white and tender green parts only, rinsed and chopped
1   onion, chopped
1/2   cup vegetable broth

1   medium potato, peeled and sliced
4   cups vegetable broth
     white pepper to taste

4   tablespoons unflavored yogurt
4   tablespoons chopped chives

In a covered saucepan, over low heat, cook together first 3 ingredients for 10 minutes, or until vegetables are softened. Add the next 3 ingredients and simmer mixture for about 30 minutes, or until vegetables are very soft Allow to cool to lukewarm and then puree mixture in a food processor Refrigerate until serving time. Serve with a dollop of yogurt, generously sprinkled with chives. Serves 6.

Lentil, Vegetable & Bulgur Soup

2   large onions, finely chopped
3   carrots, grated
3   shallots, minced
3   cloves garlic, minced

1   package (1 pound) dried lentils, picked over for foreign matter,
       rinsed and drained
1   can (1 pound) stewed tomatoes, chopped. Do not drain.
2   tablespoons tomato paste
1   tablespoon olive oil
6   cups vegetable broth
     salt and pepper to taste

1/2   cup medium-grain bulgur

In a food processor, finely chop first 4 ingredients. Place vegetables in a Dutch oven casserole and add the next group of ingredients. Cover pan and simmer soup for 50 minutes. Stir in the bulgur and continue simmering for 15 to 20 minutes, (adding a little broth, if necessary,) or until lentils are tender. This wonderful soup deserves a great crusty bread. Serves 6 to 8.

Cold Russian Beet Soup with Sour Cream & Chives

This is a simplified version of the classic "borscht". While I realize that beets are not a "national" food, this will do well for a change. Serve it with black pumpernickel with raisins and sweet butter. Soup can be made 1 day earlier and stored in the refrigerator.

1   jar (16 ounces) pickled beets (whole or sliced) and do not drain

3   cups vegetable broth, home-made or canned
2   tablespoons lemon juice (or to taste)
2   tablespoons wine vinegar (or to taste)

6   tablespoons low-fat sour cream
6   teaspoons chopped chives
     dill weed

In a food processor, blend beets until they are coarsely chopped. Alternatively, chop the beets by hand. In a large bowl, add the chopped beets, broth, lemon juice and vinegar to taste. Refrigerate for several hours. At serving time, ladle soup into bowls, top with 1 tablespoon sour cream, sprinkle with chives and dill. Serve with pumpernickel raisin bread and sweet butter. Serves 6.

Puree of Tomato & Pear Soup

The sweetness of the pears is a subtle balance to the tartness of the tomatoes. The potato thickens the soup slightly. Altogether it is a lovely balance of flavors.

2   large onions, chopped
4   shallots, minced
2   cloves garlic, minced
4   tablespoons butter

4   medium carrots, peeled and grated
1   large potato, peeled and chopped
3   ripe pears, peeled, seeded and chopped
2   pounds tomatoes, peeled, seeded and chopped
6   cups vegetable broth
     salt to taste

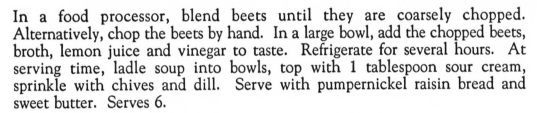

In a Dutch oven casserole, sauté together first 4 ingredients until onions are transparent, about 10 minutes. Add the remaining ingredients to the pan and simmer mixture, with cover slightly ajar, for 30 minutes or until vegetables are tender. In a food processor, puree soup in batches. Return to the pan and heat through. Serve with a teaspoon of sour cream and a sprinkling of chopped chives. Serves 8.

Country Lentil Soup with
Crispettes of Pita with Sesame Honey

This is a nice homey soup to serve family and friends on an informal Sunday night dinner. The pita crispettes are delicious flavored with honey and sesame seeds. If necessary, thin the soup with a little extra broth.

2   large onions, finely chopped
4   shallots, minced
6   cloves garlic, minced
3   carrots, peeled and grated
1   can (1 pound) stewed tomatoes, chopped. Do not drain.
1   package (1 pound) lentils, rinsed and picked over for
      foreign particles
6   cups vegetable broth
     salt and pepper to taste

In a covered Dutch oven casserole, place all the ingredients   Bring mixture to a boil, lower heat and simmer soup for about 1 hour or until lentils are very tender. Serve with Crispettes of Pita with Sesame Honey. Serves 6.

Crispettes of Pita with Sesame Honey:
3   pita breads, split in half
6   teaspoons butter
6   teaspoons honey
3   teaspoons sesame seeds

In a 12x16-inch baking pan, place pita breads in 1 layer. Spread 1 teaspoon butter and honey on each pita half. Sprinkle each with 1/2 teaspoon sesame seeds. Bake at 350° for about 10 minutes, or until edges are just beginning to brown. Careful! as there are only seconds between brown and burnt. Serves 6

Lentil & Brown Rice Soup with Carrots & Onions

Lentils with brown rice, carrots and onions produce a satisfying and robust soup. This is a very thick soup so add a little more broth if you like it thinner.

- 1 cup lentils, rinsed and picked over for foreign particles
- 2 large onions, finely chopped
- 3 carrots, peeled and grated
- 3 cloves garlic, minced
- 1 can (1 pound) stewed tomatoes, finely chopped. Do not drain.
- 6 cups vegetable broth
  salt and pepper to taste
- 1 cup long-grain brown rice

In a covered Dutch oven casserole, place all the ingredients and bring mixture to a boil. Lower heat and simmer mixture for 45 to 50 minutes or until lentils are tender. If too thick, add a little more broth to taste. Serve with black pumpernickel bread with raisins. Serves 8.

Mushroom & Barley Soup with Petite Knishes with Potatoes & Onions

This is the ultimate comfort soup. The Petite Knishes are truly delicious and I hope you enjoy them as much as my family and friends do. Please boil the egg barley separately so as to remove some of the starch.

- 1 1/2 pounds mushrooms, cleaned and very thinly sliced
- 2 large onions, finely chopped
- 6 shallots, minced
- 4 cloves garlic, minced
- 2 tablespoons butter

- 1 package (7 ounces) egg barley (barley-shaped egg noodles)
- 1 quart boiling water

- 6 cups rich vegetable broth
- 1 teaspoon dried dill weed
  salt and pepper to taste

In a Dutch oven casserole, saute together first group of ingredients until onions are soft and all the liquid rendered is evaporated.

In a separate pot, boil the egg barley in simmering water until tender and drain in a large strainer. (Don't use a collander or your barley will run down the drain.) Add the barley and the remaining ingredients to the Dutch oven and simmer soup for 15 minutes, stirring now and again. Serves 10.

Petite Knishes with Potatoes & Onions

These little knishes have to be one of the best-tasting hors d'oeuvres They are also a great accompaniment to soup or salad. Traditionally made with a heavy-duty dough, making these with puff pastry truly elevates them to gastronomical heights. I have further simplified preparation using the potato flakes. As the abundance of onions produce the dominant taste, potato flakes can be used.

Onion Potato Filling:

- 3 large onions, chopped
- 3 tablespoons margarine

- 3 cups instant mashed potato flakes
- 3 cups boiling water
- 3 tablespoons margarine
  salt and freshly ground pepper to taste

Saute onions in margarine about 20 minutes, or until onions are lightly browned. (Careful not to burn or onions will be bitter.) Meanwhile, add the boiling water to the potato flakes, stir in the margarine and salt with a good amount of pepper. Stir in the browned onions. Allow mixture to cool.

Puff Pastry:

- 1 package (17 ounces) Pepperidge Farms Puff Pastry (2 sheets)
- 1 egg, beaten
- 12 tablespoons grated Parmesan cheese

Cut pastry sheets in thirds on the fold. Cut each third in half crosswise. You will have 12 pieces. On a floured pastry cloth, roll out each piece to measure 4x8-inches. Place a few tablespoons Potato Onion Filling along the 8-inch side, fold dough over and press edges down with the tines of a fork. Scallop the edges.

Place knishes on a greased cookie sheet, brush tops with beaten egg and sprinkle with cheese. Pierce tops in 4 or 5 places with the tines of a fork. Bake at 400° for 25 to 30 minutes, or until tops are nicely browned Remove from pan and allow to cool on brown paper.

To reheat, place knishes on a cookie sheet, cut each into 4 pieces and heat in a 350° oven for 15 minutes, or until heated through. Yields 48 pieces and serves 12.

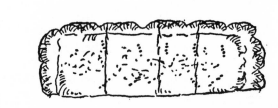

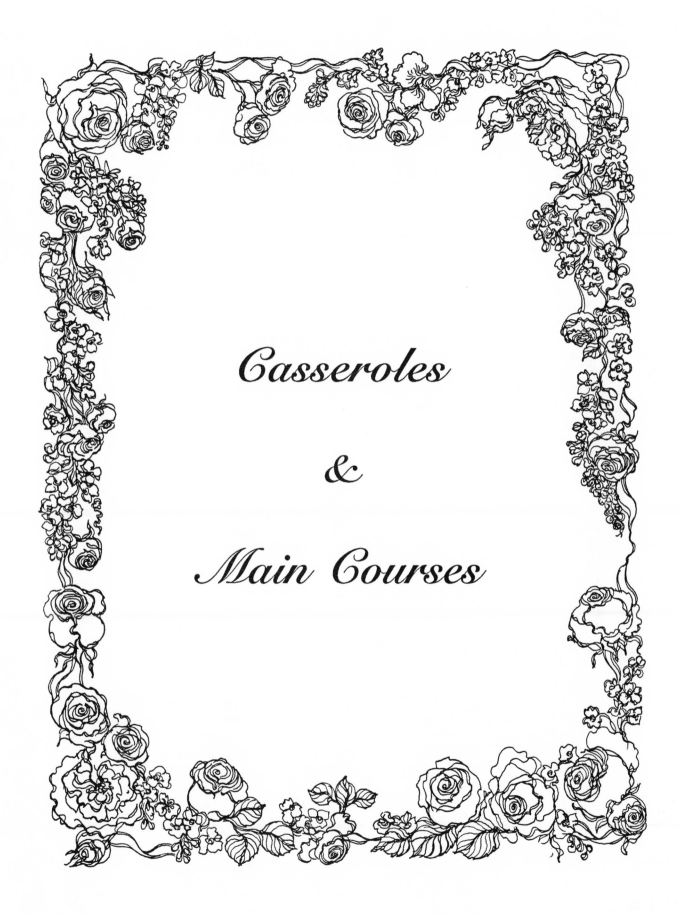

Casseroles

&

Main Courses

Eggplant Lasagna

Eggplant:
  2   eggplants, peeled and cut into 1/2-inch thick slices

Quick Tomato Sauce:
  1   can (1 pound 12 ounces) crushed tomatoes in puree
  2   tablespoons dried onion flakes
  1   tablespoon olive oil
  1   teaspoon sugar
  1/2   teaspoon dried sweet basil flakes
  1/2   teaspoon Italian seasoning flakes
  1/3   teaspoon coarse-grind garlic powder
       salt and pepper to taste

Cheese Filling:
  1/2   pound low-fat Mozzarella cheese, grated
  1/2   cup grated Parmesan cheese

Crumb-Cheese Mixture:
  1/4   cup bread crumbs
  1/4   cup grated Parmesan cheese

To Prepare Eggplant:
Place eggplant slices in a greased 12 x 16-inch pan. Cover pan tightly with foil and bake eggplant in a 400° oven for 25 minutes or until eggplant is soft

To Make Sauce:
In a saucepan, simmer together all the ingredients for 5 minutes

To Make Cheese Filling:
Stir together all the ingredients until blended.

To Make Crumb-Cheese Mixture:
Combine bread crumbs and grated cheese.

To Assemble:
In a 9 x 13-inch pan, layer 1/3 the sauce, 1/2 the eggplant slices, 1/2 the cheese filling and 1/3 the sauce. Repeat with the remaining eggplant, cheese filling and sauce. Sprinkle Crumb-Cheese Mixture evenly over the top Bake in a 350° oven until piping hot, about 35 minutes. Serves 8 to 10.

Caribbean Vegetable Jambalaya

This delicious casserole, in a Caribbean mood, is an attractive medley of textures and colors. The rice is bathed in a rich blend of herb-flavored vegetables.

For the Rice:

- 2 cups long-grain rice
- 4 cups vegetable broth
- 1 tablespoon oil
  salt to taste

For the Vegetables:

- 1 large onion, chopped
- 1 medium red bell pepper, cored and cut into 1/4-inch slivers
- 1 medium yellow bell pepper, cored and cut into 1/4-inch slivers
- 1/2 green bell pepper, chopped
- 1 stalk celery, chopped
- 4 cloves garlic, minced
- 1 can (1 pound) stewed tomatoes, chopped. Do not drain.
- 2 bay leaves
  pinch of dried red pepper flakes
- 1/2 teaspoon, each, paprika, thyme flakes, and oregano flakes
  salt and pepper to taste

To make the Rice:
In a Dutch oven casserole, stir together rice ingredients, cover pan, and simmer mixture for 30 minutes, or until rice is tender. Fluff with a fork to separate grains.

To make the Vegetables:
In an uncovered Dutch oven casserole, simmer together all the ingredients until vegetables are soft, about 30 minutes. Remove the bay leaves.

Toss the vegetables into the rice and heat through to serve. (Before serving, a nice optional is to stir in 1/2 cup of minced green onions.) Serve with Banana, Orange & Raisin Compote. Serves 8.

Banana, Orange & Raisin Compote

- 4 medium bananas, sliced on the diagonal
- 2 medium oranges, peeled and cut into 16 thin wedges
- 1/2 cup raisins
- 1/4 cup orange juice
- 2 tablespoons cinnamon sugar

In an uncovered skillet, simmer together all the ingredients for 10 minutes. Serve warm or at room temperature. Serves 8 as an accompaniment.

Spinach Lasagna with Sweet Tomato Sauce

This is a great casserole...great tasting and very satisfying. It can be assembled earlier in the day, stored in the refrigerator and heated before serving.

9 lasagna noodles, cooked and drained

1 package (10 ounces) frozen chopped spinach, defrosted and drained
1 pint non-fat cottage cheese
1 package (8 ounces) low-fat cream cheese
2 cups grated low-fat Mozzarella cheese
1/2 cup grated Parmesan cheese
2 eggs
1/2 teaspoon Italian Herb Seasoning
   salt and pepper to taste

In a 9x13-inch greased pan, place 3 cooked noodles evenly in one layer. Beat together the remaining ingredients until blended. Place 1/2 of the spinach filling evenly over the noodles. Continue with 3 more noodles and then the remaining spinach filling. Top with the remaining noodles.

Pour Sweet Tomato Sauce evenly over the noodles and sprinkle top with additional grated Parmesan cheese (optional, but nice). Heat in a 350° oven for about 45 minutes or until heated through. (It might bubble earlier, but the center will not be hot.) Cut into squares and serve with salad or cold marinated vegetables. Serves 8 to 10.

Sweet Tomato Sauce:
1 can (1 pound 12 ounces) crushed tomatoes in tomato puree.
1 onion, grated
2 tablespoons oil
1 teaspoon sugar
1/2 teaspoon Italian Herb Seasoning
   salt, pepper and garlic powder to taste

In a saucepan, combine all the ingredients and simmer sauce for 5 minutes.

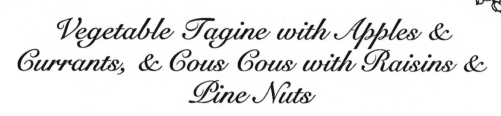

Vegetable Tagine with Apples & Currants, & Cous Cous with Raisins & Pine Nuts

Tagine is, basically, a Moroccan stew that can be made with meat, chicken, vegetables, and any combination of these. This is a vegetable tagine that uses no fat, is sweetened with apples and currants and is deliciously spiced with turmeric and cumin.

1	can (1 pound) stewed tomatoes, chopped. Do not drain.
2	onions, finely chopped
3	medium zucchini, scrubbed and sliced
2	apples, peeled, cored and grated
1/3	cup dried currants
4	cloves garlic, minced
1	can (16 ounces) garbanzo beans, rinsed and drained

Spices:
1 1/2	teaspoons ground turmeric
1	teaspoon ground cumin
1/4	teaspoon ground cinnamon
	salt and pepper to taste

In a covered Dutch oven casserole, simmer together all the ingredients for 20 minutes or until onions are tender. Remove cover and simmer for another 5 minutes, or until liquid is reduced to a sauce. Serve with Cous Cous with Raisins & Pine Nuts. Serves 6.

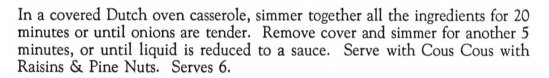

Cous Cous with Raisins & Pine Nuts:
1 1/3	cups water
	salt to taste
1	cup precooked medium-grain cous cous
1	teaspoon butter
1/3	cup plumped yellow raisins. (Raisins can be plumped in boiling water for 5 minutes and thoroughly drained.)
1/3	cup toasted pine nuts

In a saucepan, bring water and salt to a boil. In a steady stream, stir in the cous cous, cover pan and simmer mixture for 2 minutes, stirring every now and again. Stir in the butter, raisins and pine nuts and continue tossing and stirring to keep the grains separate. Serves 6.

Oven-Baked Eggplant Parmesan

It is a treat to serve this very benign eggplant casserole. Normally, Eggplant Parmesan is fried, and the thirsty eggplant can soak up over 1 cup of oil. The eggplant here is oven-fried and the casserole is light and truly delicious.

To Prepare the Eggplant:
- 1   eggplant (about 1 pound), peeled and cut into 1/4-inch slices
  light mayonnaise

- 1/4   cup savory cracker crumbs
- 1/4   cup grated Parmesan cheese

Brush each eggplant slice with a thin coating of mayonnaise. Combine crumbs and cheese and sprinkle it on the eggplant, coating both sides. Place eggplant slices on an oiled cookie sheet and bake at 400° until golden brown, about 20 minutes. Carefully turn and brown the other side, about 10 minutes.

Fresh Tomato Sauce:
- 1   onion, chopped
- 3   cloves garlic, minced
- 1   tablespoon olive oil

- 2   pounds tomatoes, chopped
- 3   tablespoons tomato paste
- 1   teaspoon Italian Herb Seasoning
- 1   teaspoon sweet basil flakes
  pinch of cayenne
  salt and pepper to taste

In a saucepan, sauté together first 3 ingredients until onion is soft. Add the remaining ingredients and simmer sauce, uncovered, for 30 minutes.

To Assemble:
- 2   cups grated part-skimmed Mozzarella cheese (4 ounces)
- 1/2   cup grated Parmesan cheese

In a 9x13-inch pan, spoon a thin layer of sauce. Top with a layer of 1/2 of the eggplant, Mozzarella, tomato sauce and Parmesan. Repeat this order for the second layer. Cover and refrigerate. Before serving, heat, uncovered, in a 350° oven for 30 minutes, or until heated through. Serve with a pink rice, orzo, or fideos. Serves 8.

Yellow Rice Paella with Artichoke Hearts & Red Peppers

This is a delicious and colorful recipe that is beautiful served in a large shallow serving dish. Green peas are a nice addition.

Yellow Rice:
-   1   cup long-grain rice
-   2   cups vegetable broth
-   1   teaspoon turmeric
-   1/2   teaspoon ground cumin
-   2   teaspoons oil
    salt and pepper to taste

Vegetables:
-   1   large onion, finely chopped
-   2   cloves garlic, minced
-   1   tablespoon oil

-   1   jar (6 or 7 ounces) marinated artichoke hearts, drained and cut into fourths. Reserve dressing (see Note below).
-   3   marinated red peppers, cut into slivers

To make the Yellow Rice:
In a covered Dutch oven casserole, simmer together all the ingredients for 30 minutes, or until rice is tender and liquid is absorbed.

Meanwhile, prepare the vegetables. Saute onion and garlic in oil until onion is soft. Stir in the artichokes and red peppers and cook for 1 minute. Stir vegetables into cooked rice, fluff with a fork and heat through. Serves 6.

Note: -This is also delicious served cold as a salad. In that case, drizzle the paella with the reserved dressing and toss until it is blended. If serving warm, reserve the dressing for another use.

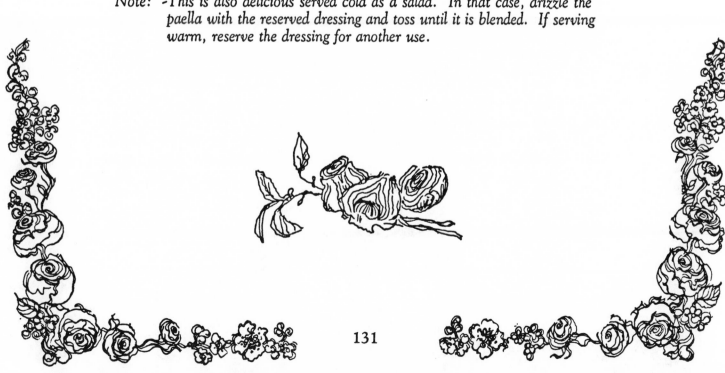

Oven-Fried Eggplant with Lemon & Chives

This is a delicious vegetable dish or a great first course. It can be prepared earlier in the day and heated before serving. The sauce is one of the best ..very fresh, pure and flavorful. It is wonderful over pasta, too.

- 1   cup unflavored low-fat yogurt
- 2   tablespoons lemon juice
- 1/4   cup chopped chives

- 1/2   cup savory cracker crumbs
- 1/2   cup grated Parmesan cheese

- 1   eggplant (about 1 pound) peeled and cut into 3/8-inch slices. Sprinkle with salt and pepper.

In a bowl, stir together yogurt, lemon juice and chives until blended. In a rimmed plate, stir together crumbs and grated Parmesan cheese.

Brush eggplant slices on both sides with yogurt mixture and coat on both sides in crumb mixture. Place eggplant slices, in one layer, on a greased jelly roll pan and bake at 400° until golden brown, about 20 minutes. Carefully turn and brown other side. Serve with a splash of lemon or a spoonful of Five-Minute Tomato Sauce. Serves 8.

Five-Minute Tomato Sauce:
- 6   cloves garlic, thinly sliced
- 2   tablespoons olive oil

- 1   can (1 pound) stewed tomatoes, chopped. Do not drain.
- 1/4   teaspoon sweet basil flakes
- 2   teaspoons onion flakes
- 1/4   teaspoon Italian Herb Seasoning
- 1   teaspoon sugar
- 1   shake red pepper flakes
-     salt and pepper to taste

Saute garlic in oil for 30 seconds. Add the remaining ingredients, cover pan and simmer sauce for 5 minutes. Yields 2 cups sauce.

Cabbage Rolls in Sweet & Sour Tomato Sauce

1	large head cabbage (about 1 pound), rinse and remove the core

1 1/2	cups raw rice, partially boiled*
1/2	small onion, grated, about 3 tablespoons
2	carrots, peeled and finely grated
1	egg
1/8	teaspoon garlic powder
	black pepper to taste

Stand cabbage up on core end and cook it in 2-inches of boiling water for 10 to 12 minutes or until softened. Remove from pan and refresh under cold water. Carefully remove the outer leaves. When the leaves are too small to roll, chop them finely and place them in a Dutch oven casserole.

Mix together the remaining ingredients until nicely blended. Place about 2 tablespoons rice mixture on the bottom of the cabbage leaf. Tuck in the sides and roll it. Place rolls on top of minced cabbage in Dutch oven and pour Sweet & Sour Tomato Sauce over all. Cover pan and simmer for 1 hour. Yields about 12 to 16 cabbage rolls and generously serves 6 to 8.

Sweet & Sour Tomato Sauce:

1	can (1 pound) stewed tomatoes, chopped. Do not drain.
1	can (8 ounces) tomato sauce
3/4	cup vegetable broth
3	tablespoons lemon juice
1	teaspoon sugar
	black pepper to taste

Stir together all the ingredients until blended.

*To partially boil rice:
Stir 1 1/2 cups rice in 2-quarts rapidly boiling water, lower heat to medium, simmer for 5 minutes and drain.

Potato & Zucchini Casserole with Onions & Bread Crumbs

     5   potatoes, peeled and grated
     3   small onions, grated
     3   medium zucchini, grated (do not peel)
     3   eggs, beaten
   3/4   cup bread crumbs
         salt and pepper to taste

Grate potatoes just before baking so that they do not darken. If you grate them earlier, cover them with cold water and drain them thoroughly before using.

Combine all the ingredients in a large bowl and stir until everything is nicely mixed. Spread mixture evenly in an oiled 9x13-inch pan and bake at 350° for about 50 minutes to 1 hour or until potatoes are tender and top is golden brown. Cut into squares to serve. Serves 8 to 10

Note: - Casserole can be baked earlier in the day and stored in the refrigerator Heat before serving.

Red Pepper, Potato & Onion Cake

This is a beautiful dish and delicious too. Potatoes prepared with sweet red peppers and green onions add excitement to a meal.

     6   medium potatoes, peeled and grated
     1   red pepper, cored, seeded and cut into dice
     6   green onions, chopped
     2   eggs
   1/2   cup cracker crumbs
         black pepper to taste

     1   tablespoon olive oil

In a large bowl, toss together first group of ingredients until nicely mixed. Place mixture into a 9x13-inch oiled non-stick baking pan. Drizzle top with a little oil. Bake at 350-degrees about 50 to 55 minutes, or until top is golden brown and crisp. Serves 6.

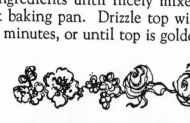

Eggplant Caponata with Tomatoes, Onions & Ricotta Cheese

This casserole yields 6 very generous servings. It is low in calories and very high in nourishment. Serve with Pink Orzo with Tomatoes for a truly satisfying and pleasurable accompaniment.

- 1   medium eggplant, cut into quarters and thinly sliced. Do not peel.
- 1   can (1 pound) stewed tomatoes, chopped. Do not drain.
- 1   can (8 ounces) tomato sauce
- 1   onion, chopped
- 3   cloves garlic, minced
- 1/2   teaspoon, each, sweet basil flakes and Italian Herb Seasoning
- 1   teaspoon sugar
-     pepper to taste

- 1   pint low-fat Ricotta cheese
- 1   egg
- 1/3   cup grated Parmesan cheese
- 1   teaspoon sweet basil flakes

- 1/2   cup grated Mozzarella cheese
- 1   tablespoon grated Parmesan cheese

In a Dutch oven casserole, simmer together first 9 ingredients for 30 minutes, or until eggplant is soft. Meanwhile, beat together the Ricotta, egg, Parmesan and sweet basil until blended.

In a 9x13-inch baking pan, spread 1/2 the eggplant mixture. Top with Ricotta cheese mixture and then, remaining eggplant mixture. Sprinkle top with grated Mozzarella and 1 tablespoon grated Parmesan (optional, but nice). Bake in a 350-degree oven for about 30 minutes, or until heated through. Cut into squares to serve. Serves 8 as a small entree or 6 for dinner.

Note: -Casserole can be baked earlier in the day and heated at serving time.

Baked Zucchini Crisps
with Marinara Sauce

Save hundreds of calories by baking, instead of frying, these zucchini crisps. These are nice to serve as an accompaniment to dinner or as small first course. The Light Marinara Sauce has only 1 teaspoon of olive oil. It is important, so don't omit it.

- 1 pound zucchini. Scrub, but do not peel. Slice on the diagonal into 1/2-inch thick slices.
- 3 tablespoons unflavored non-fat yogurt

- 1/3 cup savory cracker crumbs (like Ritz or Waverly)
- 1/3 cup grated Parmesan cheese

Spread each slice of zucchini, on both sides with a thin coating of yogurt. Combine crumbs and cheese and sprinkle on both sides of zucchini. Place zucchini on a plastic-coated cookie sheet and bake at 400-degrees until golden brown, about 20 minutes. Carefully turn and brown other side. Serve with a little Light Marinara Sauce on the side for dipping. Serves 6 to 8.

Light Marinara Sauce:
- 1 can (1 pound) stewed tomatoes, chopped. Do not drain.
- 3 tablespoons tomato paste
- 1 small onion, minced
- 2 cloves garlic, minced
- 1 teaspoon olive oil
- 1 teaspoon sugar
- 1/2 teaspoon Italian Herb Seasoning Flakes
- 1/2 teaspoon sweet basil flakes
- smallest pinch of cayenne
- salt and pepper to taste

In a saucepan, place all the ingredients, cover pan and simmer mixture for 30 minutes or until onion is soft and sauce is thickened. Yields about 2 cups.

Bean Thread Noodle & Vegetable Saute

This is a delicious one-dish meal, served in a casserole, very hearty and satisfying. It can be prepared in advance and heated before serving.

- 6 ounces bean thread noodles, cooked in boiling water for about 5 to 6 minutes, or until tender, and drained.
- 1/2 cup vegetable broth
- 2 teaspoons soy sauce

- 2 tablespoons olive oil
- 2 large red onions, peeled, cut in half and thinly sliced
- 6 cloves garlic, minced

- 1/2 pound mushrooms, sliced
- 4 large carrots, peeled and grated
  salt and pepper to taste

Place the cooked noodles in a bowl and toss with the vegetable broth and soy sauce. Set aside.

In a Dutch oven casserole, saute together next 3 ingredients, until onions are softened. Add the next 4 ingredients and continue sauteing until the carrots are tender, the onions are beginning to color, and the liquid rendered is evaporated. Toss in the noodle mixture until nicely mixed and heat through. Serves 4.

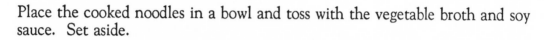

Cauliflower with Tomatoes & Potatoes

This delicious and homey casserole is attractive on a buffet for a very informal dinner. Dieters will love its blend of flavors.

- 1 can (1 pound) stewed tomatoes, chopped. Do not drain.
- 4 medium potatoes, peeled and cut into 1/2-inch slices
- 1 large onion, chopped
- 4 tablespoons lemon juice
- 1 teaspoon sugar
- 4 tablespoons chopped parsley
- 1/2 teaspoon dried dill weed
  salt and freshly ground pepper to taste

- 2 packages (10 ounces, each) frozen cauliflower florets, defrosted

- 2 tablespoons dry bread crumbs mixed with
- 2 tablespoons grated Parmesan cheese

More →

(Cauliflower with Tomatoes, Cont.)

In a Dutch oven casserole, place first 9 ingredients, and simmer mixture for 30 minutes, or until potatoes are almost tender. Stir in the cauliflower and simmer for an additional 5 minutes.

In a 12-inch oval porcelain baker, or 9x13-inch baking pan, lay cauliflower mixture in a shallow layer and sprinkle top with bread crumbs and grated cheese. Heat in a 350-degree oven until heated through. Serves 8.

Note: -This can be prepared earlier in the day, and stored in the refrigerator (except for the sprinkling of the bread crumbs and cheese, which should be done just before reheating).

Baked Vegetables with Lemon & Garlic

You are going to love the presentation of this dish. It is beautiful, served in a paella-type pan with large chunks of vegetables in a succulent lemon and garlic sauce. It is a blaze of colors and textures. Serve with a crusty, dense bread.

- 2 pounds small white onions, peeled, stemmed and left whole
- 2 pounds baby red potatoes, scrubbed
- 2 red peppers, cored, seeded and cut into 2-inch strips
- 2 yellow peppers, cored, seeded and cut into 2-inch strips
- 6 ears of corn, sliced into 2-inch rounds
- 1 large red onion, peeled and thinly sliced
- 6 cloves garlic, sliced
- 1/4 cup butter, melted
- 1/4 cup vegetable broth
- 1 teaspoon dried sage leaves
  salt and pepper to taste

- 4 tablespoons lemon juice

In a 12x16-inch baking pan, toss together first group of ingredients until vegetables are nicely coated. Cover pan tightly with foil and bake at 350° for 45 minutes or until potatoes are tender. Remove the foil and broil vegetables, turning now and again until vegetables are flecked with brown. Remove from the oven and mix in the lemon juice. Serve in a large paella-type pan with a crusty bread. Serves 8.

Cous Cous with Currants & Pine Nuts

Cous Cous is one of the easiest dishes to prepare. It is now sold precooked, so that you can prepare it in 2 or 3 minutes. Gone are the days when you needed a couscousier to steam the cous cous for 30 to 40 minutes. Cous Cous is also versatile. It can be served with any number of vegetables, dried fruits and nuts.

1	red onion, peeled, cut in half and thinly sliced
1	clove garlic, minced
2	tablespoons butter
1/2	cup dried currants
1/4	cup orange juice
1	tablespoon honey
1/2	teaspoon cinnamon
1	cup vegetable broth
1	cup precooked cous cous
1/3	cup toasted pine nuts

In a saucepan, saute onion and garlic in butter until onion is soft, but not browned. Add the next 4 ingredients and simmer mixture for 3 minutes.

In another saucepan, bring vegetable broth to a boil. Sprinkle in the cous cous, cover pan and cook mixture for 2 minutes. Remove from heat and fluff with a fork until grains are separated. Stir in currant mixture until nicely mixed. Heat to serve. Sprinkle pine nuts on top before serving. Serves 6.

Greek Frittata
with Tomatoes, Peppers & Feta Cheese

1/4	cup chopped red bell peppers
1/4	cup chopped yellow bell peppers
1/4	cup finely minced onions
1	tomato, peeled, seeded and chopped
	freshly ground black pepper to taste
4	eggs, beaten
3	ounces feta cheese, crumbled
1/4	teaspoon dried dill weed

More →

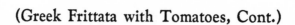

(Greek Frittata with Tomatoes, Cont.)

In a covered saucepan, cook together first 5 ingredients until vegetables are soft. Spread mixture evenly in an oiled 9x2-inch round baking pan or deep-dish pie plate. Stir together the remaining ingredients, and pour evenly over the vegetables. Bake in a 350-degree oven for about 20 minutes or until eggs are set. Serve with Onion-Flavored Baked Baby Potatoes. Serves 4.

Onion-Flavored Baked Baby Potatoes:
- 8 baby potatoes (about 1 pound), scrubbed. Peel off 1-inch of skin from around the center.
- 1 tablespoon melted butter
- 1/4 teaspoon onion powder, or to taste

In an 8-inch round baking dish, toss together all the ingredients. Bake in a 350-degree oven for about 40 minutes, or until potatoes are tender and the peeled band is golden brown. Serves 4.

Spinach Frittata with Cheese & Onions

This simple little casserole will furnish you with a fine vegetable accompaniment to dinner. It is also a very satisfying snack, and you will feel virtuous nibbling on this marvelous combination of vegetables, cheese, egg, and whole wheat bread.

- 2 packages (10 ounces, each) frozen chopped spinach, drained
- 1 pint low-fat Ricotta cheese
- 4 tablespoons grated Parmesan cheese
- 1 egg, beaten
- 2 slices fresh whole wheat bread, crumbed (1 cup fresh crumbs)
- 1/3 cup chopped green onions
- 1/2 teaspoon each, sweet basil flakes and oregano flakes
  pepper to taste

In a large bowl, stir together all the ingredients until mixture is nicely blended. Spread mixture evenly into an oiled 9x13-inch baking pan. Sprinkle top with a little grated Parmesan (optional, but nice.)

Bake at 350-degrees for about 50 to 55 minutes, or until top is browned and casserole is set. If not serving at this time, allow to cool in pan. When cool, cut into squares. This is nice served warm. Will serve 6 for lunch or 12 as an accompaniment to dinner.

Zucchini Frittata with
Onions & Cheese & Lemon Dill Sauce

This is an excellent dish, exceedingly delicious and simple to prepare. It serves well from a porcelain casserole and is a grand choice for a buffet. In the event that you do not own a porcelain casserole, then prepare the dish and let it cool. Cut it into squares, but leave it in the pan to reheat. After reheating, place squares on a lovely platter to serve. The sauce, served on the side, is lovely and delicate with just a faint hint of lemon and dill. Confetti Brown Rice or steamed baby potatoes are nice accompaniments.

```
6    medium-sized zucchini, scrubbed, peeled or unpeeled, and grated
1/2  cup chopped green onions
1/2  cup cracker crumbs (or cracker meal)
3    eggs, beaten
1    cup milk
1/4  cup grated Parmesan cheese
1/4  teaspoon dried dill weed
     pepper to taste

1    tomato, thinly sliced
1    tablespoon oil
3    tablespoons grated Parmesan cheese
```

In a bowl, toss together first group of ingredients until nicely mixed. Spread mixture evenly into a greased 9x13-inch baking pan and lay tomato slices on the top. Drizzle top with oil and sprinkle with Parmesan. Bake in a 350-degree oven for about 50 minutes or until top is crispy and golden. Cut into squares to serve. Serve with a spoonful of Lemon Dill Sauce on the top. Serves 6 to 8.

Lemon Dill Sauce:
```
6    shallots, minced
1    teaspoon butter

1/4  cup dry white wine

2    tablespoons lemon juice
1/2  cup vegetable broth
1/4  teaspoon dried dill weed
     white pepper to taste
```

In a saucepan, cook together first 2 ingredients, until shallots are tender. Add the wine and cook over high heat until it is partly evaporated. Stir together next 4 ingredients, add to saucepan, and simmer sauce, over low heat, for 10 minutes. Yields about 3/4 cup sauce.

Note: - Sauce can be prepared earlier in the day and stored in the refrigerator.

Royal Artichoke & Spinach Casserole

This serves well on a buffet, for brunch or lunch. It is a tempting combination of vegetables, cheese, eggs, yogurt, bread and a little oil...a little from each food group.

1	cup part-skimmed Ricotta cheese
1/4	cup unflavored non-fat yogurt
1	egg
1	slice bread, (1 ounce) made into crumbs
1/3	cup grated Parmesan cheese
1/4	cup chopped chives or green onions
1	package (10 ounces) frozen spinach, defrosted and drained
1	jar (6 ounces) marinated artichoke hearts, drained, rinsed and cut into fourths
	pepper to taste

Stir together first 6 ingredients until blended. Stir in spinach, artichokes and pepper. Spread mixture into an oiled 10-inch deep-dish pie plate and bake in a 350° oven for about 40 to 45 minutes or until top is golden brown. Cut into wedges to serve. Serves 8.

Artichoke and Red Pepper Frittata

4	eggs
1	cup low-fat milk
1/2	teaspoon oregano flakes
	white pepper to taste
1	jar (8 ounces) marinated artichoke hearts, drained and cut into fourths
4	marinated red peppers, drained and cut into strips
1/2	cup chopped green onions
1	clove garlic, minced
2	tablespoons grated Parmesan cheese

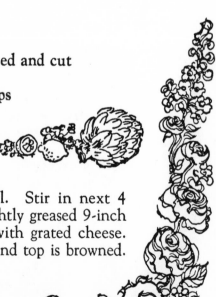

Beat together first group of ingredients in a large bowl. Stir in next 4 ingredients until blended. Pour mixture evenly into a lightly greased 9-inch quiche baker or 8x8-inch baking pan and sprinkle top with grated cheese. Bake at 350-degrees for 25 minutes, or until eggs are set and top is browned. Serves 4 for lunch.

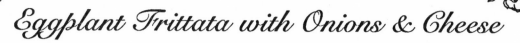

Eggplant Frittata with Onions & Cheese

This is one of my favorites. I remember it fondly, for when we were growing up, my Mom made it often. Oddly enough, we never figured out what it contained. The taste of the vegetables and cheese kept us coming back for snacks. This is a delicious vegetable dish and excellent for lunch or as an accompaniment to dinner.

1   medium eggplant (about 1 pound), peeled and sliced
1   tablespoon oil

2   cups cottage cheese
1/2 cup grated Parmesan cheese
2   ounces crumbled feta cheese
2   eggs, beaten
1/2 cup cracker crumbs
     pepper to taste

2   tablespoons grated Parmesan cheese

In a 9x13-inch baking pan, place eggplant and drizzle with oil. Cover pan tightly with foil and bake in a 350-degree oven for about 30 minutes, or until eggplant is soft.

In a large bowl, place the eggplant and the next 6 ingredients and stir until blended. Spread mixture evenly in an oiled 9x13-inch pan and sprinkle top with grated cheese. Bake at 350-degrees for about 50 minutes to 1 hour or until top is golden brown. Cut into squares to serve. Serves 12.

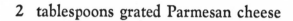

Rice with Peppers, Onion & Tomatoes

If you are planning to prepare this earlier in the day, then, cook the rice and vegetables and combine them in a casserole. The cheese is optional, but stir it in just before serving.

2   tablespoons butter or oil
2   cups vegetable broth (homemade or canned)
     salt to taste
1   cup long-grain rice

1   small yellow pepper, cut into strips
1   small red pepper, cut into strips
1   large onion, chopped
2   cloves garlic, minced
2   tablespoons butter

1/2 cup tomato sauce
1/3 cup grated Parmesan cheese (optional)

More →

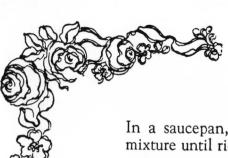
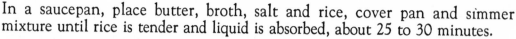

In a saucepan, place butter, broth, salt and rice, cover pan and simmer mixture until rice is tender and liquid is absorbed, about 25 to 30 minutes.

Meanwhile, in a large skillet, saute together the peppers, onion and garlic in butter until vegetables are soft. Add the tomato sauce and cook for 2 or 3 minutes, stirring.

Combine cooked rice and vegetables and heat through. Stir in the optional Parmesan cheese and serve at once. Serves 6.

Herbed Noodle Casserole with Spinach, Lemon & Green Onions

When you are thinking of serving a grand noodle dish for a buffet or informal dinner, this is a good one to consider. It presents beautifully with a crisped top sprinkled with parsley and green onions. The faint hint of lemon and herbs, combined with the melted cheeses, is simply delicious. Entire casserole can be assembled earlier in the day and baked before serving.

1   package (12 ounces) green (spinach) noodles, cooked until tender
       and drained.
1   package (10 ounces) frozen chopped spinach, defrosted and drained

1   pound low-fat Ricotta cheese
1   cup (3 ounces) grated low-fat Mozzarella cheese
1/2 cup grated Parmesan cheese
3   eggs, beaten
1/2 cup finely chopped green onion
1/4 cup finely chopped parsley
1   clove garlic minced
1/2 teaspoon Italian Herb Seasoning
3   tablespoons lemon juice
       salt and pepper to taste

In a greased 9x13-inch pan, toss noodles and spinach. Stir together the remaining ingredients until thoroughly blended. Spoon mixture on the noodles and toss and turn until everything is nicely blended.

Bake in a 350° oven for about 50 minutes or until top is golden and casserole is puffed and set. Decorate top with additional onions and parsley Serves 8

Old West Chile Rellenos Casserole
with Pink Rice

There is probably no dish that you can make that is easier than this one or more fun to eat. Everybody loves it. Serve it with some hot corn tortillas, spread with a little butter and rolled in the shape of a cigar. Entire casserole can be assembled earlier in the day and stored in the refrigerator. Heat before serving.

    3   ounces grated Jack cheese
    3   ounces grated Cheddar cheese
    1/2 cup chopped green onions

    2   cans (7 ounces, each) whole green chile peppers (about 12)

    1   can (1 pound) stewed tomatoes, drained and chopped.

    1/2 cup low-fat sour cream
    1/2 cup grated Cheddar cheese

Stir together cheeses and onions and stuff evenly into chile peppers. In a 9x13-inch porcelain baker, place filled chiles in one layer. Sprinkle tomatoes on top and dot with sour cream and additional cheddar cheese.

Bake at 350° for 20 minutes, or until cheese is melted. Broil for a few seconds to brown the top. Serve with Pink Rice. Serves 6.

Pink Rice:
    2   tomatoes, chopped
    2   teaspoons oil
    1 1/2 cups rice
    3   cups vegetable broth
           salt and pepper to taste

In a saucepan, stir together all the ingredients, cover pan, and simmer mixture for 30 minutes, or until rice is tender and liquid is absorbed. Serves 6.

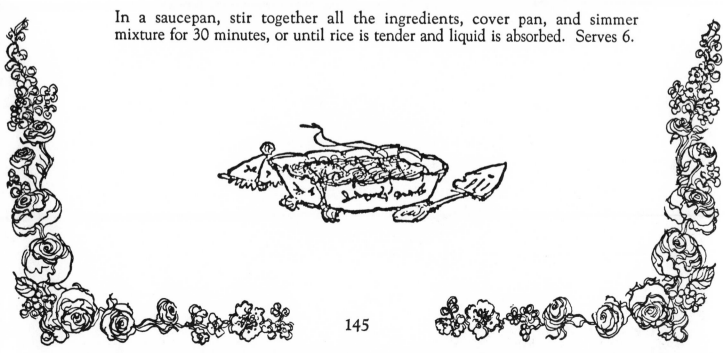

Chili with Red Beans & Pink Rice

Here's a nice healthy chili to satisfy your cravings for a strong taste   Although it contains no oil or fat, it is immensely delicious. The amounts of chili powder and cumin are average, and a lot more can be added for a more assertive taste

2	large onions, chopped (1/2 pound)
1/2	cup chopped green onions
2	tomatoes, chopped (fresh or canned)
1	can (7 ounces) diced green chiles
3	cloves garlic, minced
2	tablespoons chopped parsley
1 1/4	cups vegetable broth
1/2	teaspoon dried oregano flakes
1 1/2	tablespoons chili powder (or more to taste)
3/4	teaspoon ground cumin (or more to taste)
1/4	teaspoon black pepper
3	shakes cayenne pepper
2	cans (15 ounces, each) red kidney beans, thoroughly rinsed and drained

In a Dutch oven casserole, place all the ingredients, cover pan and simmer mixture for about 45 minutes, or until onions are very soft.   Serve on a bed of Pink Rice. Serves 8.

Pink Rice:

1 1/2	cups rice
3	cups vegetable broth
2	tablespoons tomato sauce
1	tablespoon chopped parsley

In a saucepan, stir together all the ingredients, cover pan and simmer rice for 30 minutes, or until rice is tender and liquid is absorbed Serves 8.

Quesadillos with Chiles & Cheese

Filling Ingredients:
- 1   can (3 1/2 ounces) diced green chiles
- 1   cup finely chopped green onions
- 4   ounces grated Jack cheese
- 4   ounces grated Cheddar cheese
- 1   tomato, finely diced
- 3   tablespoons minced cilantro
- 1/2 teaspoon ground cumin
  - salt and pepper to taste

- 8   8-inch flour tortillas

In a bowl, toss together Filling Ingredients until nicely mixed. Brush an 8 or 9-inch skillet with oil. Place one tortilla in pan and sprinkle top evenly with 1/4 of the filling. Top filling with a second tortilla.

Cook for several minutes, pressing top down with a spatula, until bottom is lightly browned. (By pressing the top down, the melted cheese will help keep the tortillas together when turning.) With the spatula, turn the tortilla, and brown the other side. Transfer to a baking pan and keep warm in a 250° oven. Continue with the remaining tortillas. With a sharp knife or kitchen shears, cut the quesadillo into 6 or 8 wedges to serve as a starter. Serve a whole one if it is the main course. Serves 4 to 8.

Mexican Strata with Chiles and Cheese

- 6   eggs, beaten
- 1   cup milk
- 3   slices egg bread, crusts removed, torn into 1-inch pieces

- 1   can (4 ounces) diced green chiles
- 1/2 cup Jack cheese, grated (2 ounces)
- 4   tablespoons grated Parmesan cheese
- 1/3 cup chopped chives or green onions
  - pepper to taste

- 2   medium tomatoes, peeled, seeded and thinly sliced
- 2   tablespoons grated Parmesan cheese

In a bowl, soak together first 3 ingredients until bread is evenly moistened. Stir in next 5 ingredients until blended. Pour egg mixture into a lightly oiled 9x13-inch non-stick baking pan. Lay tomato slices on top and sprinkle with grated cheese. Bake in a 350° oven for about 50 minutes or until eggs are set and top is puffy and golden brown. Serves 6.

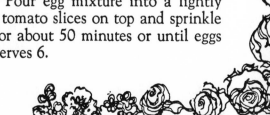

Red Hot Texas Chili with Beans

    4   cloves garlic, minced
    2   onions, finely chopped
    1   tablespoon oil

    1   can (1 pound 12 ounces) crushed tomatoes in tomato puree
    1   cup vegetable broth
    1   can (6 ounces) tomato paste
    1   can (7 ounces) diced green chiles
    3   cans (1 pound, each) kidney beans, rinsed and drained
    4   tablespoons chili powder
    1   teaspoon cumin
    1   teaspoon oregano
  1/4   teaspoon red pepper flakes
        salt and pepper to taste

Toppings:
    2   cups grated Cheddar cheese (8 ounces)
        finely minced onion (optional)

In a Dutch oven casserole, saute together first 3 ingredients until onions are just beginning to brown. Add the remaining ingredients and simmer mixture, with cover slightly ajar, for about 45 minutes, or until it is very thick. Serve chili in bowls with grated Cheddar and finely chopped onion on top. Corn Bread or with Cheese & Garlic Bread is a nice accompaniment. Serves 8.

Cheese & Garlic Bread:
   16   1/2-inch slices French Bread

   16   teaspoons low-fat mayonnaise
    2   cloves garlic, put through a press
  1/2   cup grated Parmesan cheese
        paprika

Stir together mayonnaise, garlic and grated Parmesan until blended. Spread mixture on one side of each bread slice and sprinkle lightly with paprika. Place on a cookie sheet and broil for a few minutes until top is bubbly and lightly browned. Serve at once. Serves 8.

Note: - Bread can be assembled earlier in the day, covered tightly with foil and stored in the refrigerator. Broil before serving.

Tomatoes Stuffed with Spinach in Light Tomato Sauce

This is a good dish to consider serving with rice as a main course or as an accompaniment to dinner.

8 medium-sized firm tomatoes

1 package (10 ounces) frozen chopped spinach, defrosted and pressed dry in a strainer
1/2 cup fresh bread crumbs
1/2 cup non-fat cottage cheese
1/4 cup grated Parmesan cheese
1 egg, beaten
1 tablespoon chopped parsley
pepper to taste

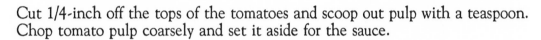

Cut 1/4-inch off the tops of the tomatoes and scoop out pulp with a teaspoon. Chop tomato pulp coarsely and set it aside for the sauce.

Combine the remaining ingredients until blended and stuff tomatoes loosely with spinach mixture.

In an 10-inch round oven-proof casserole, place the tomatoes in one layer. Spoon Light Tomato Sauce over the top and bake in a 350-degree oven for about 30 minutes. Serves 4.

Light Tomato Sauce:
1 tablespoon oil
reserved chopped tomato pulp
1 can (1 pound) stewed tomatoes, chopped and drained
1/4 teaspoon, each Italian Herb Seasoning and sweet basil flakes
1/8 teaspoon, each, garlic powder and onion powder
pinch of cayenne pepper
freshly ground black pepper to taste

Stir together all the ingredients until blended.

Italian Zucchini
Stuffed with Tomatoes, Onions & Cheese

Stuffed vegetables are a little more work, but well worth the extra effort. This is a great main course. It is excellent served with pink rice or orzo as an accompaniment.

6   zucchini, (about 1 1/2 pounds). Trim stem, leaving about 1/2-inch. Cut the zucchini in half, lengthwise, and scoop out the centers (a melon-ball cutter does the job nicely) leaving a 1/4-inch shell. Chop and reserve the pulp.

1/2   cup water

Stuffing Mixture:
     Reserved pulp
2   medium onions, chopped
2   shallots, minced
2   tomatoes, seeded and chopped
2   garlic cloves, minced
1   tablespoon olive oil
     salt and pepper to taste

1/4   pound goat cheese, crumbled
1/2   cup fresh bread crumbs
1/2   teaspoon dried dill weed

12   teaspoons grated Parmesan

Place water in a 9x13-inch baking pan and set the zucchini, cut side up. Cover pan tightly with foil and bake at 350° for 10 minutes or until shells are just firm tender. Remove zucchini from pan and drain on paper towelling. Clean pan and brush bottom with a little oil.

In an uncovered Dutch oven casserole, simmer the next 8 ingredients until onions are soft and juices rendered have evaporated. Allow to cool. When cool, toss in the cheese, bread and dill until blended. Divide stuffing into prepared shells and place in baking pan. Sprinkle tops with grated cheese. Just before serving, heat zucchini in a preheated oven and broil for about 3 to 4 minutes, or until tops are flecked with brown and heated through. Serves 6 as a main course or 12 as an accompaniment.

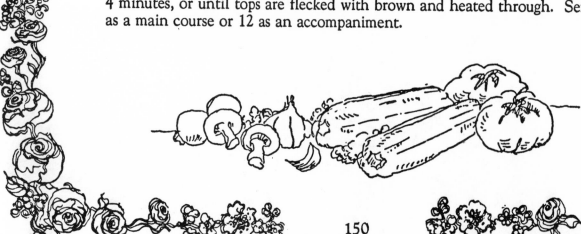

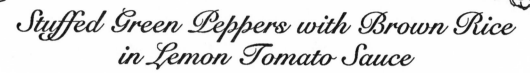

Stuffed Green Peppers with Brown Rice in Lemon Tomato Sauce

We were raised on every manner of stuffed vegetables. My Mom stuffed green and red peppers, eggplant, zucchini, tomatoes, squash and any vegetable that could be scooped and stuffed. Fillings also varied from a simple rice to rice mixed with any number of complimentary vegetables. Grains varied from brown or white rice, bulgur, lentils, or cous cous.

6   large green peppers, cut in half lengthwise, seeds and membranes removed. You will have 12 halves.

Stuffing:
- 3   medium tomatoes, seeded and coarsely chopped
- 2   medium onions, finely chopped
- 3   cloves garlic, thinly sliced
- 1   tablespoon olive oil

- 3   cups cooked brown rice
- 3   tablespoons lemon juice
- 1/4   cup chopped parsley leaves
- 1   teaspoon sweet basil flakes
- salt and freshly ground pepper to taste

In a 9x13-inch baking pan, spread Lemon Tomato Sauce and place peppers on top. In a saucepan, simmer together next 4 ingredients until onions are soft. Place mixture in a large bowl and stir in the remaining ingredients. Divide mixture between the peppers and spoon some of the sauce on the tops. Cover pan with foil and bake at 350° for 40 minutes. Remove foil and continue baking for 10 to 15 minutes or until peppers are tender. Serves 6.

Lemon Tomato Sauce:
- 1   can (1 pound 12 ounces) crushed tomatoes in puree
- 3   tablespoons lemon juice
- 1   clove garlic, minced
- 1   small onion, minced
- 1   teaspoon sugar
- 1   teaspoon sweet basil flakes
- 1/2   teaspoon Italian Herb Seasoning
- 2   teaspoons oil
- salt and pepper to taste

Stir together all the ingredients until blended.

The Best Rice-Stuffed Tomatoes with Garlic & Herbs

I love these stuffed tomatoes. While this recipe appeared in one of my earlier cookbooks, it is so good, it bears repeating. The simplicity of the preparation, and the purity of taste is truly wonderful.

12   medium tomatoes (about 3 pounds). Cut a thin slice off the tops, scoop out the centers with a grapefruit knife and then a teaspoon. Reserve the tomato pulp.

Tomato & Rice Filling:
- 2 1/2 cups cooked rice (see below)
  Reserved tomato pulp from above
- 1 tablespoon oil
- 1 small onion, grated
- 2 cloves garlic, minced
- 1 teaspoon sweet basil flakes
- 3 tablespoons minced parsley
  salt and freshly ground pepper to taste

Prepare tomatoes. Mix together all the filling ingredients until blended. Stuff the tomatoes loosely with filling and place any leftover rice mixture on the bottom of a 9x13-inch porcelain baker. Settle the tomatoes over the rice Pour Tomato, Garlic & Herb Sauce over the tops.

Cover pan loosely with foil, and bake in a 350° oven for about 40 minutes or until tomatoes are tender, but not mushy. (Cooking time will vary, so check after 30 minutes.) Serve warm not hot. Yields 12 stuffed tomatoes.

Tomato, Garlic & Herb Sauce:
- 1 tablespoon oil
- 1 can (1 pound) stewed tomatoes, finely chopped
- 4 tablespoons tomato paste
- 1 small onion, grated
- 2 cloves garlic, minced
- 2 teaspoons sugar
- 1 teaspoon sweet basil flakes
- 1 teaspoon Italian Herb Seasoning flakes
  salt and pepper to taste

Stir together all the ingredients until blended.

To precook rice:
Cook 1 cup rice in 3 cups of rapidly boiling water until tender and drain.

Eggplant Stuffed with Ricotta

This delicious dish is a fine entree for vegetarian lunch or light supper. It is exceedingly low in calories when you consider the huge portion. It is rather a complete food, too, as it contains vegetables, eggs, cheese and bread. If serving for dinner, pasta is a nice accompaniment.

3 medium eggplants, (about 3/4 pound, each), cut in half lengthwise. Scoop out the vegetable, leaving a 1/3-inch thick shell. Finely chop the scooped out eggplant.
1 teaspoon, each, oil and water

1 pound low-fat Ricotta cheese (also called "part-skimmed")
1/2 cup grated Parmesan cheese
2 eggs, beaten
1 cup fresh bread crumbs (2 slices)
1/2 teaspoon Italian Herb Seasoning
1 tablespoon minced parsley leaves
   white pepper to taste

3 tablespoons grated Parmesan cheese for topping

In a 9x13-inch baking pan, place chopped eggplant. Drizzle with 1 teaspoon of oil and 1 teaspoon of water, cover pan tightly with foil and bake in a 400-degree oven for about 25 minutes or until eggplant is very soft.

In a large bowl, mix together cooked eggplant and next 7 ingredients until blended and divide mixture between the 6 eggplant shells. Sprinkle tops with grated cheese. Place in a baking pan and bake, uncovered, for 45 minutes, or until tops are browned. Serves 6.

Old-Fashioned Stuffed Peppers in Tomato Sauce

6 medium green bell peppers, cut in half lengthwise (top to bottom). Remove seeds and membranes. You will have 12 halves.

2 tomatoes, peeled, seeded and chopped (fresh or canned)
1 cup rice (par-boiled in 3 cups water for 15 minutes), drained
1 tablespoon minced parsley leaves
1/2 teaspoon sweet basil flakes
   salt and pepper to taste

Place peppers in a 9x13-inch baking pan. In a bowl, combine the remaining ingredients and divide stuffing between the peppers, smoothing the tops. Pour Quick Tomato Sauce over the tops, cover pan with foil, and bake at 350-degrees for 30 minutes. Uncover pan and continue baking for 20 minutes, basting now and again. Serves 6 as a main course or 12 as a side dish. More

(Old-Fashioned Stuffed Peppers, Cont.)

Quick Tomato Sauce:
- 1   can (1 pound) stewed tomatoes, chopped. Do not drain.
- 3   tablespoons tomato paste
- 1   small onion, grated
- 1   teaspoon sugar
- 1   clove garlic, minced
- 1   tablespoon minced parsley leaves
- 1/2   teaspoon sweet basil flakes
- 1/2   teaspoon Italian Herb Seasoning flakes
-     pinch of cayenne pepper

In an uncovered saucepan, simmer together all the ingredients for 10 minutes.

Noodle Pudding with Cottage Cheese & Chives

Serve this with a green vegetable for a very enjoyable dinner. Casserole can be assembled earlier in the day and stored in the refrigerator. Bring to room temperature before heating.

- 1/2   pound wide noodles, cooked tender and drained
- 2   tablespoons melted butter or margarine

- 4   eggs
- 2   cups non-fat cottage cheese
- 1/2   cup chopped chives
- 1/2   cup Parmesan cheese, grated
-     pepper to taste

Toss noodles in melted butter. Beat together next 5 ingredients until blended. Combine noodles and egg mixture and toss to mix well. Place mixture into a buttered 9x13-inch baking pan and bake in a 350° oven for about 45 minutes or until pudding is set and top is browned. Serve with Quick-Cook Tomato Sauce on the side. Serves 6 for dinner or 12 as an accompaniment.

Quick-Cook Tomato Sauce:
- 1   can (1 pound 12 ounces) crushed tomatoes in tomato puree
- 2   tablespoons onion flakes
- 1/4   teaspoon coarse ground garlic powder
- 1   teaspoon sugar
- 1   teaspoon olive oil
- 1   teaspoon, each, sweet basil flakes and Italian Herb Seasoning

In a saucepan, cook together all the ingredients for 5 minutes.

Bread Pudding with Chiles & Cheese & Fresh Salsa

I have given you many such recipes in the past. I used to call them "mini-souffles", for these are close to their sophisticated cousins. There is no end to the different combinations you could use. This serves nicely for brunch or lunch with a Mexican theme.

8	slices sourdough bread, crusts removed and cut into cubes
2	cups grated Jack cheese (about 4 ounces)
1/2	cup chopped green onions
1	can (4 ounces) diced green chiles

4	eggs
1 1/4	cups milk
4	tablespoons grated Parmesan cheese
	salt and pepper to taste

In an 8x12-inch greased porcelain baker, spread half the bread. Sprinkle top evenly with cheese, onions and chiles. Cover with remaining bread and press down gently. Beat together the remaining ingredients and pour over the casserole, pressing down any bread that floats to the top. When bread appears to have absorbed the egg mixture (about 15 minutes), bake at 350° for about 45 minutes, or until puffed and golden brown. Serve with Fresh Salsa on the side (optional.) Serves 6.

Fresh Salsa:

3	medium tomatoes, peeled, seeded and chopped
3	ounces diced green chiles (see note)
1/4	cup minced red onion
1	tablespoon minced cilantro
1	tablespoon minced parsley
1	teaspoon oil
2	tablespoons lemon juice
1	tablespoon vinegar

Stir together all the ingredients until blended. Refrigerate until serving time. Yields 2 cups salsa.

Note: -If you are planning to serve this with the salsa, then purchase a 7-ounce can of diced green chiles and divide it between the pudding and the salsa.

Parmesan Bread Pudding with Tomatoes & Artichokes

This little invention is a lovely choice for an informal luncheon. It can be assembled earlier in the morning and baked before serving. Using the richer half and half adds a little more flavor.

12   thin slices (about 1/4-inch thick) crusty French bread. Toast lightly at 350° for 10 minutes, or until crisped. Break bread into small pieces.

6   eggs
1   cup milk or half and half
1/2   cup grated Parmesan cheese
1/4   cup chopped chives
     salt and pepper to taste

1   jar (7 ounces) marinated artichoke hearts, drained and coarsely chopped

2   medium tomatoes, peeled, seeded and thinly sliced
2   tablespoons grated Parmesan cheese

Prepare bread. In a bowl, beat together next 6 ingredients until blended. In a 10x3-inch round porcelain baker, layer half the bread, half the egg mixture, artichokes and remaining bread. Pour remaining egg mixture over the bread and set tomato slices evenly on top. Sprinkle top with grated Parmesan. Bake at 350° for about 40 to 45 minutes, or until puffed and golden. Serves 6.

Old-Fashioned Cornbread Pudding

2   onions, peeled and chopped
2   stalks celery, scraped and chopped
3   tablespoons minced parsley leaves
1   teaspoon each sage, thyme and sweet basil flakes
4   tablespoons butter (1/2 stick)
     salt and pepper to taste

6   cups packaged seasoned cornbread stuffing
1   cup vegetable broth

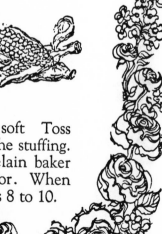

In a skillet, sauté together first 7 ingredients until vegetables are soft Toss in the cornbread stuffing. Add enough vegetable broth to soften the stuffing. Spread pudding evenly in a 10-inch round baking pan (a porcelain baker works nicely for this), cover with foil and store in the refrigerator. When ready to serve, bake uncovered at 350° until heated through Serves 8 to 10.

Eggplant & Cheese Pie with Marinara

You'll love this pie. Layers of eggplant surround a savory cheese filling and flavored with a yummy sauce make this casserole memorable. Casserole can be assembled earlier in the day and heated before serving.

>2   eggplants (about 1 pound, each)
>   pepper
>1   teaspoon oil
>
>2   eggs, beaten
>1   pound low-fat Ricotta cheese
>1/4 pound part skim milk Mozzarella cheese, grated
>1/2 cup grated Parmesan cheese
>1/2 teaspoon dried basil flakes
>
>   Quick Marinara Sauce
>2   tablespoons grated Parmesan cheese

Peel and slice eggplant in 1/4-inch slices. Sprinkle with pepper. Place eggplant slices on a cookie sheet, brush lightly with oil, cover with foil and bake in a 400° oven for about 20 minutes or until eggplant slices are soft. Remove from oven and set aside.

Beat together eggs, cheeses and basil until blended. Set aside. In a 9x13-inch baking pan, layer 1/2 the Quick Marinara Sauce, 1/2 the eggplant and all of the cheese mixture. Top with remaining eggplant and sauce. Sprinkle top with additional Parmesan cheese. Bake at 375° for about 40 minutes or until piping hot. Serves 8 to 10.

Quick Marinara Sauce:
>1   can (1 pound 12 ounces) crushed tomatoes in puree
>1   onion, very finely chopped
>3   cloves garlic, minced
>1   teaspoon, each sweet basil flakes and Italian Herb Seasoning
>1   teaspoon olive oil
>1   bay leaf

In a saucepan, simmer together all the ingredients for 10 minutes. Remove bay leaf.

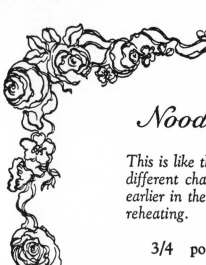

Noodle & Cheese Pie with Italian Sauce

This is like the Greek Pastitsio in an Italian mood. The egg noodles gives a totally different character to this lasagna-type dish. Entire casserole can be assembled earlier in the day and stored in the refrigerator. Bring to room temperature before reheating.

3/4   pound wide egg noodles, cooked until tender and drained

Italian Sauce:
- 1   onion, finely chopped
- 2   cloves garlic, minced
- 1   teaspoon oil

- 1   can (1 pound 12 ounces) crushed tomatoes in puree
- 1   teaspoon sugar
- 1   teaspoon Italian Herb Seasoning
-    pepper to taste

Cheese Filling:
- 1   pound low-fat Ricotta cheese
- 3   eggs
- 1/2   cup grated Parmesan cheese
- 1   teaspoon sweet basil flakes
- 1/4   cup chopped chives

To make Sauce:
Saute onion and garlic in oil until onion is soft. Add tomatoes, sugar and seasonings and simmer sauce gently for 20 minutes. Set sauce aside.

To make Cheese Filling:
Beat together the Ricotta cheese and next 4 ingredients until blended.

To Assemble:
Spread 1/3 of the sauce in a 9x13-inch porcelain baking pan. Place half the noodles over the sauce. Next, spoon the cheese mixture on top. Continue with the remaining noodles and sauce. Sprinkle top with a little more grated Parmesan cheese. Bake casserole at 350° for about 35 minutes or until piping hot. Serves 8.

Winter Tart with Onions & Apples

This lovely winter tart can be prepared earlier in the day, stored in the refrigerator and heated before serving.

1   frozen deep dish 9-inch pie crust, baked for 8 minutes in a 350°
     oven or until crust is set and just beginning to take on color.

3   medium onions, cut in half and thinly sliced thinly sliced.
2   medium apples, peeled, cored and grated
4   cloves garlic, minced
2   tablespoons butter
2   teaspoons sugar
     salt and pepper to taste

2   eggs
1/2 cup half and half
1/2 teaspoon dried sage flakes
1/4 teaspoon dried thyme flakes

Prepare pie crust.   In a skillet saute together next group of ingredients until onions and apples are soft, about 20 minutes.   Place mixture into prepared pie shell.   Beat together next 4 ingredients until blended and pour over the onion mixture, easing it gently until egg mixture is evenly dispersed.   Place tart on a cookie sheet and bake at a 350° oven for about 40 minutes, or until filling is set. Serves 6.

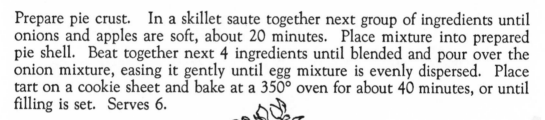

Cheese Lover's Pie
with Cheese Crumb Butter Crust

This lovely quiche is an excellent choice for lunch.   The cheese crumb crust is outstanding and harmonizes with the cheesy filling.   And to add to its virtues, it can be prepared earlier in the day.

3   eggs, beaten
1/2 cup half and half or milk
3   tablespoons grated Parmesan cheese
     pinch of prepared mustard

2   ounces Gruyere cheese, grated
4   ounces cream cheese, cut into 1/2-inch cubes
     salt and pepper to taste

6   paper-thin slices of tomato, seeded and drained

Beat together first 4 ingredients until blended.   Stir in the next 4 ingredients until blended.

More →

Pour egg mixture into Cheese Crumb Butter Crust and place tomato slices decoratively on top. Bake in a 350° oven for about 25 minutes or until custard is just set and top is lightly browned. Do not overbake. To serve, cut into wedges. Serve hot, warm or at room temperature. Serves 6.

Cheese Crumb Butter Crust:
- 3/4 cup cracker crumbs. (Use a tasty cracker like Butter Sesame or French Onion.)
- 3/4 cup grated Parmesan cheese
- 4 tablespoons melted butter

Combine all the ingredients until blended. Pat mixture on the bottom of an 8-inch porcelain quiche baker and bake in a 350° oven for 8 minutes. Allow shell to cool a little before filling.

Note: -Pie can be prepared earlier in the day and stored in the refrigerator. Heat in a 350° oven for 10 minutes before serving.
-This is not a traditional quiche, but a firm, dense cheese pie.

French Brie Quiche with Strawberries & Toasted Almonds

Brie, served with fresh fruit and almonds, is a lovely combination of flavors and colors. Here, they are combined in a quiche that has flair and panache and is a good choice for a very special brunch. It can be prepared in advance and stored in the refrigerator. Heat through before serving.

- 1 deep dish frozen pie shell, baked in a 400° oven for about 8 minutes, or until just beginning to take on color. Leave shell in pan.

- 6 ounces French Brie. Remove the outer moldy rind and cut the remaining Brie into small dice.
- 1 package (3 ounces) cream cheese, cut into 1/2-inch dice

- 4 eggs
- 1 cup half and half

- 1/3 cup sliced almonds
- 1 cup strawberries sliced in halves

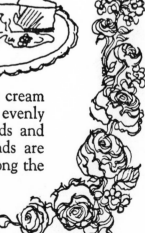

Place pie shell on a cookie sheet. Place Brie evenly in shell. Place cream cheese evenly in shell. Beat together eggs and half and half and pour evenly in shell. Bake at 350° for 30 minutes. Sprinkle top with almonds and continue baking for 15 minutes or until custard is set and almonds are toasted. Remove from the oven and place strawberries decoratively along the rim. Serves 6.

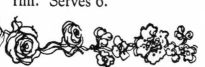

Ricotta Tart with Raisins & Pine Nuts

This very Italian pie is much denser than a quiche and is a nice first course for an informal dinner. It is a lovely choice for lunch with a vegetable salad and spiced apples or apricots.

2   9-inch frozen shallow pie shells (not the deep-dish variety). Place shells on a cookie sheet and bake in a 400° oven for 8 minutes or until just beginning to take on color.

3   eggs
1   cup low-fat ricotta cheese
1   cup half and half
1   package (frozen spinach) defrosted and pressed in a strainer to drain
1   tablespoon sugar
    pinch of salt, pepper and nutmeg

1/2   cup raisins
1/2   cup toasted pine nuts

Prepare pie shells and leave them on the cookie sheet. Beat together next group of ingredients until blended. Stir in raisins and pine nuts. Divide mixture evenly between the two pie shells and bake at 350° for 40 to 45 minutes or until pie is set and top is golden brown. Each pie serves 6.

Artichoke, Tomato & Chevre Cheese Pie

1   deep dish 9-inch frozen pie shell
1   jar (6 ounces) marinated artichoke hearts, drained and cut into small pieces. Reserve the marinade for another use.
1/3   cup chopped chives
4   ounces Chevre cheese, diced

2   eggs
1   cup milk
2   tablespoons grated Parmesan

6   thin tomato slices to lay on top
1   tablespoon grated Parmesan

Place pie shell on a cookie sheet. Place artichokes, chives and cheese evenly in pan. Beat together eggs, milk and Parmesan until blended and pour evenly into the pie shell. Lay the tomatoes slices on the top and sprinkle with the Parmesan. Bake at 350° for 45 minutes, or until custard is set. Serves 6.

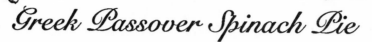

Greek Passover Spinach Pie

This is a good choice for lunch during the Passover holidays. A few Greek olives, and a slice of feta cheese are nice accompaniments. To thoroughly wet the matzas, submerge them in a large bowl of water. Do not wait until they fall apart. They should be softened through and through, but not to the point where they cannot be removed from the water almost whole. Next place them on a thirsty towel, let them drain a little and then crumble them.

- 3   packages (10 ounces, each) frozen chopped spinach, defrosted and thoroughly drained by placing it in a strainer and pressing out the juices
- 2   cups grated Parmesan cheese
- 6   eggs
- 6   matzas, soaked in water, squeezed dry and crumbled

- 3   tablespoons oil
- 3   tablespoons grated Parmesan for top

In a large bowl, stir together spinach, grated cheese, eggs and matzas until mixture is nicely combined. Spread oil into a 9x13-inch baking pan and spread spinach mixture evenly in pan. Sprinkle top with additional grated Parmesan. Bake in a 350° oven for about 1 hour, or until top is browned. Cut into squares and serve warm. Serves 16.

California Cheese Pie with Chevre, Pine Nuts & Sun-Dried Tomatoes

This delicious pie is filled with all manner of good things...goat cheese, sun-dried tomatoes, pine nuts...and faintly scented with dill. Nice to serve at a luncheon.

- 3   eggs, beaten
- 1 1/2   cups low-fat or regular milk
- 2   tablespoons grated Parmesan cheese

- 1   package (8 ounces) Chevre goat cheese, cut into 1/4-inch dice
- 4   ounces cream cheese, cut into 1/4-inch dice
- 1/3   cup finely chopped sun-dried tomatoes
- 1/3   cup pine nuts
- 1/3   cup finely chopped chives
- 1   teaspoon dried dill weed

- 1   9-inch deep dish frozen pie crust

Beat together eggs, milk and grated cheese until thoroughly blended. Stir in next 6 ingredients until blended. Pour mixture into frozen pie crust and bake at 350° for 40 to 45 minutes or until custard is set. Serves 8.

Gratin of Vegetables

Richly flavored with garlic, onions, peppers and tomatoes, this is a great dish to serve with Yellow Rice with Tomato & Chiles..

2	large red onions, cut into halves and thinly sliced
2	red peppers, cored and cut into 1-inch slices
2	yellow peppers, cored and cut into 1-inch slices
10	garlic cloves, minced
1	can (1 pound) stewed tomatoes, chopped and drained
1	teaspoon ground turmeric
1/2	teaspoon ground cumin
1	tablespoon olive oil
2	tablespoons grated Parmesan cheese

In a foil-covered baking pan, bake together all the ingredients (except the cheese) for 20 minutes or until vegetables are almost tender. Remove cover and continue baking for 20 minutes or until vegetables are tender. Sprinkle vegetables with grated cheese and place pan under the broiler for 2 to 3 minutes to brown the top. Serves 8.

Stir-Fried Mixed Vegetable Platter

The following can take on a totally different character with different seasonings. To take on an Oriental mood, add 1 tablespoon low-sodium soy and 1/4 teaspoon ground ginger. Herbs are nice. Sweet basil flakes, oregano or thyme add interest. Curry to taste is another good choice. Other vegetables can be used...cauliflower, broccoli, asparagus. Keep it varied and you will never feel bored.

8	green onions, cut into 1-inch strips, on the diagonal
4	carrots, peeled and sliced on the diagonal
1	sweet red bell pepper, cut into 1/2-inch slices
1	yellow bell pepper, cut into 1/2-inch slices
4	stalks celery, cut into thin slices
4	cloves garlic, sliced
	seasoning of your choice
2	teaspoons oil
2	tablespoons vegetable broth

Prepare the vegetables. In a wok or large skillet, over high heat, heat the oil and broth until bubbling. Add the vegetables, and continue cooking, over high heat, tossing and turning, until vegetables are tender, but still firm. Serves 4.

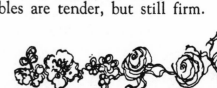

Broiled Mixed Vegetable Platter

The beauty of this dish lies in the myriad of colors and shapes, and the large cuts of vegetables. Using vegetable broth, instead of oil, makes this truly low calorie. Other vegetables can be used, broccoli, cauliflower, carrots, asparagus. Potatoes are also good, but should be cooked before using. Baby vegetables are especially attractive.

2   leeks, white and tender green part only. Cut in half, lengthwise, and rinse off every trace of sand.
8   green onions. Trim the whiskers and any frayed tops and leave whole.
4   zucchini, about 1 pound. Scrub and do not peel. Cut into long 1/2-inch slices on the diagonal.
1   sweet red bell pepper, cut into 1-inch slices
2   cloves garlic, sliced
1/2 teaspoon dried dill weed
1   cup rich vegetable broth

In a 9x13-inch broiling pan, place all the vegetables, sprinkle with dill and pour vegetable broth over all. Place pan under the broiler and broil, 4-inches from the heat, turning the vegetables now and again, for 20 minutes or until they are tender and browned. Serves 4.

Roasted Vegetable Platter with Eggplant, Onion Rings & Mixed Peppers

This is an attractive and exciting vegetable presentation. Vegetables should be served al dente, not too raw, nor mushy, either. Serve on a large platter. Green or yellow zucchini are nice; mushrooms can be added; and keep the onions in rings.

2   Japanese eggplants, cut into 1/2-inch slices. Do not peel.
2   medium red onions, cut into 1/4-inch slices and separated into rings
4   zucchini, cut on a sharp diagonal into 1/4-inch slices. Do not peel.
1   red pepper, stemmed, cored and cut into 1/2-inch strips
1   yellow pepper, stemmed, cored and cut into-1/2 inch strips
1/2 cup rich vegetable broth
2   tablespoons olive oil
2   tablespoons lemon juice
    salt and freshly ground pepper to taste

In a 9x13-inch pan, toss together all the ingredients. Cover pan with foil and bake at 350° for 20 minutes. Remove foil and continue baking for about 20 minutes, turning now and again until vegetables are tender. Place pan under the broiler for 1 to 2 minutes to brown the tops. Serve warm. Add a splash of lemon juice to taste. Serves 8.

Pastas

&

Pizzas

Baked Ziti with Ricotta & Mozzarella in Instant Tomato Sauce

This is a very abbreviated version of a classic dish. The sauce is fresh, light and truly delicious and no one will guess it took 5 minutes to prepare. This yields a very generous serving.

1/2   pound ziti pasta (tube pasta), cooked in boiling water
        until tender (al dente), and drained thoroughly

Cheese Mixture:
    1   pound low-fat Ricotta cheese
    4   ounces grated Mozzarella cheese
    1   egg
  1/2   cup grated Parmesan cheese

Instant Tomato Sauce:
    1   can (1 pound 12 ounces) crushed tomatoes in puree
    2   teaspoons oil
    2   tablespoons minced dried onions
  1/2   teaspoon coarse grind garlic powder
    1   teaspoon sugar
    1   teaspoon Italian Herb Seasoning flakes
    1   teaspoon sweet basil flakes
       salt and pepper to taste
    1   sprinkle cayenne pepper

Have everything ready before you assemble the dish. Prepare ziti and set aside to drain in a collander, shaking occasionally to remove all water. Stir together Cheese Mixture and set aside. Place Instant Tomato Sauce ingredients in a saucepan and heat for 5 minutes.

In a 9x13-inch porcelain baker, place half the ziti. Spoon Cheese Mixture over the top and cover evenly with remaining ziti. Pour sauce evenly over all and sprinkle with additional grated Parmesan cheese. Bake at 350° for 30 minutes or until piping hot. Serves 6.

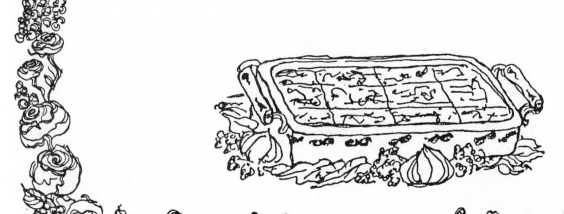

Pastitsio a la Grecque
(Greek Pasta & Cheese Casserole)

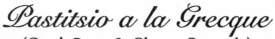

Pastitsio is a Greek version of pasta and cheese in casserole. It is basically easy to prepare and very easy to serve.

Tomato Sauce:
- 2 large onions, chopped
- 6 cloves garlic, minced
- 2 tablespoons olive oil

- 1 can (1 pound 12 ounces) chopped tomatoes in puree
- 1 can (8 ounces) tomato sauce
- 3 tablespoons chopped parsley leaves
- 1/4 teaspoon, each, cinnamon and nutmeg
  salt and pepper to taste

In a Dutch oven casserole, saute onions and garlic in olive oil until onions are transparent. Stir in tomatoes, parsley and seasonings, cover pan and simmer mixture for 15 minutes or until sauce has thickened slightly.

Cheese Mixture:
- 2 cups grated Mozzarella mixed with 1 cup low-fat Ricotta Cheese

Cheese/Crumb Mixture:
- 1/4 cup grated Parmesan cheese mixed with 1/4 cup stale bread crumbs

Pasta:
- 1 pound pasta (small ziti or small penne), cooked in boiling water until tender, but firm, and thoroughly drained.

To Assemble:
In a 9x13-inch baking pan, layer half the sauce, half the pasta, half the cheese mixture. Continue layering with the remaining pasta, cheese mixture and sauce. Pat top down to settle the casserole. Sprinkle top with Cheese/Crumb Mixture. Bake in a 350° oven for 30 minutes, or until heated through and top is a little crusty. Serves 8 to 10.

Cheese Tortellini with Garlic Pesto Sauce

Spinach tortellini is equally delicious with the pesto sauce. In fact, the sauce is excellent with linguini, fettuccini or any pasta. Pesto Sauce is traditionally made with pine nuts. This recipe is made with walnuts and is adapted in the style of Northern Italy. This is a great hors d'oeuvre, a lovely small entree and a good choice for dinner.

1   package (12 ounces) frozen cheese or spinach tortellini. Cook these in a spaghetti cooker in 2 quarts boiling water until tender but firm. Remove the strainer with the tortellini and shake from time to time to keep them separate. When ready to serve, plunge the tortellini into boiling water until hot.

Garlic Pesto Sauce:
6   cloves garlic, finely minced
1   tablespoon butter
1   pint half and half

2   tablespoons minced basil leaves
1/2   cup grated walnuts (use a nut grater)
1/4   cup chopped chives
      salt and white pepper to taste

In a saucepan, saute garlic in butter for 2 minutes. Add the half and half and simmer mixture until sauce is reduced by 1/3. Stir in the remaining ingredients and simmer mixture for 2 minutes, stirring now and again.

Plunge tortellini in boiling water for 2 minutes, or until heated through and pass the sauce at the table. Serves 4 for dinner or 8 as a small entree.

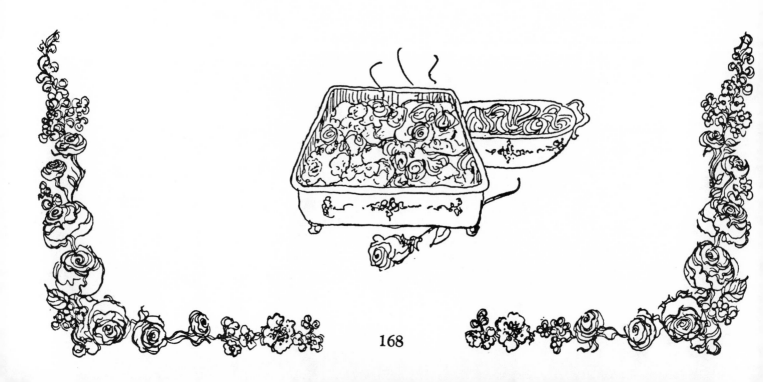

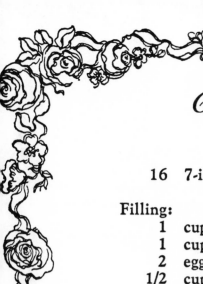

Cheese Cannelloni Firenzi with Instant Marinara Sauce

16   7-inch Herb Crepes

Filling:
- 1   cup cottage cheese
- 1   cup Ricotta cheese
- 2   eggs
- 1/2   cup fresh bread crumbs
- 1   cup grated Swiss cheese
- 1/2   cup grated Parmesan cheese
- 1   teaspoon Italian Herb Seasoning
    salt and white pepper to taste

Combine all the filling ingredients and beat until blended. Divide the filling between the crepes, (about 2 heaping tablespoons on each). Roll and place filled crepes , seam side down, and in one layer, in a 12x16-inch pan. (You can also arrange 2 filled crepes in 8 individual au gratin dishes.) Spread Instant Marinara Sauce over the top. Sprinkle tops with

- 4   ounces grated Mozzarella cheese, (1 cup)
- 1/3   cup grated Parmesan cheese

Heat cannelloni in a 350° oven for about 20 to 25 minutes or until piping hot. Broil for a few seconds to brown top. Serves 8.

Instant Marinara Sauce:
- 1   can (1 pound 12 ounces) crushed tomatoes in tomato puree
- 1   teaspoon sugar
- 1   tablespoon oil
- 2   tablespoons instant onion flakes
- 1 1/2   teaspoons Italian Herb Seasoning
- 1/4   teaspoon garlic powder
    salt and pepper to taste

Combine all the ingredients and simmer sauce for 10 minutes.

Note: - Can use non-fat cottage cheese and low-fat Ricotta and Mozzarella.

More →

(Cheese Cannelloni, Cont.)

Herb Crepes:

1 1/2   cups flour
1 1/2   cups milk
1/4   cup water
5   eggs
2   tablespoons oil
1   tablespoon minced parsley
2   tablespoons minced chives
   pinch of salt

In a large bowl, combine all the ingredients and with a whisk or hand beater, beat until mixture is blended and smooth.

Heat a small omelet-type pan with rounded sides, (7 to 8-inches) and butter bottom with a paper napkin or paper towel. When pan is very hot, but butter is not browned, pour about 1/8 cup batter into the pan. Tilt and turn pan immediately to evenly coat the bottom with a thin layer of batter. Pour out any excess batter.

Cook on one side for about 45 seconds or until bottom is golden and top is dry Turn and cook other side for about 15 seconds. Makes about 16 to 20 crepes.

Pasta with Artichoke, Red Pepper & Sun-Dried Tomato Sauce

This is a great sauce to serve over pasta. Mostacciola, a medium tube pasta, is a good choice, although any shape will do. Sauce can be prepared earlier in the day or 1 day earlier and stored in the refrigerator. Cook the pasta and heat the sauce just before serving.

1   jar (6 ounces) marinated artichoke hearts, chopped.
   Do not drain.
1   jar (8 ounces) roasted red peppers, drained and cut into strips
2   tablespoons chopped sun-dried tomatoes
2   shallots, minced
2   cloves garlic, minced
1/4   teaspoon, each, Italian Herb Seasoning and sweet basil flakes
   black pepper to taste

8   ounces pasta, cooked al dente
4   teaspoons grated Parmesan cheese (optional)

In a saucepan, heat together first group of ingredients and simmer for 10 minutes or until shallots are soft. Serve hot over pasta and sprinkle with optional cheese. Serves 4 to 6.

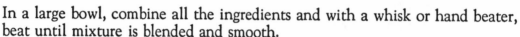

Fresh Linguini with Basil & Sun-Dried Tomato Sauce

1   pound fresh linguini, cooked in 4 quarts boiling water until
    al dente and drained. Fresh linguini cooks in minutes, so
    watch the time carefully.

Basil & Sun-Dried Tomato Sauce:
8   shallots, minced
8   cloves garlic, minced
2   tablespoons olive oil

4   sun-dried tomatoes (packed in oil) drained and chopped
2   cans (1 pound, each) stewed tomatoes, chopped. Do not drain.
6   tablespoons tomato paste (1/2 of a 6-ounce can)
1/3 cup chopped fresh basil
    salt and pepper to taste
    pinch of cayenne pepper

Saute shallots and garlic in olive oil until shallots are transparent. Add the
remaining ingredients and simmer sauce for 10 minutes. Serve sauce over
linguini. A teaspoon of grated cheese is nice, but optional. Serves 6 to 8.

Note: -Sauce can be prepared earlier in the day and stored in the refrigerator.
        Heat before serving.

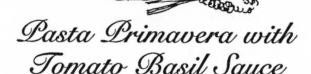

Pasta Primavera with Tomato Basil Sauce

*One of the tricks in lowering calories is to take a marvelous pasta dish and build it
up with a gorgeous array of vegetables. In this Primavera, the pasta is halved and
the vegetables are tripled. The sauce is light and fresh and delicious. Using fresh
vegetables is, of course, preferred. But the Del Sol mixture of vegetables makes this
dish simple to prepare and economical, too. The carrots are pre-cut into perfect
strips and only the florets of the cauliflower and broccoli are included.*

1   pound bag frozen Del Sol vegetables (carrot strips, cauliflower
    and broccoli florets). Cook vegetables in boiling water for
    5 minutes and drain.
1/4 pound whole wheat pasta (fresh or fresh-frozen is best). Cook
    in boiling water until firm but tender. Drain.

More →

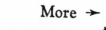

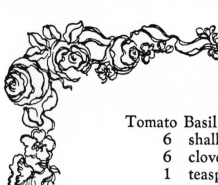

(Pasta Primavera, Cont.)

Tomato Basil Sauce:
- 6   shallots, minced
- 6   cloves garlic, minced (or more to taste)
- 1   teaspoon olive oil

- 4   medium tomatoes, peeled, seeded and diced
- 1   tablespoon tomato paste
- 1/4   cup minced fresh basil (or 1 teaspoon dried basil leaves)
    pinch of cayenne pepper

- 4   teaspoons grated Parmesan cheese

In a Dutch oven casserole, saute shallots and garlic in olive oil until shallots are transparent. Add the tomatoes, tomato paste, basil and pepper and simmer sauce for 10 minutes. Add the prepared vegetables and pasta to the sauce, toss to blend and heat through. Serve with a spoonful of cheese on top Serves 4.

Pasta with Eggplant, Red Pepper & Sun-Dried Tomato Sauce

- 1   medium eggplant (1 pound), peeled and chopped
- 2   red bell peppers, cut into strips
- 1   can (1 pound) stewed tomatoes, chopped. Do not drain.
- 3   sun-dried tomatoes cut into strips
- 1   small onion, minced
- 2   cloves garlic, minced
- 1   tablespoon vinegar
- 1   teaspoon sugar
- 1   teaspoon oil
- 1/2   teaspoon sweet basil flakes
- 1/2   teaspoon oregano flakes
    freshly ground black pepper
    pinch of cayenne pepper

- 1/4   cup sliced black olives (optional)
- 2   tablespoons capers, thoroughly rinsed (optional)

- 1   pound linguini, cooked al dente
- 6   teaspoons grated Parmesan cheese

In a Dutch oven casserole, place first group of ingredients, cover pan and simmer mixture for about 40 to 50 minutes, or until eggplant is tender. Add the olives and capers (optional). Serve over a bed of linguini and spoon a little cheese on top. Yields 8 generous portions.

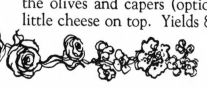

The Best Dilled Mushroom Ravioli in Light Beurre Blanc

The Dilled Mushroom Filling is simply marvelous and the Light Beurre Blanc sparkles this dish to gastronomical heights. This is a majestic first course or main course and I hope it brings you as much pleasure as it has brought to our family and friends. The Beurre Blanc (Butter Sauce) has been lightened with the addition of broth. The Pepper, Mushroom & Red Onion Saute is a lovely accompaniment.

Dilled Mushroom Filling:

6	shallots, minced, (1/2 cup)
1	clove garlic, minced
2	tablespoons butter
3/4	pound mushrooms, sliced
3	tablespoons flour
1/2	teaspoon dried dill weed
	salt to taste
3/4	cup low-fat sour cream
1	package won ton wrappers, fresh or frozen. If frozen, defrost in the refrigerator. (1 package contains 55 to 60 wrappers.)

Saute together first 3 ingredients until shallots are transparent. Add mushrooms and continue sauteing until mushrooms are tender and liquid rendered is evaporated. Add flour and seasonings and cook, stirring, for 2 minutes. Add sour cream and cook, stirring, for 2 minutes. Mixture will be very thick. Place filling in a food processor bowl, and pulse until mushrooms are coarsely chopped. Place mixture in a bowl, allow to cool and then refrigerate.

Light Beurre Blanc:

3	tablespoons minced shallots
1	tablespoon butter
1/3	cup white wine
3/4	cup rich vegetable broth
2	tablespoons minced chives
1	tablespoon lemon juice
1/3	teaspoon dried dill weed
	salt and white pepper to taste

In a skillet, saute shallots in butter until shallots are tender. Add the white wine and simmer mixture until wine is almost evaporated. Add the remaining ingredients and simmer mixture for 2 minutes. Set aside.

More →

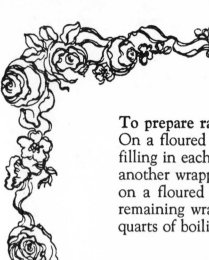

Mushroom Ravioli, (Continued)

To prepare ravioli:
On a floured pastry cloth, lay 6 won ton wrappers. Place 1/2 tablespoon of filling in each center, moisten the edge of each wrapper with water, and place another wrapper on top. Press the edges securely to seal, place filled ravioli on a floured plate and cover plate with plastic wrap. Continue with the remaining wrappers. When ready to assemble, place 6 ravioli at a time in 2 quarts of boiling water for 2 minutes, or until tender. Yields 27 to 30 ravioli

To assemble casserole:
In a 12x16-inch porcelain casserole or baker, spread 1/4 cup Beurre Blanc Place cooked ravioli, slightly overlapping, in the pan, and drizzle remaining sauce on the top. Sprinkle top with

2   tablespoons chopped chives
2   tablespoons grated Parmesan cheese.

Heat in a 350° oven for 20 minutes, or until heated through. Serve with Pepper, Mushroom & Red Onion Saute. Serves 6 as a main course or 10 as a small entree.

Note: -Won ton wrappers come in squares and rounds. If you use the rounds, it eliminates trimming the edges. If you use the squares, then place the top ravioli at an angle, and it will produce a beautiful star.

Pepper, Mushroom & Red Onion Saute

1   red bell pepper, remove seeds and cut into strips
1   yellow bell pepper, remove seeds and cut into strips
1/2   pound medium mushrooms caps, cleaned and stems discarded
1   medium red onion, cut in half vertically, and thinly sliced

4   tablespoons salted butter
1   tablespoon lemon juice

In a skillet, saute each vegetable separately in 1 tablespoon butter, until vegetables are tender. Place vegetables in a 9x13-inch pan, keeping each vegetable separate. Before serving, broil vegetables for a few minutes, or until tops are flecked with brown. Again, place vegetables in a low bowl, keeping each vegetable separate. Drizzle top with a splash of lemon juice.

Note: -As the peppers and onion have strong, assertive flavors, I prefer to saute each separately so that the flavor of the delicate ravioli is not overpowered.

Ricotta & Chevre Ravioli in Sun-Dried Tomato Sauce

Won ton wrappers, sometimes called "Won ton skins" are a good substitute for fresh pasta in the making of ravioli. It cuts preparation time to the minimum and the results are very satisfactory. The combination of goat cheese and sun-dried tomatoes is especially delicious. Won ton wrappers come in squares and rounds. If you use the rounds for ravioli, it eliminates trimming down the won tons to size. If you use the squares, then place the top ravioli at an angle, and it will produce a beautiful star.

Cheese Filling:

1/2	pound low-fat Ricotta cheese
1/2	pound Chevre (goat cheese, such as Montrachet)
1	egg, beaten
1/4	cup chopped chives
1	teaspoon sweet basil flakes or
	2 tablespoons fresh basil, chopped
1	teaspoon grated lemon peel
	white pepper to taste

1 package round won ton wrappers, fresh or frozen. Defrost in refrigerator if frozen. (1 package contains 55 to 60 wrappers.)

In a bowl, stir together Cheese Filling ingredients until blended. On a floured pastry cloth, lay 1 won ton wrapper. Place 1 tablespoon Cheese Filling in the center, moisten the edge of the wrapper with water, and place another won ton wrapper on top. Press the edges gently to seal and place filled ravioli on a floured plate. Continue with the remaining wrappers. (Can be held, at this point, for several hours, stored in the refrigerator, covered with plastic wrap.)

When ready to serve, in a spaghetti cooker, bring 4-quarts water and 1 tablespoon oil to a gentle boil. Add the ravioli in 2 batches, and allow to simmer for 3 to 4 minutes, or until ravioli are tender and float to the top. Serve with Sun-Dried Tomato Sauce on top and a sprinkling of grated Parmesan. Yields 30 ravioli and serves 8 to 10.

Sun-Dried Tomato Sauce:

1	medium red pepper, cut into slivers
6	cloves garlic, minced
1	tablespoon olive oil
1	can (28-ounces) Italian plum tomatoes, drained and chopped. Use 1/2 cup juice and reserve the rest for another use.
4	sun-dried tomatoes (packed in oil), drained and chopped
1	teaspoon dried sweet basil flakes or
	2 tablespoons fresh basil, chopped

In a saucepan, saute together first 3 ingredients until peppers are tender. Add the remaining ingredients and simmer sauce for 5 minutes.

Cheese Ravioli in Light Tomato Sauce

Using non-fat cottage cheese, markedly reduces the fat content of this recipe. The taste difference is hardly perceptible from the regular cottage cheese. These can be frozen, uncooked, in separated layers of plastic wrap.

Cheese Filling:
- 1   pint non-fat small curd cottage cheese
- 1/2 cup grated Parmesan cheese
- 1   egg, beaten
- 1/3 cup bread crumbs

- 1   package round won ton wrappers, fresh or frozen. Defrost in refrigerator if frozen. (1 package contains 55-60 wrappers.)

Mix together first 4 ingredients until nicely blended.

On a floured pastry cloth, lay 1 won ton wrapper. Place 1 tablespoon Cheese Filling in the center, moisten the edge of the wrapper with water, and place another won ton wrapper on top. Press the edges gently to seal and place filled ravioli on a floured plate. Continue with the remaining wrappers. (Can be held, at this point, for several hours, stored in the refrigerator, covered with plastic wrap.)

When ready to serve, in a spaghetti cooker, bring 4-quarts water and 1 tablespoon oil to a gentle boil. Add the ravioli in 2 batches, and allow to simmer for 3 to 4 minutes, or until ravioli are tender and float to the top. Serve with Light Tomato Sauce on top and a sprinkling of grated Parmesan. Yields 30 ravioli and serves 8 to 10.

Light Tomato Sauce:
- 1   medium onion, chopped
- 6   cloves garlic, minced
- 1   tablespoon olive oil

- 1   can (1 pound 12 ounces) Italian plum tomatoes, chopped. Do not drain.
- 1/4 cup tomato paste (4 tablespoons)
- 1   teaspoon, each, Italian Herb Seasoning and dried sweet basil flakes

  salt and pepper to taste

In a saucepan, saute onion and garlic in oil until onion is soft. Add the remaining ingredients and simmer sauce for 5 minutes.

Spinach & Cheese Ravioli in Pesto Sauce

The combination of spinach and cheese with pesto is a delicious blend of flavors. Each serving of pesto contains 1 tablespoon oil. This can be reduced by substituting 6 tablespoons of vegetable broth for 3 tablespoons of oil. The results are a little lighter and less caloric.

Spinach & Cheese Filling:

- 1   package (10 ounces) frozen chopped spinach, defrosted and pressed dry in a strainer
- 1/2   pound low-fat Ricotta cheese
- 1/2   cup grated Parmesan cheese
- 1   egg, beaten
- 4   tablespoons bread crumbs
-     pepper to taste

- 1   package round won ton wrappers, fresh or frozen. Defrost in refrigerator if frozen. (1 package contains 55 to 60 wrappers.)

In a bowl, stir together filling ingredients until blended. On a floured pastry cloth, lay 1 won ton wrapper. Place 1 tablespoon Spinach & Cheese Filling in the center, moisten the edge of the wrapper with water, and place another won ton wrapper on top. Press the edges gently to seal and place filled ravioli on a floured plate. Continue with the remaining wrappers. (Can be held, at this point, for several hours, stored in the refrigerator, covered with plastic wrap.)

When ready to serve, in a spaghetti cooker, bring 4-quarts water and 1 tablespoon oil to a gentle boil. Add the ravioli in 2 batches, and allow to simmer for 3 to 4 minutes, or until ravioli are tender and float to the top. Serve with 2 tablespoons of Pesto Sauce on top and a sprinkling of grated Parmesan. Yields 30 ravioli and serves 8 to 10.

Pesto Sauce:

- 8   cloves garlic
- 1/4   cup pine nuts
- 1/2   cup chopped fresh basil leaves
- 2   ounces grated Parmesan cheese (about 2/3 cup)

- 6   tablespoons olive oil

In the bowl of a food processor, blend together first 4 ingredients, until finely chopped. With the motor running, slowly drizzle in the oil until thoroughly blended. Yields about 3/4 cup pesto.

Olive Oil Pizza Dough

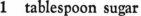

1   tablespoon sugar
1   cup warm water (110°)
1   package (2 1/2 teaspoons) active dry yeast

3   cups flour, bread or unbleached all-purpose flour
3/4   teaspoon salt
1/4   cup olive oil

      extra flour as needed
      olive oil to coat

To proof the yeast:
In the large bowl of an electric mixer, dissolve sugar in water. Stir in the yeast and allow to stand for 5 minutes, or until yeast start to foam. If yeast does not foam, it is not active and should be discarded.

To make the dough:
Add the flour, salt and oil and beat for 2 minutes. Continue beating with the dough hook for 5 minutes. If the dough is sticky or tacky, knead in a little flour, a tablespoon at a time. Place dough into an oiled bowl, and turn to coat completely. Cover the bowl with plastic wrap and a towel and allow to stand in a warm place (75° to 80°) until dough has doubled in bulk, about 1 hour. Punch dough down.

To shape the dough:
Place dough on a floured surface and lightly flour the top. With floured hands shape dough into a circle or rectangle.. With a floured rolling pin, roll dough out to 1/4-inch thickness. With your palm, press in 1/2-inch of the rim to form a small lip around the edge. Sprinkle a pizza pan with cornmeal and place dough on the top. Dough is now ready for filling and baking.

Note: Dough recipe using 3 cups of flour will serve 6 and yield:
       2 12-inch round pizzas   or
       4 8-inch round individual-sized pizzas

To Make Flatbreads:
This dough can be used to make flat breads of many styles. In this case, follow directions above. After placing dough into a 12-inch pan, brush it with a little oil, sprinkle and lightly press into the dough, either garlic powder, Parmesan cheese, poppy seeds, onion flakes, hot pepper, Cajun seasoning, sesame seeds, chives, green onions, herbs, or any combination that will harmonize with your meal. Bake for 15 minutes for a chewy bread or 20 minutes for a very crisp one.

Pizza with Sun-Dried Tomatoes & Chevre

A marvellous combination of flavors and colors, this is one of my family's favorites. If you are only serving 4, freeze the second pizza in double thicknesses of plastic wrap and foil.

2   12-inch pizza crusts

2   teaspoons olive oil
1   teaspoon red pepper flakes (or to taste)
1/2   cup sun-dried tomatoes (packed in oil) drained and chopped
8   ounces crumbled chevre cheese
1/4   cup minced chives
2   teaspoons sweet basil flakes (or 2 tablespoons fresh basil)

8   ounces grated part-skim Mozzarella cheese (2 cups)

Preheat oven to 450-degrees. Brush crusts with oil, sprinkle with red pepper, tomatoes, chevre, chives and basil and bake for 10 minutes. Sprinkle top with Mozzarella and continue to bake for 10 minutes longer, or until edges are browned and cheese is bubbling. Yields 16 slices.

Mediterranean Pizza with Sun-Dried Tomatoes, Pine Nuts & Mozzarella

The sun-dried tomatoes add an intense flavor and color to this fresh and delicious-tasting pizza. The flavor is so rich and satisfying, that a small amount delivers a lot of pleasure. Mozzarella cheese can be sprinkled on top before baking, but it develops a crust, which is not satisfactory for my taste. I like the cheese melted and bubbling and not crusty brown.

1   12-inch pizza crust
2   teaspoons olive oil
1/2   teaspoon red pepper flakes (or to taste)

1/2   cup sun-dried tomatoes, cut into strips
1   clove garlic, peeled
3   tablespoons pine nuts, (about 1 ounce)
2   tablespoons grated Parmesan cheese

6   ounces Mozzarella cheese, grated
12   fresh basil leaves

Preheat oven to 450-degrees. Brush crust with oil and sprinkle with red pepper. In a food processor, blend together next 4 ingredients until blended and spread over prepared crust. Bake for 10 minutes. Sprinkle top with Mozzarella cheese and basil leaves and continue to bake for 10 minutes longer, or until edges are browned and cheese is bubbling. Yields 8 slices.

Pizza with Eggplant, Mushrooms, Leeks & Feta Cheese

Very Greek in feeling with the flavors of eggplant, leeks and feta cheese. Feta is a low-calorie cheese, at only 76 calories per ounce. If you are only serving 4, freeze the second pizza in double thicknesses of plastic wrap and foil.

2	12-inch pizza crusts
4	small Japanese eggplants, unpeeled, cut into 1/4-inch slices, or 1 pound eggplant, cut in half and into 1/4-inch slices
1/2	pound mushrooms, sliced
2	leeks, white parts and 1-inch of tender green parts, thoroughly washed and thinly sliced
2	cloves garlic, minced
1	tablespoon olive oil
2	tablespoons lemon juice
2	tomatoes, thinly sliced
8	ounces feta cheese, crumbled (2 cups)
2	teaspoons sweet basil flakes (or 2 tablespoons fresh basil)

Prepare pizza crusts as directed and have them ready in their prepared pans.

Place next 4 ingredients in a 9x13-inch pan and toss with oil and lemon juice. Broil for 8 to 10 minutes, turning once, until eggplant is softened and tops are beginning to brown.

Preheat oven to 450-degrees. Divide vegetables between the pizza crusts Top each with sliced tomatoes, feta cheese and sweet basil and bake for about 20 minutes, or until edges are browned. Truly delicious. Yields 16 slices

Calzones Margherita with Tomatoes & Cheese

This is an exciting adaptation of pizza. It is basically a pizza-style pie with a double crust. Traditionally made with bread dough, I enjoy making it with puff pastry, producing a lighter, crisper and far more delicious Calzone.

- 1 package frozen patty shells (6 shells), thawed
- 1 egg, beaten
- 4 tablespoons grated Parmesan cheese

Roll out patty shell to measure a 6-inch circle. Place 1/6 of the Tomato Cheese Filling in the center and fold over. Press the edge down with the tines of a fork and scallop the edge. Continue with remaining patty shells. Place Calzones on a greased cookie sheet.

Brush tops with beaten egg and sprinkle with grated Parmesan cheese. Pierce tops in 4 places with the tines of a fork. Bake at 400° for 25 to 30 minutes, or until pastry is puffed and top is a deep golden brown. Serve with an antipasto-type salad. Serves 6.

Tomato & Cheese Filling:
- 1 pound Mozzarella cheese, grated
- 1/2 cup grated Parmesan cheese
- 1 clove garlic, minced
- 1 can (1 pound) stewed tomatoes, thoroughly drained. Reserve juice for another use.
- 1 teaspoon Italian Herb Seasoning
- 1 teaspoon Sweet Basil Flakes
- 1/4 teaspoon red pepper flakes
  salt and pepper to taste

Place all the ingredients in a bowl and toss and turn until blended.

California Pizzas with Tomatoes & Cheese

This is an exciting adaptation of Pizza. Traditionally made with bread dough, I enjoy making it with puff pastry. I find it lighter, crisper and frankly, much more delicious.

- 1 package frozen patty shells (6 shells), thawed
- 6 tablespoons grated Parmesan cheese

More →

(California Pizzas, Cont.)

Roll out each patty shell to measure a 6-inch circle. Sprinkle 1/6 of the Tomato & Cheese Filling on top. Sprinkle with grated Parmesan cheese. Place pizza on a greased cookie sheet. Repeat with the remaining patty shells.

Bake in a 400° oven for 25 minutes or until pastry is puffed and top is a deep golden brown. Yields 6 pizzas and serves 6 as a light lunch.

Tomato & Cheese Filling:

 1   onion, sliced into the thinnest rings
 2   cloves garlic, minced
 2   tablespoons oil

 1   can (1 pound) stewed tomatoes, thoroughly drained and chopped.
       Reserve juice for another use.
 1   teaspoon Italian Herb Seasoning
 1   teaspoon sweet basil flakes
 6   ounces Mozzarella cheese, grated
     pinch of red pepper flakes
     salt and pepper to taste

In a skillet, saute onions and garlic in oil until onions are soft Stir in the remaining ingredients. Will top 6 pizzas .

Vegetable Pizza on Flour Tortillas

Using the flour tortillas as a base, makes this light pizza easy to prepare in minutes. It is also very delicious and satisfying.

 6   flour tortillas, (6-inch rounds)

 6   ounces low-fat Mozzarella cheese, grated
1/2 pound mushrooms, cleaned and sliced
 2   medium tomatoes, cut into thin slices
 4   tablespoons sliced black olives (1/4 cup)
 1   teaspoon oregano flakes
     cayenne pepper to taste
     freshly ground black pepper to taste
 6   teaspoons grated Parmesan cheese

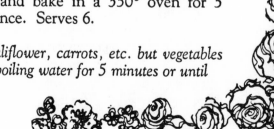

Place tortillas on a 12x16-inch cookie sheet and toast in a 350° oven for about 2 minutes, or until lightly crisped. Now, divide the remaining ingredients, in order listed, equally over the tortillas and bake in a 350° oven for 5 minutes or until cheese is bubbly. Serve at once. Serves 6.

Note: -This is also delicious with broccoli, cauliflower, carrots, etc. but vegetables must first be blanched by placing in boiling water for 5 minutes or until firm tender.

Accompaniments

Noodles

Rice

Legumes & Grains

Vegetables

Fruits

Puddings

Pink Rice with Artichokes & Cheese

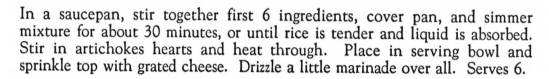

1 1/2	cups long-grain rice
3	cups vegetable broth
1	medium tomato, peeled, seeded and chopped
1	tablespoon oil
	salt and pepper to taste

| 1 | jar (6 ounces) marinated artichoke hearts, drained, and cut into fourths. Reserve marinade. |
| 3 | tablespoons grated Parmesan cheese |

In a saucepan, stir together first 6 ingredients, cover pan, and simmer mixture for about 30 minutes, or until rice is tender and liquid is absorbed. Stir in artichokes hearts and heat through. Place in serving bowl and sprinkle top with grated cheese. Drizzle a little marinade over all. Serves 6.

Herbed Rice with Tomatoes and Onions

1	onion, finely chopped
2	tablespoons oil
1 1/2	cups rice

3	cups vegetable broth
1	tomato, peeled, seeded and chopped
2	tablespoons chopped chives
2	tablespoons chopped parsley
	salt and pepper to taste
	pinch of thyme

Sauté onion in oil until onion is soft. Add rice and cook and stir for 2 minutes. Stir in the remaining ingredients carefully. Cover pan and simmer rice until liquid is absorbed and rice is tender, about 35 minutes. Serves 6.

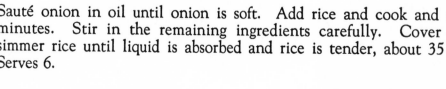
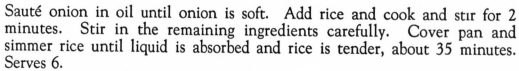

Yellow Rice with Raisins & Pistachios

A delicious combination of spices, color and texture. Rice can be prepared earlier in the day and heated before serving. Sprinkle with a few teaspoons of broth when reheating.

1	cup rice
2	cups vegetable broth
2	tablespoons oil
1	teaspoon ground turmeric or more to taste
1/2	teaspoon ground cumin
	salt and pepper to taste

1/2	cup raisins, plumped in boiling water for 5 minutes, and drained
1/2	cup toasted shelled pistachio nuts or almonds, coarsely chopped

In a covered saucepan, simmer together first 7 ingredients for 30 minutes, or until rice is tender and liquid is absorbed. Stir in raisins and nuts. Serves 6.

Emerald Rice with Parsley & Chives

1	cup rice
2	cups vegetable broth
1	teaspoon oil
	white pepper to taste

1/4	cup minced chives
2	tablespoons minced parsley

In a covered saucepan, simmer together first 4 ingredients, until rice is tender and liquid is absorbed. Stir in chives and parsley and heat through. Serves 6.

Casserole of Rice, Onions, Carrots & Cicis

This is an unusual casserole that is especially pretty to serve on a buffet. It is a lovely blend of tastes, textures and colors. Casserole can be prepared earlier in the day and stored in the refrigerator. Sprinkle with a few drops of water before reheating over low heat for about 20 to 25 minutes. Stir now and again to prevent rice from sticking to the pan.

- 2 medium carrots, grated
- 1 onion, chopped
- 1 clove garlic, minced
- 1 can (1 pound) cici peas (garbanzos), rinsed and drained
- 1 tablespoon oil

- 1 cup rice
- 2 cups vegetable broth, homemade or canned
- 1 tablespoon oil
  salt and pepper to taste

- 1 tablespoon parsley leaves

In a skillet, over low heat, saute together first 5 ingredients until onion and carrots are soft, but not browned.

Meanwhile, in a saucepan, stir together rice, broth, oil and seasonings, cover pan and simmer mixture for 30 minutes, or until rice is tender and liquid is absorbed. Fluff rice with a fork as you stir in carrot/onion mixture and parsley. Serves 6.

Risotto with Tomatoes, Onion & Garlic

Rice, flavored with onion, tomato and garlic is a great accompaniment to Eggplant Parmesan. It can be prepared earlier in the day and reheated, over low heat, before serving. Sprinkle rice with a few drops of water or broth before reheating.

- 1 tablespoon olive oil
- 1 small onion, finely chopped

- 1 1/4 cups rice
- 2 1/2 cups vegetable broth
  1 teaspoon ground turmeric
- 1 large tomato, peeled, seeded and chopped
  salt and pepper to taste

Saute onion in butter until onion is soft. Stir in next 6 ingredients, cover pan and simmer rice for about 30 minutes or until rice is tender and liquid is absorbed. Serves 6.

Curry Rice Indienne with Raisins & Almonds

    2   cups vegetable broth
    1   cup long grain rice
    1   tablespoon oil
         salt and pepper to taste
    1   teaspoon curry powder or more to taste

In a covered saucepan, simmer together first 5 ingredients until liquid is absorbed and rice is tender, about 30 minutes. When rice is cooked, toss in the following:

    1/4   cup golden raisins, plumped in orange juice
    1/4   cup slivered or chopped toasted almonds
    1/4   cup chopped chives

Sprinkle top with additional minced chives. Serves 6.

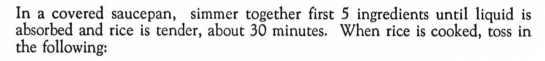

Curried Rice with Mushrooms & Peas

    1   cup rice
    2   cups vegetable broth
    1   tablespoon oil
    2   teaspoons curry powder
         salt and pepper to taste

    1/2   pound mushrooms, sliced
    1   tablespoon butter

    1   package (10 ounces) frozen petit peas

In a covered saucepan, simmer together first 6 ingredients for 30 minutes, or until rice is tender and liquid is absorbed.

Meanwhile, in a skillet, saute mushrooms in butter until mushrooms are tender and liquid rendered is evaporated. Stir in the frozen peas and cook and stir for 2 minutes. Add the vegetable mixture to the rice and heat through. Serves 6.

Rice & Peas with Onions & Tomatoes

While in Italy, we had a wonderful dish that resembled this one. Rice and peas, sometimes called "Risi e Bisi" is a delightful casserole. The addition of onions and tomatoes adds a certain depth to this dish.

1	cup rice
2	cups vegetable broth
1	medium tomato, peeled, seeded and chopped
2	tablespoons butter or oil
1	large onion, chopped
1	tablespoon butter
1	package (10 ounces) frozen peas
1/4	cup grated Parmesan cheese (or more to taste)
	salt and pepper to taste

In a saucepan, place first 5 ingredients, cover pan and simmer mixture until liquid is absorbed and rice is tender.

Meanwhile, saute onion in butter until onion is soft. Add the peas and saute for several minutes or until peas are tender. In the pan with rice, add the onion mixture, cheese, and seasonings and heat through. Serves 4 as a main dish or 6 as an accompaniment.

Note: - Casserole can be prepared earlier in the day and stored in the refrigerator. Add a few drops of water when reheating, and stir, now and then, to prevent scorching.

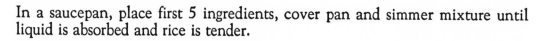

Rice with Raisins & Toasted Pine Nuts

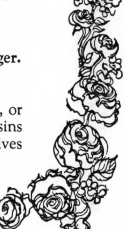

1	cup rice
2	cups vegetable broth
1	tablespoon butter
	salt to taste
1/2	cup yellow raisins, plumped in boiling water for 5 minutes and drained
1/2	cup pine nuts, toasted in a flat baking pan at 350° for 4 to 5 minutes, or until just beginning to take on color and no longer.
1/2	cup minced chives

In a covered saucepan, simmer together first 4 ingredients for 30 minutes, or until rice is tender and liquid is absorbed. Meanwhile, prepare the raisins and pine nuts. When rice is cooked, toss with raisins, pine nuts and chives and heat through. Serves 6.

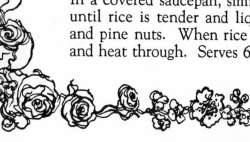

Golden Mexican Rice with Tomatoes & Chiles

1	medium tomato, chopped
1	can (3 ounces) diced green chiles
1	tablespoon oil

1 1/2	cups rice
3	cups vegetable broth
1	teaspoon turmeric
1/2	teaspoon ground cumin
	salt and pepper to taste

In a saucepan, cook tomato and chiles in oil for 2 minutes, stirring. Stir in the remaining ingredients, cover pan, and simmer mixture for 30 minutes, or until rice is tender and liquid is absorbed. This is excellent to serve with Red Hot Texas Chili. Serves 8.

Lemon Rice with Tomato & Chives

1 1/3	cups rice
1	tablespoon oil

2 1/2	cups vegetable broth
2	tablespoons lemon juice
1	tomato, peeled, seeded and finely chopped (or 1 canned tomato, finely chopped)
	salt and pepper to taste

1	tablespoon chopped parsley
3	tablespoons chopped chives

In a saucepan, saute rice in oil for 1 minute, stirring. Stir in the next 5 ingredients, cover pan and simmer mixture for 30 minutes, or until rice is tender and liquid is absorbed. Stir in the parsley and chives and heat through. Serves 6.

Pink Rice with Tomatoes & Chives

This is a very tasty way to prepare rice. Do not use any more than 3 tablespoons tomato sauce, or the rice can get sticky.

- 2 cups vegetable broth
- 1 tablespoon oil
- 1 tomato, seeded and coarsely chopped.
- 3 tablespoons tomato sauce
- 1 tablespoon chopped parsley
- 3 tablespoons chopped chives
  salt and pepper to taste

- 1 cup long-grain rice

In a saucepan, bring first group of ingredients to a boil. Stir in rice, cover pan and simmer mixture over low heat, until liquid is absorbed and rice is tender, about 30 minutes. Serves 6.

Rice with Red Pepper, Onion & Sun-Dried Tomatoes

This recipe can be expanded with extra vegetables and will serve 6 as a main course.

- 2 cups vegetable broth
- 1 tablespoon oil
  salt and pepper to taste
- 1 cup long-grain rice

- 1 red bell pepper, seeded and cut into strips
- 1 onion, chopped
- 2 sun-dried tomatoes, chopped
- 1 tablespoon oil

In a saucepan, stir together first 5 ingredients and bring mixture to a boil. Lower heat, cover pan and simmer mixture for about 30 minutes, or until rice is tender and liquid is absorbed.

Meanwhile, in a skillet, saute pepper, onion and sun-dried tomatoes in oil until pepper and onion are soft. Stir vegetables into the rice and heat through. Serves 6.

Yellow Rice with Tomatoes & Chiles

This rice is an excellent accompaniment to a Mexican-style dinner. If you like a stronger chili taste, add 1 teaspoon chili powder. It can be prepared earlier in the day, and reheated at time of serving. Do not freeze.

2	cups vegetable broth, home-made or canned
	salt and pepper to taste
1	teaspoon chili powder
1/2	teaspoon turmeric (or more to taste)
1/4	teaspoon ground cumin
1	large tomato, skinned, seeded and chopped coarsely
3	tablespoons oil
1	cup long-grain rice
3	tablespoons canned diced green chiles (these are mild)

In a saucepan, bring first group of ingredients to a boil. Stir in rice, cover pan and lower heat. Simmer rice until liquid is absorbed and rice is tender, about 30 minutes. Stir in diced green chiles. Serves 6.

Lemon Rice with Leeks & Herbs

1	cup rice
2	cups vegetable broth
2	tablespoons lemon juice
1	teaspoon oil
1	leek, (white and 1-inch of the tender green parts) cut into thin slices
2	shallots, minced
1	clove garlic, minced
1	tablespoon minced parsley
1/2	teaspoon thyme flakes
1	teaspoon oil

In a covered saucepan, simmer together first 4 ingredients for 30 minutes, or until rice is tender and liquid is absorbed. Meanwhile, in a covered skillet, saute together the remaining ingredients for 20 minutes, or until leeks are soft. Toss together rice and vegetables and heat through. Serves 6.

Noodles Primavera
with Zucchini & Tomatoes

Pasta Primavera is also delicious served with egg noodles. The sauce can be enriched with any number of other vegetables.

Zucchini & Tomato Sauce:
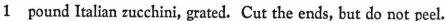
    1   large onion, chopped
    3   cloves garlic, minced
    4   shallots, minced
    2   tablespoons olive oil

    1   pound Italian zucchini, grated. Cut the ends, but do not peel.
    4   carrots, grated
    1   can (1 pound 12 ounces) crushed tomatoes in puree
    1   package (10 ounces) frozen peas
         salt and freshly ground pepper to taste

    1   package (1 pound) medium egg noodles cooked al dente
             according to directions on the package and drained

    1/2   cup grated Parmesan cheese (or more to taste)

Saute onion, garlic and shallots in olive oil until the onion is transparent. Add the zucchini and carrots and continue sauteing until the vegetables are tender. Add the tomatoes, peas and seasonings and simmer mixture for 10 minutes. Sauce should be very thick and not soupy. To serve, toss hot cooked noodles with sauce and sprinkle with cheese.

To Make as a Casserole:
Place noodles and sauce in a 9x13-inch baking pan. Sprinkle top with 4-ounces of grated Mozzarella cheese. Sprinkle grated cheese over the top. Heat in a 350° oven for 25 minutes or until heated through. Serves 12.

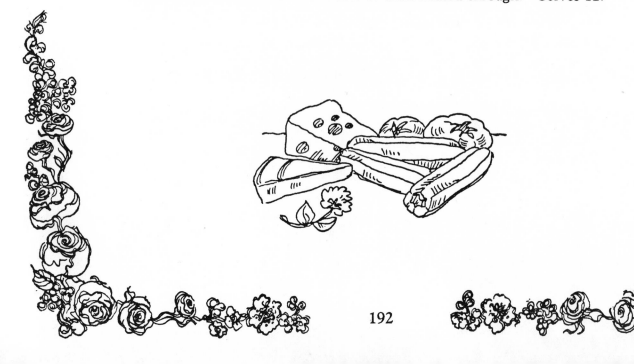

The Best Velvet Noodle Pudding

This is my favorite noodle pudding trimmed down a little. It is not as rich as the original, but the texture and taste is still wonderful.

8 ounces (1/2 pound) medium noodles, cooked and drained
4 tablespoons butter (1/2 stick)

4 eggs
1 pint (2 cups) low-fat sour cream
1/2 cup milk
2 teaspoons vanilla
3/4 cup sugar
salt to taste

1 cup yellow raisins
1 tablespoon cinnamon sugar

In a 9x13-inch pan, melt the butter. Add the cooked and drained noodles and toss them in the butter until they are evenly coated. Beat together next 6 ingredients until blended. Stir in the yellow raisins.

Pour the egg mixture evenly over the noodles and bury the raisins into the custard. Sprinkle top with cinnamon sugar. Bake in a 350° oven for 1 hour or until custard is set and top is brown. Cut into squares and serve warm. Serves 12.

Divine Noodle Pudding

3/4 pound broad noodles, cooked and drained
1/4 cup butter (1/2 stick)

5 eggs
8 ounces low-fat cream cheese, at room temperature
3/4 cup sugar
1/2 cup orange juice concentrate
1 1/2 cups milk

1 cup golden raisins
3 teaspoons cinnamon sugar

In a 9x13-inch roasting pan, melt butter and toss the cooked noodles to coat evenly. In mixer bowl, beat eggs with cream cheese until well blended. Beat in sugar, juice and milk until smooth. Stir in raisins. Toss egg mixture with cooked noodles and spread evenly. Sprinkle top with cinnamon sugar. Bake in a 350° oven for about 1 hour. Serves 12.

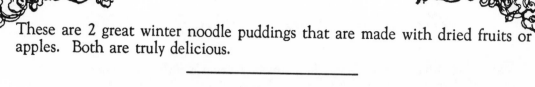

These are 2 great winter noodle puddings that are made with dried fruits or apples. Both are truly delicious.

Noodle Pudding with Apricots & Raisins

- 1 package (12 ounces) wide noodles, cooked in boiling water until tender and drained
- 4 tablespoons butter, melted
- 1 cup dried apricots, chopped
- 1/2 cup mixed yellow and dark raisins

- 4 eggs, beaten
- 1/2 cup sugar
- 1 cup low-fat sour cream
- 1/2 cup milk
- 1/2 orange, grated, about 3 tablespoons. Use fruit, juice and peel.
- 2 tablespoons cinnamon sugar

In a 9x13-inch pan, toss together first 4 ingredients until nicely mixed. Beat together the next 5 ingredients and pour evenly over the noodles. Sprinkle top with cinnamon sugar. Bake at 350° for about 55 minutes, or until eggs are set and top is golden brown. Serves 12.

Noodle Pudding with Apples & Raisins

- 2 large apples, peeled, cored and grated
- 1/2 cup yellow raisins
- 1 tablespoon grated orange peel
- 4 tablespoons cinnamon sugar
- 1/4 cup orange juice

- 1 package (8 ounces) medium noodles, cooked and drained
- 1/4 cup melted butter

- 4 eggs, beaten
- 1/2 cup sugar
- 1 1/2 cups low-fat sour cream
- 2 teaspoons vanilla
  salt to taste

In a saucepan, simmer together first 5 ingredients until apples are tender, about 10 minutes. In a 9x13-inch pan, toss together noodles and butter. Toss in apple mixture.

Beat together the remaining ingredients until blended and pour evenly over the noodles. (Ease the noodles, here and there, so that the egg mixture is evenly distributed.) Bake at 350° for about 1 hour or until top is golden and custard is set. Cut into squares to serve. Serves 12.

Royal Crown Noodle & Apple Pudding with Cinnamon & Pecans

Noodle pudding is a homey, family dish, but when baked in a ring mold, masked with cinnamon and pecans, it is dressed for the most formal occasions. The apples, baked in the custard are a great addition. To facilitate unmolding, use a non-stick coated mold and generously butter the mold.

3	tablespoons melted butter
3	tablespoons cinnamon sugar
1	cup pecan halves
1	apple, peeled, cored and grated
1/4	cup melted butter (1/2 stick)
4	tablespoons cinnamon sugar
1	package (8 ounces) medium noodles, cooked tender, but firm
2	eggs
1/2	cup sour cream
1/2	cup sugar
1/2	teaspoon vanilla

Generously butter a 2-quart ring mold. Drizzle bottom of mold with melted butter and sprinkle evenly with cinnamon sugar and pecans.

In a skillet, saute apple in butter until apple is tender. Toss apple with cinnamon sugar and cooked noodles and place evenly in the mold.

Beat together eggs, sour cream, sugar and vanilla until blended and pour this over the noodles so that it is distributed evenly. Place mold on a cookie pan and bake in a 350° oven for 1 hour, or until top is golden and custard is set. Unmold onto a serving platter and decorate with spiced peaches or spiced apricots. Serves 8.

Note: -If you prepare this earlier in the day, store it, in the mold, in the refrigerator. However, it must be reheated in a pan with 1-inch water, for about 25 minutes, or until heated through, or pecans can burn.

Old-Fashioned Cracker Pudding

This is a version of an old-fashioned stuffing, but this is a bit softer and more moist. It is a fine accompaniment to most vegetables.

      3   onions, chopped
      2   stalks celery, finely chopped
      4   shallots, minced
      4   cloves garlic, minced
      1   carrot, grated
      1   teaspoon each, sage flakes and thyme flakes
      4   tablespoons butter

      9   cups soda cracker crumbs (about 12 ounces)
      2   eggs, beaten
          salt and pepper to taste

      1   quart vegetable broth (use only enough to make a soft pudding)

In a Dutch oven casserole, sauté together first group of ingredients until onions are soft. Place mixture in a large bowl and toss in crumbs, eggs and seasonings. Add enough broth to make a soft pudding (not too dry, but not soggy, either.) Place pudding in a 9x13-inch porcelain baker, and bake at 350° for 30 minutes or until heated through and top is crusty. Serves 8.

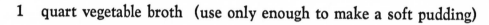

Raisin Cornbread Pudding with Apricots & Pecans

    1/2   cup chopped dried apricots
    1/2   cup yellow raisins
      2   apples, peeled, cored and grated
    1/2   cup sugar
      2   teaspoons pumpkin pie spice
          pinch of ground nutmeg and ground cloves
      2   tablespoons butter

      1   package (8 ounces) corn bread stuffing mix
      2   eggs, beaten
  1 1/2   cups apple juice
    1/2   cup chopped pecans

In a skillet, sauté together first group of ingredients until apples are tender and apricots are softened, about 12 to 15 minutes. Place mixture in a large bowl and stir in the remaining ingredients until blended. Place pudding in a 10-inch round porcelain baker and bake at 350° for 30 minutes, or until top is beginning to crisp. Serves 8.

Confetti Brown Rice with Scallions & Red & Yellow Peppers

This casserole is a blaze of color and very delicious, too. It is wonderful with grilled vegetables.

1	cup brown rice
2 1/4	cups vegetable broth
1	teaspoon oil
1	teaspoon low-sodium soy sauce
1/2	cup finely chopped red bell pepper
1/2	cup finely chopped yellow bell pepper
1/4	cup finely chopped green onion
1	teaspoon oil

In a covered saucepan simmer together first 4 ingredients for about 35 minutes, or until rice is tender and liquid is absorbed.

Meanwhile in a skillet, saute together next 4 ingredients, for about 10 minutes, stirring, until vegetables are tender. Toss vegetables with rice and heat through. Serves 6.

Brown Rice with Lentils, Mushrooms & Onions

Brown rice and lentils are a wonderful pair. Add mushrooms and onions and the combination is truly delicious...and healthy, too.

3/4	cup brown rice
1/2	cup lentils, rinsed and picked over for foreign particles
2 1/4	cups vegetable broth
2	teaspoons oil
1/2	pound mushrooms, sliced
1	large onion, sliced
1	teaspoon oil

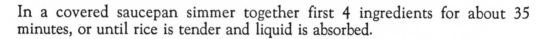

In a covered saucepan, simmer together first 4 ingredients for about 40 minutes, or until lentils are tender. Meanwhile, in a skillet, saute mushrooms and onion in oil until onion is tender. When rice is cooked, stir in mushrooms and onions and heat through. Serves 6.

Wild Rice with Apricots & Pecans

This is a great winter dish, hardy, robust and very delicious. It is also quite attractive and a good choice around the holidays. For a festive presentation, press the hot, cooked rice into a mold and invert it onto the serving platter.

1 1/2	cups wild and brown rice
4	tablespoons butter
3 1/4	cups vegetable broth
	salt to taste
4	tablespoons butter
1	onion, finely chopped
2	stalks celery, finely chopped
6	shallots, minced
4	cloves garlic, minced
1	cup coarsely chopped pecans
3/4	cup dried apricots, chopped

In a saucepan, bring the first 4 ingredients to a boil, cover pan, lower heat, and simmer mixture for about 40 to 45 minutes, or until rice is tender.

Meanwhile, in a skillet, saute together next 5 ingredients until vegetables are tender. Add the pecans and apricots and continue cooking for 5 minutes, stirring every now and again. When rice is cooked, stir in the apricot mixture. Serves 8.

Wild & Brown Rice with Apricots, Currants & Pine Nuts:
Prepare the recipe as indicated above except, omit the pecans and add 1/4 cup dried currants and 1/4 cup toasted pine nuts. Serves 8.

Wild Rice with Apricots & Chestnuts:
Prepare the recipe as indicated above except, omit the pecans and add 1 can (1 pound) chestnuts, packed in water, drained and sliced. Serves 8.

Toasted Vermicelli

Vermicelli is a nice change from rice or potatoes and I do hope you make it soon. Instead of browning fideos in oil, these are browned in the oven. It is a lot easier, far less caloric and every bit as good.

8	ounces vermicelli coils, also called "fideos"
2 1/4	cups vegetable broth, home-made or canned
2	tablespoons olive oil
	salt and pepper to taste

In a roasting pan, bake vermicelli in a 350° oven for about 8 minutes or until it is golden. Careful not to burn it. Set aside.

Combine broth, oil and seasonings and bring mixture to a boil. Add toasted vermicelli, cover pan and reduce to low heat. Simmer mixture until vermicelli is tender and liquid is absorbed, about 10 minutes. Serves 6.

Fideos with Onions & Mushrooms

Fideos, also known as vermicelli, are so nice to serve. Even though everyone seems to love them, they are not served often. If you do not toast them, or saute them in a little oil, they can get sticky. Here they are sparkled with mushrooms and onions...a delicious treat.

8	ounces fideo or vermicelli coils
1	tablespoon oil
2 1/2	cups vegetable broth
	salt and pepper to taste
1	tablespoon oil
1/2	onion, finely chopped
1/4	pound mushrooms, thinly sliced

Toast fideos in a shallow pan in a 350° oven, or until beginning to color. Careful not to burn it. In a saucepan, bring next 4 ingredients to a boil and add fideos. Cover pan, lower heat and simmer mixture until fideos are tender and liquid is absorbed, about 10 minutes. Fluff with a fork.

In a skillet, saute onion and mushrooms in oil until onion is tender. Add to fideos, tossing until nicely mixed. Serves 6.

Pastina with Fresh Tomato & Basil Sauce

Pastinas are little dots of pasta that are an interesting starch accompaniment to a meal. Here, I pair it with fresh tomatoes and basil...truly delicious.

    3   tomatoes, peeled, seeded and chopped
    1   teaspoon olive oil
    1   teaspoon sweet basil flakes (or 1 tablespoon fresh basil)
  1/4   cup chopped chives
          pinch of cayenne

    8   ounces pastina

In a skillet, cook together first 5 ingredients until liquid is absorbed and tomatoes are soft, about 10 minutes.

Cook the pastina in 2-quarts of rapidly boiling water, until tender, about 10 minutes. Drain thoroughly in a strainer or a colander with very small holes, or your pastina will disappear down the drain. Stir pastina into tomato sauce, heat through and serve at once. Serves 6 to 8.

Toasted Pastina with Mushrooms & Onions

Pastina is an interesting alternative to rice or noodles. With mushrooms and onions it is truly delicious.

  1/2   pound mushrooms, thinly sliced
    1   onion, minced
    1   tablespoon butter
          pepper to taste
    1   package (8 ounces) pastina

In a saucepan, sauté together first 4 ingredients until onion is soft. Meanwhile, toast pastina in a 350° oven for about 5 minutes, or until it is just beginning to take on color. Place it in a pot with 2-quarts of rapidly boiling water, and cook it until it is tender, about 10 minutes. Drain thoroughly in a large strainer, with small holes. Don't use a colander with large holes or the pastina will slip through. Stir pastina into saucepan with mushroom mixture and heat through. Serves 6 to 8.

Bulgur with Lemon & Chives

This is a basic recipe for bulgur. You can add to it any number of minced cooked vegetables...onions, carrots, cauliflowerets, baby peas and the like.

2	shallots, minced
2	teaspoons margarine

1 1/2	cups bulgur (cracked wheat)
1 1/2	tablespoons margarine
3	cups vegetable broth
2	tablespoons lemon juice
	salt and pepper to taste

1/2	cup chopped chives

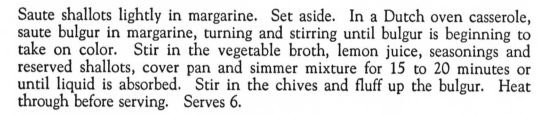

Saute shallots lightly in margarine. Set aside. In a Dutch oven casserole, saute bulgur in margarine, turning and stirring until bulgur is beginning to take on color. Stir in the vegetable broth, lemon juice, seasonings and reserved shallots, cover pan and simmer mixture for 15 to 20 minutes or until liquid is absorbed. Stir in the chives and fluff up the bulgur. Heat through before serving. Serves 6.

Bulgur, Red Pepper & Pine Nut Pilaf

1	medium onion, finely chopped
1	small red pepper, cut into thin slivers
1	clove garlic, minced
1	tablespoon oil

2	cups bulgur
4	cups vegetable broth
	salt and pepper to taste

1/4	cup toasted pine nuts
2	tablespoons minced chives

In a Dutch oven casserole, saute together first 4 ingredients until onions are soft. Stir in the next 4 ingredients, cover pan and simmer mixture for 20 minutes or until bulgur is tender and liquid is absorbed. Fluff with a fork and add pine nuts and chives before serving. Serves 8.

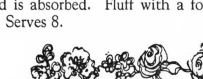

Lemon Bulgur with Currants & Pine Nuts

    1   cup bulgur (also called "cracked wheat")
    1   teaspoon oil

1 1/4   cups vegetable broth
  1/2   cup water
    3   tablespoons lemon juice
         black pepper to taste

  1/2   cup chopped green onions
    3   tablespoons dried black currants
    3   tablespoons pine nuts (about 1 ounce)

In a saucepan, cook cracked wheat in oil, stirring now and again, for 2 minutes. Carefully (it could splatter), add the next 4 ingredients, cover pan, lower heat and simmer mixture for about 15 minutes, or until liquid is absorbed. Stir in remaining ingredients and heat through. Serves 6.

Kasha with Mushrooms & Red Peppers

Your guests will love this flavorful kasha. I recommend that you prepare an extra amount as I have found that most of our friends tend to have seconds.

    1   cup kasha (also known as cracked-wheat bulgur)
    1   tablespoon oil

1 1/4   cups vegetable broth
  3/4   cup water
         salt and pepper to taste

    1   large onion, chopped
  1/4   pound mushrooms, sliced
  1/3   cup chopped sweet red pepper
    1   tablespoon oil

In a saucepan, cook kasha in oil, stirring now and again, for 2 minutes. Carefully (it could splatter), stir in the broth, water and seasonings. Cover pan, lower heat, and simmer mixture for about 15 minutes, or until liquid is absorbed.

Meanwhile in another covered saucepan, saute together next 4 ingredients until onion is soft. Uncover pan and cook for another few minutes or until juices have evaporated. Toss mushroom mixture into cooked kasha and heat through. Decorate with a little chopped parsley on top. Serves 6.

Kasha & Bow Tie Noodles with Mushrooms & Onions

This is a Middle European specialty that you might enjoy. While it is an old recipe, it is not one I knew as a child. I discovered this dish in a Hungarian restaurant many years ago, and was surprised to know it is a Hungarian classic. It is very tasty when made with a rich vegetable broth. The mushrooms and onions were my addition.

1	cup medium-grain kasha
1	egg, beaten
2	cups rich vegetable broth
2	tablespoons butter or margarine
	salt and pepper to taste
4	ounces bow-tie egg noodles, cooked until tender and drained
2	onions, chopped
1/2	pound mushrooms, sliced
2	tablespoons butter or margarine

In a Dutch oven casserole, stir together kasha and beaten egg until blended. Cook, over medium heat, stirring and turning until the egg has dried, and grains are separated, about 2 minutes. Stir in the broth, butter and seasonings, cover pan and cook, over low heat, until liquid is absorbed, about 20 minutes. Fluff with a fork.

Cook bow-tie noodles in briskly boiling water until tender and drain. Set aside. In a skillet, saute onions and mushrooms in butter until onions are tender and beginning to brown. Add the cooked noodles and onion mixture to the kasha, and fluff everything nicely with a fork. Heat through. Serves 8.

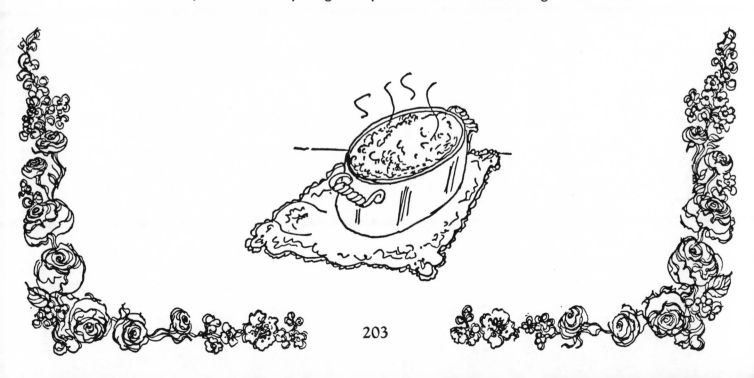

Cous Cous with Raisins & Pine Nuts

Precooked cous cous can be purchased in most markets and it takes minutes to prepare. I urge you to try it soon.

1   clove garlic, minced
1   tablespoon butter

1   cup vegetable broth
1   cup precooked cous cous
    pinch of salt

1/4   cup toasted pine nuts
1/4   cup raisins, plumped in orange juice and drained

In a saucepan, saute garlic in butter for 1 minute, or until garlic is softened. Add vegetable broth and bring to a boil. Stir in cous cous and salt, cover pan, lower heat, and cook for 2 or 3 minutes, or until cous cous is tender. Fluff with a fork and stir in pine nuts and raisins. Serves 6.

Cous Cous with Dates & Almonds:
Substitute chopped dates and almonds for the raisins and pine nuts.

Vegetable Cous Cous with Chick Peas

Cous cous with vegetables and chick peas is practically a complete meal. Add a few nuts and raisins for a feast.

1   onion, chopped
2   zucchini, unpeeled and sliced
2   carrots, thinly sliced
1   can (15 ounces) chick peas (garbanzos), rinsed and drained
1/2   cup vegetable broth

2   cups vegetable broth
2   cups precooked cous cous
    pinch of salt

In a covered saucepan, simmer together first 5 ingredients until vegetables are tender. Uncover pan and cook until broth is almost evaporated.

In another saucepan, bring vegetable broth to a boil. Slowly, stir in cous cous, cover pan, lower heat and cook for 2 minutes, or until cous cous is tender. Fluff with a fork until grains are separated and, then, stir in vegetable mixture. Serves 8.

Red Lentils with Tomatoes & Fried Onions

This is a most delicious accompaniment to dinner in an Indian mood. It is beautiful to behold and the fried onions add the nicest flavor.

1	onion, coarsely chopped
4	cloves garlic, minced
2	tablespoons butter

1	cup red lentils, rinsed and picked over for foreign particles
2	cups vegetable broth
1	can (1 pound) stewed tomatoes, drained and chopped
1	teaspoon ground turmeric or more to taste
1/2	teaspoon ground cumin
	salt and pepper to taste

In a saucepan, saute onion and garlic in butter until onion is beginning to take on color. Stir in the remaining ingredients, cover pan, and simmer mixture for 45 minutes, or until lentils are tender and most of the liquid is absorbed. Stir in the fried onions and heat through. Serves 6.

To make Fried Onions:
Cut 1 medium onion in half lengthwise. Thinly slice each half into thin half rings. Dust lightly with flour. Fry onions in 2 tablespoons oil until golden brown. Remove from pan and drain on paper towels.

Brown Lentil Stew

This is a delicious dish to serve with rice or orzo. Brown rice or bulgur or kasha is another good choice.

1	pound brown lentils, rinsed and picked over for foreign particles
4	cups vegetable broth
1	large red onion, peeled, cut in half and thinly sliced
1	can (1 pound) stewed tomatoes, chopped. Do not drain.
4	cloves garlic, minced
1	tablespoon olive oil
	salt and pepper to taste

In a Dutch oven casserole, stir together all the ingredients. Bring to a boil and then lower the heat. Simmer mixture, with cover slightly ajar, for 45 to 50 minutes, or until lentils are tender. Serves 6 to 8.

Spiced Lentils with Tomatoes & Onion

Lentils are delicious and healthy, too. As a soup, or side-dish, the combinations are endless. This recipe produces a nice thick lentil accompaniment.

- 1 onion, chopped
- 4 cloves garlic, minced
- 2 tablespoons butter

- 1 cup brown lentils, rinsed and picked over for foreign particles
- 2 cups vegetable broth
- 1 can (1 pound) stewed tomatoes, chopped. Do not drain.
- 1 teaspoon ground turmeric
- 1/2 teaspoon ground cumin
- salt and pepper to taste

In a saucepan, saute onion and garlic in butter until onion is transparent. Stir in the remaining ingredients, cover pan, and simmer mixture for 45 minutes, or until lentils are tender and most of the liquid is absorbed. Depending on the number of dishes you are serving, this will serve 6 as an accompaniment.

Lentils with Tomatoes, Carrots & Onions

Lentils are a healthy and delicious accompaniment to an informal dinner with family and friends. After cooking, if there is a little extra broth, then drain it off. This is not a soup, but an accompaniment to dinner. I recommend that you serve this in a separate, small bowl.

- 1 cup lentils, washed and picked over for any foreign particles
- 3 carrots, peeled and thinly sliced
- 2 cloves garlic, minced
- 1 large onion, minced
- 2 shallots, minced
- 1 can (1 pound) stewed tomatoes, chopped. Do not drain.
- 3 cups vegetable broth
- 1 tablespoon olive oil
- pepper to taste

In a Dutch oven casserole, stir together all the ingredients, cover pan and simmer mixture for 45 minutes to 1 hour, or until lentils are tender and most of the broth is absorbed. Serves 6.

Easiest & Best Barbecued Baked Beans

This is a vegetarian version of my best baked beans. Starting with canned beans simplifies preparation. This can be prepared a day in advance and stored in the refrigerator. Make certain you have a pan with a tight-fitting lid that will safely go into the oven. Aluminum foil can be used as a cover, but it is a bit of a bother to remove and reseal when you check that the sauce doesn't run low.

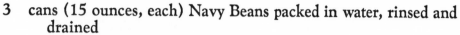

3	cans (15 ounces, each) Navy Beans packed in water, rinsed and drained
1	large onion, minced
3/4	cup barbecue sauce. (Chris' & Pitt's Original BBQ Sauce)
3/4	cup dark brown sugar
1/4	cup dark molasses (Brer Rabbit Dark Molasses)
3/4	cup tomato juice

In an oven-proof Dutch oven or lidded pan, add all the ingredients and stir until nicely mixed. Cover pan and bake in a 325° oven for 1 1/2 hours or until the sauce has thickened. Check after 1 hour and if sauce looks dry, add a little juice. (Normally, this is not necessary.) This should serve 8 to 10, but allow for extras. Enjoy!

Sweet Potatoes, Carrots with Dried Fruits

This is actually very simple to prepare...boil the carrots, soften the dried fruit and assemble the casserole. It can be prepared 1 day earlier, stored in the refrigerator and heated before serving.

1	package (1 pound) baby carrots
1	can (1 pound 12 ounces) sweet potatoes, drained and cut into 1-inch thick slices
1	package (1 pound) mixed dried fruits - a combination of dried apricots, peaches, apples, pears and prunes. (Make certain that the prunes are pitted.)
1 1/2	cups orange juice
4	tablespoons cinnamon sugar
6	sprinkles ground cinnamon or to taste

In a saucepan, cook carrots in boiling water until tender, about 15 minutes. Place carrots evenly in a 9x13-inch baking pan. Place sweet potatoes evenly over the carrots. In a saucepan, simmer together next three ingredients until fruits are tender, about 10 minutes. Place fruits and juice evenly over the sweet potatoes. Sprinkle top lightly with cinnamon.

Can be held at this point, covered, in the refrigerator. Before serving, add a little orange juice if casserole appears dry. Heat, loosely tented with foil, in a 350° oven for 30 minutes, or until piping hot. Serves 12.

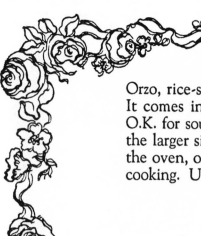

Orzo, rice-shaped pasta, can be found in some markets or in Greek groceries. It comes in 3 sizes. The smallest size is found is most supermarkets and is O.K. for soup, but it lacks the glamor of the larger size for casseroles. I prefer the larger size for soups, too. In the recipes that follow, the orzo is toasted in the oven, or sauteed in a little oil. This helps to reduce the starchiness when cooking. Use the method you prefer as both work well.

Pink Orzo with Tomatoes

1   cup orzo (large-size rice-shaped pasta)
1   tablespoon oil

2   cups vegetable broth
    salt and pepper to taste

2   tomatoes, peeled, seeded and chopped
1   small onion, chopped
2   cloves garlic, minced
1   teaspoon oil

In a Dutch oven casserole, saute orzo in oil, stirring all the while, until orzo is just beginning to take on color. Carefully pour in (it will splatter) the vegetable broth and seasonings. Cover pan, and simmer mixture for 40 minutes, or until orzo is tender and liquid is absorbed. Meanwhile in a covered saucepan, simmer together last 4 ingredients until onion is soft. Stir tomato mixture into cooked orzo until nicely mixed and heat through to serve. Serves 6.

Toasted Orzo with Mushrooms & Onions

1   cup large-size orzo (rice-shaped pasta)

1   tablespoon oil
2   cups vegetable broth
    salt and pepper to taste

1   onion, chopped
1   pound mushrooms, sliced
1   tablespoon oil

Place orzo in a shallow pan and toast in a 350° oven for 8 minutes, or until orzo is beginning to take on color. In a Dutch oven casserole, place toasted orzo with the next 4 ingredients, cover pan and simmer orzo for 40 minutes, or until orzo is tender and liquid is absorbed. Meanwhile, in a large skillet, saute together onion and mushrooms in oil until onion is tender and liquid rendered is evaporated. Stir mushroom mixture into cooked orzo and heat through. Serves 6.

Honey Spiced Acorn Squash with Pineapple & Cinnamon

3	medium acorn squash, cut into halves. Remove strings and seeds.
	hot water
1	can (8 ounces) crushed pineapple, drained
1/4	cup honey
1/4	cup brown sugar
1/4	cup butter, melted
2	tablespoons finely grated orange (use fruit, juice and peel)
1	tablespoon finely grated lemon (use fruit, juice and peel)
1/4	teaspoon cinnamon
	pinch of nutmeg
	pinch of powdered cloves
	salt to taste

Place acorn squash, cut side down in a baking pan. Add about 1/4-inch hot water to pan. Bake squash in a 350° oven for about 40 minutes or until squash is tender.

Into a large bowl, scoop out the pulp and mash it. Add the remaining ingredients and stir until thoroughly blended. Spoon mixture into a greased porcelain baker and bake in a 350° oven for 20 minutes or until casserole is heated through. Sprinkle a little cinnamon sugar on top when serving. Serves 6.

Broccoli, Mushroom & Tomato Frittata

2	packages (10 ounces, each) frozen chopped broccoli, defrosted
2	medium tomatoes, peeled, seeded and chopped
1/2	pound mushrooms, sliced
1/2	cup chopped green onions
2	tablespoons grated Parmesan cheese
2	eggs beaten
1/2	cup cracker crumbs
1/2	teaspoon Italian Herb Seasoning

In a large bowl, mix together all the ingredients until nicely blended. Place in an oiled 8x12-inch porcelain baker and bake at 350-degrees for about 40 minutes, or until casserole is set and top is browned. Serves 6.

Asparagus with Lemon, Garlic & Cheese

1 pound fresh thin asparagus spears. Trim the ends and if the stalks are coarse, peel them with a vegetable peeler. Tie asparagus and stand it up in a steamer. Steam for 5 to 7 minutes or until firm tender and drain.

2 tablespoons low-fat unflavored yogurt
4 tablespoons chopped chives
2 teaspoons lemon juice
2 tablespoons garlic croutons, crushed into crumbs
2 tablespoons grated Parmesan cheese
1 tablespoon melted butter

Arrange cooked asparagus in a porcelain baking dish. Brush asparagus with yogurt, sprinkle with chives and drizzle with lemon. Sprinkle with crumbs and Parmesan. Drizzle top with melted butter.

Bake in a 350-degree oven until heated through. Broil for a few seconds to brown top. Serves 8.

Note: *-Entire dish can be assembled earlier in the day and brought to room temperature before heating.*

Brussels Sprouts with Lemon Chive Sauce

2 packages (10 ounces, each) frozen Brussels sprouts
1/2 cup vegetable broth
4 tablespoons lemon juice
1/4 teaspoon thyme flakes
2 tablespoons minced parsley leaves
white pepper to taste

2 tablespoons half and half cream
4 tablespoons minced chives

In a saucepan, simmer together first group of ingredients until sprouts are tender, and drain. Add the cream and cook until it is reduced by half. Sprinkle with chopped chives at serving time. Serves 6.

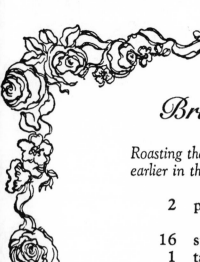

Brussels Sprouts with Roasted Shallots

Roasting the shallots adds a wonderful flavor to the sprouts. This can be prepared earlier in the day and heated before serving.

2	packages (10 ounces, each) frozen Brussels sprouts or
	1 quart fresh sprouts, trimmed
16	small shallots, peeled and left whole
1	tablespoon butter
1	tablespoon lemon juice
1/2	cup dry white wine
1/2	cup vegetable broth
	salt and pepper to taste

In a 9x13-inch baking pan, evenly spread all the ingredients. Cover pan with foil and bake in a 350° oven for 30 minutes or until vegetables are tender. Remove the foil and stir and toss vegetables. Return pan to the oven and bake another 10 minutes. Serves 8.

Brussels Sprouts, Mushrooms & Shallots

2	packages (10 ounces, each) frozen Brussels sprouts
1/2	cup vegetable broth
1/4	pound mushrooms, sliced
3	shallots, minced
2	cloves garlic, minced
1/4	cup vegetable broth
1/2	teaspoon Italian Herb Seasoning
1	tablespoon minced parsley

In a saucepan, cook sprouts in vegetable broth until they are tender and drain. In a skillet, cook together remaining ingredients until mushrooms are tender and all the liquid rendered is evaporated. Combine sprouts and mushroom mixture and heat through. Serves 6.

Sweet & Sour Red Cabbage with Apples and Raisins

1   onion, chopped
1   clove garlic, minced
1   tablespoon butter

1   small head red cabbage, (about 1 1/4 pounds), cored and
        finely shredded
2   apples, peeled, cored and grated
1   cup drained sauerkraut
2   tablespoons brown sugar
3/4 cup apple juice
1/2 cup raisins
      salt and pepper to taste

In a Dutch oven casserole, saute together first 3 ingredients until onions are transparent. Stir in the remaining ingredients, cover pan, lower heat and simmer mixture for about 45 minutes or until cabbage is tender. To prevent scorching, add a little apple juice if cabbage appears dry. Serves 8.

Sweet & Sour Red Cabbage with Apples & Currants

1   onion, chopped
2   cloves garlic, minced
1   teaspoon oil

1   cup vegetable broth
4   tablespoons lemon juice
1   small head red cabbage (about 1 pound), cored and shredded
2   apples, peeled, cored and grated
2   tablespoons dried black currants

In a Dutch oven casserole, saute onion and garlic in oil until onions are soft. Add the remaining ingredients, cover pan, and simmer mixture for about 30 minutes, or until cabbage is tender. Serves 8.

Pureed Carrots with Cinnamon

This is a beautiful dish to serve for a dinner party. It can be prepared earlier in the day and heated before serving.

- 1 pound carrots, peeled and sliced. Cook in boiling water for about 15 minutes or until soft. Thoroughly drain and pat dry with paper towelling.

- 1/2 teaspoon cinnamon
- 1 teaspoon sugar
- 3 eggs
- 1/2 cup milk

Line the bottoms of 6 individual ramekins with parchment paper. (This will make for easy removal.) Puree carrots in food processor. Beat together the remaining ingredients and add to carrots and pulse for 2 or 3 seconds until blended.

Divide mixture between the 6 prepared ramekins and place in a baking pan with boiling water coming halfway up the sides. Bake at 350-degrees for about 30 to 40 minutes or until mold is firm. Remove from pan and allow to set for 2 or 3 minutes. Run a knife around the edge, and invert on a plate, remove paper and allow some of the liquid rendered to drain. Place onto a porcelain server. Can be held at this point. Before serving, heat in a 350-degree oven for 10 to 12 minutes. Plant a small parsley leaf on each top. Serves 6.

Lemon Carrots with Butter & Honey

Even if you are so-so about carrots, you will enjoy the delicate flavor of this dish. It is also pretty to look at, glazed and flecked with parsley

- 1 bag (1 pound) baby carrots
- 1/2 cup water

- 1 tablespoon butter
- 2 tablespoons honey

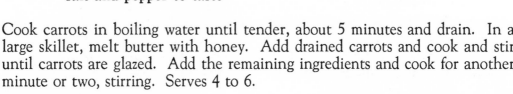

- 1 tablespoon lemon juice
- 3 tablespoons chopped parsley leaves
  salt and pepper to taste

Cook carrots in boiling water until tender, about 5 minutes and drain. In a large skillet, melt butter with honey. Add drained carrots and cook and stir until carrots are glazed. Add the remaining ingredients and cook for another minute or two, stirring. Serves 4 to 6.

Spicy Cauliflower, Potatoes & Tomatoes

The seasonings will not produce a hot dish. If you like it "hot" then add a sprinkle of cayenne pepper to taste.

1   large onion, coarsely chopped
1   clove garlic, minced
2   tablespoons butter

1   can (1 pound) stewed tomatoes, chopped. Do not drain.
1/2   cup vegetable broth

Seasonings:
1/2   teaspoon chili powder
1   teaspoon turmeric
1   teaspoon ground cumin
1/2   teaspoon ground coriander
     salt to taste

1   pound potatoes, peeled and cut into 1-inch pieces
1   small head cauliflower, cut into small florets

In a Dutch oven casserole, saute onion and garlic in butter until onion is soft. Stir in the tomatoes, broth and seasonings and bring mixture to a simmer. Add the potatoes and cauliflower, cover pan and simmer for 30 minutes, or until vegetables are tender. Add a little broth if mixture appears dry. Serves 8.

Cauliflower with Tomatoes & Onions

1   can (1 pound) stewed tomatoes, chopped. Do not drain.
1   onion, chopped
1   clove garlic, minced

2   packages (10 ounces, each) frozen cauliflower, cut into
         small florets
3   tablespoons lemon juice
1   teaspoon sugar
1   tablespoon minced parsley
     white pepper to taste

In a saucepan, cook together first 3 ingredients until onions are soft. Stir in the remaining ingredients and continue cooking until cauliflower is tender, about 7 minutes. Serves 6.

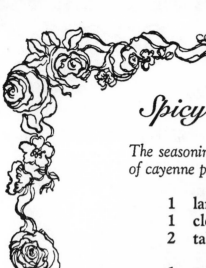

Celery in Lemon Dill Sauce

Celery is one of the many ignored vegetables. It is used as an accompaniment to stuffings or soups, but it is not often served alone. It is so low in calories that it is a good vegetable to consider serving when a little dessert is around the bend.

1	large bunch celery (1 pound). Remove leaves, scrub the stalks, and cut on the diagonal into 1/2-inch thick slices.
1/2	cup vegetable broth
2	tablespoons dry white wine
2	tablespoons lemon juice
3	shallots, minced
1	clove garlic, minced
1/2	teaspoon dried dill weed

In a Dutch oven casserole, with cover slightly ajar, simmer together all the ingredients until celery is tender, about 7 to 10 minutes. Serves 6.

Country Corn Pudding

2	packages (10 ounces, each) frozen corn kernels, defrosted and patted with paper towelling to soak up moisture
3	eggs
1	cup half and half
1	tablespoon sugar
	salt to taste

Prepare corn. With a fork, beat eggs with the remaining ingredients just until blended. Stir in the corn. Place mixture into a 12x2-inch oval porcelain baker and bake at 350° for 35 to 40 minutes, or until custard is set. To serve, spoon it directly from the porcelain baker. Serves 8.

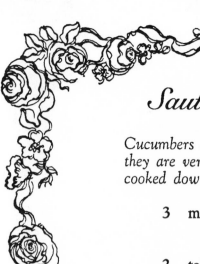

Sauteed Cucumbers with Chives & Dill

Cucumbers are not often used as a vegetable course, and it is really a shame, as they are very satisfying. They do render a great deal of liquid which should be cooked down.

3 medium cucumbers, peeled and cut in half, lengthwise.
       Scoop out the seeds with a spoon and slice the cucumbers,
       crosswise, into thin slices.
2 tablespoons butter
2 tablespoons white wine

3 tablespoons chopped chives
1 tablespoon chopped parsley
1/4 teaspoon dry dill weed
       salt and white pepper to taste

In a saucepan, simmer cucumbers with butter and wine until wine is almost evaporated. Add the remaining ingredients and toss mixture to combine. Serves 6.

Cucumbers with Lemon, Parsley & Chives

Cucumbers are wonderful served as a warm vegetable. They prepare in minutes and are an interesting accompaniment to dinner.

3 medium cucumbers, peeled and halved (about 1 pound). With a
       spoon, scoop out the seeds.
4 tablespoons vegetable broth
1 tablespoon lemon juice or more to taste

1 tablespoon chopped parsley leaves
3 tablespoons chopped chives

In a saucepan, cook together first 3 ingredients until cucumbers are limp, about 3 minutes. Stir in parsley and chives. Serves 4.

Roasted Chinese Eggplants

2   tablespoons oil
1   teaspoon sesame oil
2   tablespoons soy sauce
1   tablespoon crushed dried rosemary
6   Chinese eggplants, (5x1-inch approximately), stems trimmed and
        cut into halves lengthwise

In a 9x13-inch baking pan, mix the oils and soy sauce and spread evenly.
Sprinkle evenly with rosemary on top and lay the eggplant slices, cut side
down. Bake at 400° for 30 minutes or until eggplants are soft. Serve with
Bean Thread Noodles & Vegetable Saute. Serves 6.

Herbed Green Beans with Tomatoes & Garlic

1   onion, finely chopped
2   cloves garlic, minced
1   tablespoon olive oil

1   pound green beans. Snap off ends and remove any strings.
1   can (1 pound) stewed tomatoes, finely chopped. Do not drain.
2   tablespoons tomato paste
1   tablespoon lemon juice
3   tablespoons chopped parsley leaves
1/2 teaspoon sweet basil flakes
     salt and pepper to taste

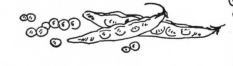

In a Dutch oven casserole, saute onion and garlic in oil until onions are
transparent. Add the remaining ingredients, cover pan and simmer mixture
until green beans are tender. (Green beans should not be too firm for this
dish.) Serves 6.

Green Beans with Parsley Sauce

- 1/2 cup vegetable broth
- 1/4 cup dry white wine
- 4 shallots minced
- 3 cloves garlic, minced
- 1/4 cup minced parsley leaves
- 2 teaspoons butter
- white pepper to taste

- 1 pound green beans, ends snapped off

In a Dutch oven casserole, simmer first 7 ingredients until shallots are softened, about 5 minutes. Add the green beans, cover pan and cook green beans until tender, about 8 minutes. If sauce appears soupy, remove green beans and cook sauce over high heat until reduced to 1/3 cup. Serves 6.

Buttered Italian Green Beans with Onions

- 2 packages (10 ounces, each) broad Italian Green Beans

- 1 medium onion, finely chopped
- 1 tablespoon butter
- 1/4 cup vegetable broth
- salt and pepper to taste

Cook vegetables in boiling water for 6 minutes or until firm-tender. Drain and refresh under cold running water.

Meanwhile, saute onion in butter until onion is just beginning to brown. Add the broth, seasonings and green beans, and continue cooking and turning until beans are tender. Serves 12.

Lima Beans with Onions & Tomatoes

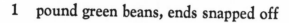

- 2 packages (10 ounces, each) frozen lima beans
- 1 onion, minced
- 1 can (1 pound) stewed tomatoes, chopped. Do not drain.
- 2 tablespoons lemon juice
- pepper to taste

In a saucepan, stir together all the ingredients. Cover pan and simmer mixture until onion is soft and beans are tender, about 30 minutes. Serves 6.

Onion & Mushroom Saute

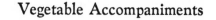
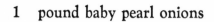

1 pound baby pearl onions

1 pound mushrooms, sliced
1 tablespoon butter

1/4 cup vegetable broth
2 tablespoons chopped parsley

Cook onions in boiling water for 10 minutes and drain. Allow to cool and slip off the skins. In a Dutch oven casserole, saute the mushrooms in butter until tender. Add the onions and the broth. Cook for a few minutes, uncovered, until the broth is almost evaporated. Stir in the parsley and serve. Serves 8.

Mushrooms & Tomatoes in Wine Sauce

1 pound mushrooms, sliced
2 medium tomatoes, peeled, seeded and chopped
3 shallots, minced
3 cloves garlic, minced
1/4 teaspoon thyme flakes
1 tablespoon minced parsley leaves
1/4 cup dry white wine
pinch of cayenne pepper

In a saucepan, cook together all the ingredients until mushrooms are tender. Increase the heat and cook rapidly until liquid rendered is evaporated. Serves 6.

Mushrooms in Wine & Herb Sauce

This is a delicious vegetable side dish. It is also excellent, served as a first course on small squares of puff pastry.

1 pound mushrooms, thinly sliced
6 cloves garlic, minced
1 teaspoon butter
1/4 cup red wine
1 teaspoon red wine vinegar
1 teaspoon dried thyme flakes
pepper to taste

In a covered saucepan, place all the ingredients and over low heat, simmer mushrooms for 10 minutes. Remove cover and continue simmering for about 10 minutes, or until liquid is absorbed. Serves 4.

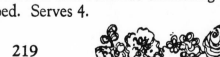

Confit of Onions with Raisins

2   onions, thinly sliced
2   teaspoons sugar
1/4   cup vegetable broth

1/4   cup vegetable broth
1/4   cup raisins
1   tablespoon parsley

In a covered skillet, over very low heat, cook onions in sugar and broth until onions are soft and just beginning to take on color, about 30 minutes. Do not allow to brown. Add the remaining ingredients, and simmer mixture, uncovered, until broth is almost evaporated. Serves 4.

French-Style Buttered Peas & Onions

1   tablespoon butter
1/2   cup sliced green onions (use only the white bulbs)
2   packages (10 ounces, each) baby peas
1   cup finely shredded Boston or Butter lettuce
1   tablespoon minced parsley leaves
1/4   cup vegetable broth
     salt and pepper to taste

1   tablespoon lemon juice

In a saucepan, simmer together first 8 ingredients until peas are tender. Stir in the lemon juice. Serves 8.

Peas with Shallots & Parsley

2   tablespoons butter
3   shallots, finely chopped
1/2   teaspoon sugar
3   tablespoons finely chopped parsley
     salt and pepper to taste

2   packages (10 ounces, each) frozen baby peas

In a saucepan, saute together first 6 ingredients until shallots are tender. Add the peas and cook for 2 minutes, or until peas are tender but firm. Serves 6.

Glazed Onions with Yellow Raisins

```
4    tablespoons vegetable broth
6    medium onions, peeled and cut in half horizontally
4    tablespoons olive oil
     salt and pepper to taste

1/2  cup golden raisins, plumped in boiling water
       for 5 minutes and drained
```

In a 9x13-inch baking pan spread vegetable broth and set the onions cut side up. Drizzle onions with olive oil and season with salt and pepper. Bake at 350° for 30 minutes. Broil onions for a few minutes, or until flecked with brown. Sprinkle raisins on top and continue baking for 10 minutes. Serves 6.

Peas with Mushroom & Lemon Sauce

```
1/2  pound mushrooms, sliced
1    small onion, minced
1    clove garlic
1    tablespoon butter

1/4  cup vegetable broth
2    tablespoons lemon juice
1/8  teaspoon ground poultry seasoning
     salt and pepper to taste

2    packages (10 ounces, each) frozen baby peas
```

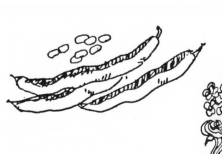

In an uncovered saucepan, saute together first 4 ingredients until onion is soft. Add the next 5 ingredients and simmer sauce for 2 minutes. Add the peas and simmer peas for 3 minutes or until they are tender. Serves 8.

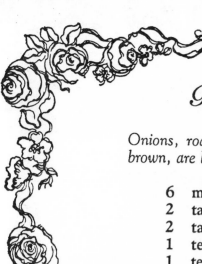

Baked Red Onions with Thyme

Onions, roasted with herbs, sparkled with a splash of vinegar and flecked with brown, are beautiful to serve on a buffet.

- 6 medium red onions, peeled and cut into 1/2-inch slices
- 2 tablespoons olive oil
- 2 tablespoons vinegar
- 1 teaspoon sugar
- 1 teaspoon dried thyme flakes
  salt and pepper to taste

In a large bowl, toss together all the ingredients until onions are nicely coated. Place mixture in a 9x13-inch baking pan, and bake at 400° for 20 minutes, turning now and again, until onions are tender. Broil onions, about 4-inches from the heat for a few minutes on each side, or until onions are flecked with brown. Serves 6.

To Make Onion Chrysanthemums:
Instead of slicing the onions as described above, cut the onions 3/4 the way down lengthwise, and continue slicing around the onion every 1/4-inch. When the onions cook, the slices will open up like a flower and they are just beautiful and decorative..

Confit of Onions with Herbs

Deeply rich and aromatic, this can be served as a vegetable side dish. It is also excellent, thinly spread on toast points, to accompany soup or salad. Please cook this on very low heat (this process is called "sweating") so that the onions are cooked very slowly and do not burn.

- 6 medium onions, cut in half and very thinly sliced
- 6 cloves garlic, minced
- 1/2 cup red wine
- 2 tablespoons red wine vinegar
- 1 tablespoon honey
- 2 teaspoons dried thyme flakes
  pepper to taste

In a covered Dutch oven casserole, place all the ingredients and cook over very low heat for about 1 hour, stirring every now and again. Remove the cover and cook for another few minutes until liquid is evaporated. Serves 6.

French Potato, Onion & Apple Torte

Potato cakes are usually served with a dollop of sour cream and applesauce. In this recipe, the apple is added before baking and adds a very pleasant sweetness. This can be baked earlier in the day and stored in the refrigerator. Cut into squares and then reheat. It is easier to cut the potato torte into squares when it is cold. These can be prepared as pancakes (called "galettes"); instructions follow the recipe.

6   potatoes, peeled and grated
3   onions, peeled and grated
1   apple, peeled, cored and grated

2   eggs, beaten
1/2   cup cracker crumbs
     salt and pepper to taste

1   tablespoon oil
1   tablespoon oil

So that the potatoes and apple do not darken, potatoes, onions and apple should be grated in food processor just before baking. Place in a large bowl and stir in eggs, crumbs and seasonings until blended.

Spread 1 tablespoon oil in a 9x13-inch baking pan, place potato mixture evenly in pan, and drizzle top with 1 tablespoon oil. Bake at 350° for about 1 hour or until top is golden brown. Cut into squares to serve. Serve 12 generously.

Potato, Onion & Apple Pancakes

In a very hot oiled skillet, form pancakes with 2 tablespoons of potato mixture. Flatten to form a 3-inch pancake. Cook until bottom is golden brown, then turn, and brown the other side. Place pancakes on a cookie sheet and heat through in a 300° oven before serving.

Steamed Baby Potatoes with Parsley & Dill

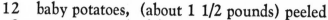

12   baby potatoes, (about 1 1/2 pounds) peeled
2   teaspoons melted butter
2   tablespoons chopped parsley
1/2   teaspoon dried dill weed

Line a 10-inch round baking pan with foil, extending the sides 6-inches. Toss together all the ingredients, place in pan, and fold the foil to seal the potatoes. Bake in a 350-degree oven for 25 minutes or until potatoes are tender. Serves 6.

Country Baked Potatoes

6   medium potatoes (about 1 1/2 pounds), peeled
2   tablespoons melted margarine
   onion powder and paprika

Brush the peeled potatoes with melted margarine and sprinkle generously with onion powder and paprika. Bake uncovered at 350-degrees until potatoes are tender and golden brown, about 45 minutes. Can be held in a 300-degree oven for 20 minutes. However, do not prepare these in advance. Serves 6.

Potato Frittata with Onions & Cheese

6   medium potatoes, peeled and grated
2   onions, grated
1/2   cup bread crumbs
3/4   cup grated Parmesan cheese
2   eggs, beaten
   salt and pepper to taste

Combine first 7 ingredients in a large bowl and stir until mixture is well mixed. Spread mixture evenly in an oiled 9x13-inch baking pan. Bake at 350° for about 55 minutes or until potatoes are tender and top is golden brown. Cut into squares and serve with a dollop of low-fat sour cream and a spoonful of applesauce. Serves 10.

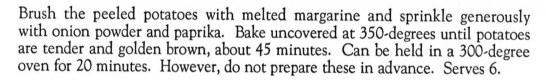

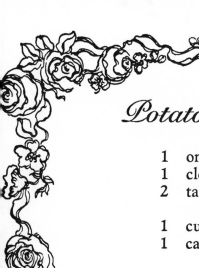

Potato Casserole with Tomatoes & Onions

        1   onion, chopped
        1   clove garlic, put through a press
        2   tablespoons butter

        1   cup vegetable broth
        1   can (1 pound) stewed tomatoes, chopped. Do not drain

        2   pounds potatoes, peeled and cut into 3/4-inch thick slices
             salt and pepper to taste

In a Dutch oven casserole, saute onion and garlic in butter until onions are soft. Add broth and tomatoes and stir until blended. Add potatoes and seasonings. Cover saucepan and simmer mixture for 30 to 40 minutes or until potatoes are tender. Serves 6 to 8.

Note: -*This dish can be baked in the oven. In that case, delete butter, spread the remaining ingredients evenly in a 9x13-inch pan, cover pan loosely with foil and bake at 350° for 40 minutes, or until potatoes are tender.*
       - Can be made earlier in the day and heated before serving.

Potatoes & Onions Baked in Broth

This is a delicious way to serve potatoes. It can be prepared ahead and heated before serving...and assembling couldn't be easier.

        6   medium potatoes, peeled and cut into 1/2-inch thick slices
        2   cups chopped onions
    1 1/4   cups vegetable broth
        1   teaspoon oil
             salt and pepper to taste

In a 9x13-inch baking pan, place all the ingredients and toss them around so that they are nicely mixed. Cover pan loosely with foil and bake in a 350° oven for 1 hour or until potatoes are tender. Broth should almost be absorbed. Serves 6.

Garlic Potatoes with Onions & Rosemary

The success of this dish rests mainly with the tastiness of the broth. The richer the broth, the more succulent the taste. Prepare this in a porcelain baker (one with its own serving tray) and it will go from oven to table without the bother of transferring to a serving platter.

- 1 onion, chopped
- 6 cloves garlic, minced
- 1/2 cup vegetable broth
- 1 teaspoon oil
- 1 teaspoon dried rosemary

- 6 medium baking potatoes, (about 1 1/2 pounds), scrubbed and cut into 1/4-inch thick slices. Do not peel.
- freshly ground black pepper
- 1/4 cup vegetable broth

Stir together first 5 ingredients until nicely mixed. In a 9x13-inch non-stick baking pan, toss together the potatoes and onion mixture and spread evenly. Cover pan tightly with foil and bake at 375-degrees for 30 minutes.

Remove the foil and drizzle remaining vegetable broth evenly over all. Return to oven, uncovered and bake for another 20 to 30 minutes, or until potatoes are tender, top is browned and broth is almost absorbed. Serves 6.

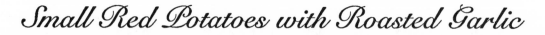

Small Red Potatoes with Roasted Garlic

Roasted garlic is sweet and mild and when paired with small baked red potatoes it is truly delicious.

- 16 small red potatoes, cut into quarters
- 16 cloves garlic, peeled and thinly sliced
- 1/3 cup olive oil
- 4 tablespoons melted butter
- salt and pepper to taste

In a 9x13-inch baking pan, toss all the ingredients together until nicely blended and spread evenly. Bake at 350° for about 40 minutes, turning 3 or 4 times or until potatoes are tender and browned. Serves 8.

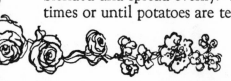

Garlic Mashed Potatoes

These are delicious. Using the non-fat cream cheese, eliminates a stick of butter. The cream cheese also adds a wonderful flavor.

- 2 pounds potatoes, peeled and cut into chunks. Boil for about 30 minutes, or until tender, and drain. Mash at once.

- 2 tablespoons butter
- 8 cloves garlic, minced

- 1/2 package (4 ounces) non-fat cream cheese, at room temperature
  salt and pepper to taste

While potatoes are boiling, saute garlic in butter until garlic is softened and just beginning to color. Add to the mashed potatoes. Mash in the cream cheese and seasonings until nicely blended. Serves 6 to 8.

Yellow Potatoes with Mushrooms & Onions

These potatoes are an attractive addition to a buffet. They are also truly delicious.

- 4 medium potatoes, peeled and cut into 3/4-inch dice
- 1 cup vegetable broth
- 1 teaspoon ground turmeric
- 1/2 teaspoon ground cumin
  salt and pepper to taste

- 2 onions, chopped
- 4 cloves garlic, minced
- 2 tablespoons butter

- 1/2 pound mushrooms sliced

In a saucepan, over low heat, cook together first 6 ingredients until potatoes are tender, about 20 minutes.

In a skillet, saute onions and garlic in butter until onions are transparent. Add the mushrooms and continue sauteing until liquid rendered is evaporated. Add mushroom mixture to potatoes and stir until nicely blended. Cover pan and heat through. Serves 6.

Potatoes & Artichokes with Green Onions

Instead of browning the vegetables in large quantities of oil, broiling them with a little butter produces a similar effect, with a saving of calories. The small amount of butter adds a good deal of flavor.

       2   packages (10 ounces, each) frozen artichoke hearts
     1/2   pound baby red-skinned potatoes, peeled or unpeeled

       6   green onions, cut into 1-inch lengths
       1   tablespoon butter, melted
       1   teaspoon dried crushed rosemary

Cook the artichokes in boiling water for 5 to 7 minutes or until tender and drain. Cook the potatoes in boiling water for 12 to 15 minutes or until tender and drain. Cut the artichokes and potatoes in quarters and place them in a bowl. Add the remaining ingredients and toss together until nicely mixed.

Place vegetable mixture in 1 layer in a broiler pan and broil, 4-inches from the heat, turning until nicely browned on all sides. Serves 8.

Creamed Spinach Casserole with Chives & Cheese

This is a lovely way to serve spinach, sparkled with nutmeg, chives and cheese. Entire casserole can be assembled earlier in the day and heated at time of serving.

       1   package (10 ounces) frozen chopped spinach,
                 defrosted and drained
       1   package (3 ounces) low-fat cream cheese, at room temperature
       3   tablespoons chopped chives
       2   tablespoons grated Parmesan cheese
     1/8   teaspoon nutmeg
              salt and pepper to taste

In a saucepan and over very low heat, simmer together all the ingredients, stirring, until heated through. Do not allow to boil. Serves 4 to 6.

Sweet Potato Casserole with Cinnamon, Orange & Apples

Grated sweet potatoes, flavored with orange and apples and sparkled with cinnamon is truly fit for a king. Potatoes and apples can be grated in a food processor. Orange should be grated, with short strokes, on the 3rd largest side of a 4-sided grater.

2	pounds sweet potatoes, peeled and grated.
2	medium apples, peeled, cored and grated
1	medium orange, grated, (about 6 tablespoons fruit, juice and peel)
1/2	cup orange juice
1/2	cup cracker crumbs
3	eggs, beaten
1/2	cup Cinnamon Brown Sugar
	salt to taste
1/4	cup melted margarine
4	tablespoons Cinnamon Brown Sugar

In a large bowl, mix together first 8 ingredients until blended. Place melted margarine into a buttered 9x13-inch baking pan and spread potato mixture evenly in pan. Sprinkle top with Cinnamon Brown Sugar. Bake at 350° for 1 hour, or until potatoes are tender and top is browned. Cut into squares to serve. Serves 12.

To Make Cinnamon Brown Sugar:
In a glass jar with a tight-fitting lid, shake together 1 cup sifted brown sugar and 1 tablespoon sifted cinnamon.

Sweet Potatoes Baked with Honey & Spice

This is a nice dish to serve on Thanksgiving. It is slimmed down a lot using only 1 tablespoon of butter.

2	large sweet potatoes, peeled and cut into 1/2-inch slices, (3/4 pound)
1	tablespoon butter or margarine, melted
2	tablespoons honey
1/2	teaspoon cinnamon
	pinch of ground nutmeg

Place potatoes in one layer in a non-stick baking pan. Drizzle top with butter and honey and sprinkle with cinnamon and nutmeg. Bake at 350-degrees until potatoes are tender, about 30 minutes. Serves 4.

Broiled Tomatoes with Herbed Crumbs, Lemon & Cheese

12   tomato slices, cut 1-inch thick
2   tablespoons low-fat mayonnaise
1   tablespoon lemon juice

12   teaspoons fresh bread crumbs
12   teaspoons grated Parmesan cheese
2   tablespoons chopped chives
1   tablespoon chopped parsley
1   tablespoon chopped sweet basil
    salt and pepper to taste

Place tomato slices on a cookie sheet. Mix together mayonnaise and lemon juice and brush tomato slices. Combine the remaining ingredients in a bowl and mix until blended. Divide mixture between the tomato slices and pat it down, covering the tops. Broil 6-inches from the heat until lightly browned on top and heated through. Serves 6.

Baked Zucchini with Tomatoes & Cheese

2   pounds zucchini. Do not peel. Cut into 1/4-inch slices.
3   tomatoes, peeled, seeded and thinly sliced

1   clove garlic, minced
2   tablespoons, each, chopped parsley and chives
1/2   teaspoon sweet basil flakes
2   tablespoons cracker crumbs
2   tablespoons grated Parmesan cheese
    black pepper to taste
    pinch of cayenne

2   teaspoons olive oil

In a 9x13-inch pan, place zucchini. Top with sliced tomatoes. Toss together the remaining ingredients and sprinkle on top of the tomatoes. Drizzle with olive oil. Bake in a 350-degree oven for 30 minutes, or until zucchini are tender. Broil for a few minutes to brown the top. Serves 8.

Yam Casserole with Apples, Prunes & Pecans

2	apples, peeled, cored and sliced
1	cup pitted prunes
1/2	cup yellow raisins
1/4	cup butter (1/2 stick)
1/2	cup honey or to taste
2	slices of lemon
1	can (1 pound 12 ounces) yams, drained. Discard liquid and cut into 1-inch slices.
1/3	cup chopped pecans

Combine first 6 ingredients in a saucepan and cook over low heat for about 15 minutes or until apples are almost tender. In a buttered 9x13-inch porcelain casserole, place yam slices and spread apple mixture evenly over them. Sprinkle top with chopped pecans. Bake in a 350° oven for about 15 minutes or until casserole is heated through. Serves 8.

Gingersnap Yam Pudding with Honey & Raisins

1	can (1 pound 16 ounces) yams, drained. Discard liquid.
3	eggs
1	cup milk
2/3	cup honey
1/2	cup yellow raisins
1/2	cup gingersnap cookie crumbs
1	teaspoon cinnamon
1/4	teaspoon nutmeg

Combine all the ingredients in the large bowl of an electric mixer and beat for about 1 minute or until mixture is thoroughly blended. Spread mixture into a buttered 10-inch oval porcelain baking dish and bake at 350° for 30 minutes. Sprinkle top with Cinnamon Sugar Topping and continue baking for 10 minutes, or until casserole is puffed and set. Serves 6 to 8.

Cinnamon Sugar Topping:
Combine 1 tablespoon cinnamon sugar with 1/4 cup chopped walnuts and mix until blended.

Zucchini Frittata with Onions & Cheese

This is an excellent dish, exceedingly delicious and simple to prepare. It serves well from a porcelain casserole and is a grand choice for a buffet. In the event that you do not own a porcelain casserole, then prepare the dish and let it cool. Cut it into squares, but leave it in the pan to reheat. Then place it on a lovely platter to serve.

1 1/2	pounds zucchini, scrubbed and grated
2	medium onions, grated
1/4	cup cracker crumbs (or cracker meal)
1	egg, beaten
	pepper to taste
3	tablespoons grated Parmesan cheese
1	teaspoon oil

In a bowl, toss together first 5 ingredients until nicely mixed. Spread mixture evenly into a non-stick 9x13-inch baking pan, sprinkle top with cheese and drizzle with oil. Bake in a 350-degree oven for about 50 minutes or until top is crispy and golden. Cut into squares to serve. Serves 8.

Zucchini with Tomatoes & Onions

1	medium onion, minced
1	clove garlic, minced
1	can (1 pound) stewed tomatoes, chopped. Do not drain.
1	teaspoon parsley flakes
1/2	teaspoon Italian Herb Seasoning
1	tablespoon lemon juice
1	tablespoon olive oil
	pepper to taste
6	medium zucchini, (about 1 1/2 pounds), ends cut and sliced 1/4-inch thick

In a Dutch oven casserole, place first group of ingredients. Bring mixture to a boil, cover pan, and lower heat. Simmer mixture for 15 minutes. Add the zucchini and continue to simmer for 15 minutes, or until onion is soft and zucchini is tender. Serves 8.

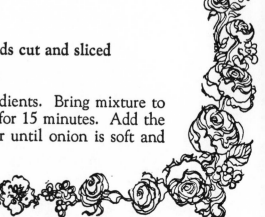

Zucchini with Mushrooms & Onions

This is a rather simple, but by no means plain, method of preparing zucchini. The vegetables are cooked in their own juice and this intensifies the flavor.

6	medium zucchini, peeled and thinly sliced
1/2	pound mushrooms thinly sliced
1	small onion, minced
1	tablespoon olive oil
	salt and pepper to taste
1	tablespoon minced parsley leaves

In a large skillet, over medium-high heat, saute together all the ingredients until vegetables are tender and liquid rendered is evaporated, about 15 minutes. Serves 6.

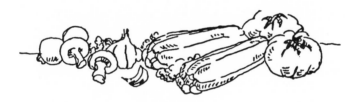

Zucchini with Onion, Garlic & Lemon

6	medium zucchini, cut into very thin slices. Do not peel.
4	cloves finely minced garlic
2	tablespoons finely minced onion
1	tablespoon olive oil
1	tablespoon lemon juice
1	tablespoon Italian Herb Seasoning
1	teaspoon minced parsley
	salt and pepper to taste

In a large skillet, saute together first 4 ingredients until zucchini are tender. Stir in the remaining ingredients and continue cooking for 1 or 2 minutes or until heated through. Can be served hot as a vegetable accompaniment or cold as part of an antipasto platter. Serves 6.

Compote of Summer Fruits & Berries

This lovely compote is satisfying and refreshing. Serve with a thin butter cookie or other plain cookie.

- 4 ripe peaches, rinsed and patted dry with paper towelling
- 4 ripe apricots, rinsed and patted dry
- 1 cup fruity wine, Riesling or Chablis
- 2 tablespoons sugar
- 1 teaspoon vanilla

- 1 cup strawberries, rinsed and hulled
- 1 cup raspberries, rinsed and patted dry
- 1 cup blueberries, rinsed and patted dry

In a saucepan, simmer together first 5 ingredients for 5 minutes, or until fruit is firm tender. Remove fruit with a slotted spoon, peel the fruit by slipping off the skins (optional), cut it in half and remove the stones.

To the poaching liquid, add the berries and simmer for 3 minutes. Return the peaches and apricots to the poaching liquid, allow to cool and refrigerate until serving time.

Serve with a spoonful of Creme Fraiche Vanilla and a drizzle of the poaching liquid. Serves 8.

Creme Fraiche Vanilla:
- 1/2 cup half and half
- 1/2 cup low-fat sour cream
- 1 tablespoon sugar
- 1 teaspoon vanilla

In a glass jar, with a lid, stir together all the ingredients and allow to stand at room temperature for 2 hours. Refrigerate until serving time. Yields 16 tablespoons.

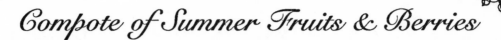

Rhubarb & Apricot Compote

- 1 package (20 ounces) frozen sliced rhubarb
- 4 apricots, peeled, pitted and sliced
- 3/4 cup orange juice
- 2 tablespoons lemon juice
- 1/3 cup sugar

In a saucepan, combine all the ingredients and simmer mixture for 10 minutes or until rhubarb is soft. Serve as a fruit accompaniment or as a lovely dessert with frozen yogurt. Serves 8.

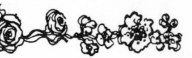

Spiced Peaches with Walnuts

This very versatile spicy fruit is nice to serve as an accompaniment to dinner. It is also great to serve as a topping for ice cream or non-fat yogurt. It is attractive and colorful on a buffet. Can be prepared earlier in the day and heated before serving. Apples or apricots can be substituted for the peaches. Can be served warm or chilled..

8 peaches, (about 2 pounds) peeled, pitted and cut in half
1/2 cup orange juice

2 tablespoons sugar
1/2 teaspoon cinnamon
3 sprinkles, each, ground nutmeg and ground cloves

1/2 cup coarsely cut walnuts

Place peaches in one layer in a shallow baker and pour orange juice on top. Stir together sugar, cinnamon, nutmeg and cloves and sprinkle evenly over the fruit.

Bake peaches in a 350° oven, basting every now and again, about 20 minutes. Sprinkle top with walnuts and bake another 10 minutes. Serve warm or at room temperature. Serves 8.

To make Spiced Apples with Walnuts:
Substitute 2 pounds apples, peeled, cored and sliced, for the peaches. Total baking time is 45 minutes. Sprinkle with walnuts after 35 minutes, and then bake 10 minutes longer.

To make Spiced Apricots with Walnuts:
Substitute 2 pounds apricots, peeled, halved and stoned, for the peaches. Baking time is the same as for the peaches.

Honey Spiced Apples with Orange & Walnuts

3 apples, peeled, cored and thinly sliced
1/2 cup orange juice
1/2 cup honey
1 teaspoon pumpkin pie spice

1/2 cup chopped walnuts

In a saucepan, cook together first 4 ingredients for 20 to 25 minutes, or until apples are softened. Add the walnuts and continue cooking for about 2 minutes or until juice is syrupy. Serve warm or slightly chilled.

Apple, Orange & Cranberry Winter Compote

Using the lovely fruits of winter, this tart and mouth-watering compote is a great fruit accompaniment. If you are looking for a fruity topping for sponge cake or ice cream, this is a good one to consider. It can be prepared 1 day earlier and stored in the refrigerator. It is exceedingly delicious served warm or cold.

- 3 apples, peeled, cored and thinly sliced
- 1/2 orange, grated. Use fruit, juice and peel, about 3 tablespoons.
- 1/2 cup orange juice
- 6 tablespoons cinnamon sugar

- 3/4 cup fresh or frozen cranberries

In a 9x13-inch baking pan, place the first 3 ingredients and sprinkle with the cinnamon sugar. Bake at 350° for 25 minutes. Stir in the cranberries and continue baking for 15 minutes, or until cranberries are popped and tender. Serve warm or cold. Serves 6.

Fresh Cranberry Relish with Apricots, Currants & Walnuts

- 1 pound fresh cranberries
- 1 cup chopped dried apricots
- 1/2 cup yellow raisins
- 1/4 cup black currants
- 1 cup sugar
- 3/4 cup orange juice
- 2 tablespoons lemon juice

- 3/4 cup chopped toasted walnuts
- 1/2 teaspoon vanilla

Combine first 7 ingredients in a saucepan and simmer mixture for about 20 minutes or until apricots are tender and liquid is syrupy. Stir in the walnuts and vanilla. Yields about 3 cups relish.

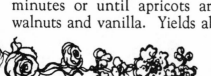

Glazed Cinnamon Apple Rings

4 large apples, cored and sliced into 3/4-inch rings
1/2 cup apple juice
3 tablespoons cinnamon sugar
   pinch of nutmeg and cloves

1/2 cup chopped pecans

Place apple rings in a 9x13-inch baking pan, drizzle with apple juice, sprinkle with cinnamon sugar and spices. Bake in a 350° oven for 20 minutes, sprinkle top with pecans and continue baking for 10 minutes. Serves 8.

Royal Rhubarb & Strawberry Compote

Everybody loves this simple but very delicious compote. It is tart, fruity and refreshing. Make extras as almost everyone takes seconds. Any leftover compote can be stored in the refrigerator.

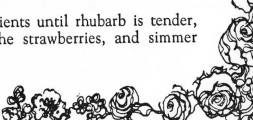

1 bag (20 ounces) frozen rhubarb
1/2 cup orange juice
1/3 cup sugar
2 tablespoons lemon juice

1 package (12 ounces) frozen strawberries

In a saucepan, simmer together first 4 ingredients until rhubarb is tender, but not mushy, about 10 minutes. Add the strawberries, and simmer compote for 2 minutes. Serves 8 to 10.

Apples Poached in Orange Honey

Some apples render more juice than others, so if the apples appear dry, add a little more orange juice. Bake for an extra 10 minutes and it will produce a delicious apple sauce.

- 6 medium apples, peeled, cored and sliced
- 3/4 cup orange juice
- 1/4 cup honey
- 2 teaspoons cinnamon sugar

Place apples in a deep-dish 10-inch round porcelain baker. Drizzle apples with orange juice and honey. Sprinkle top with cinnamon sugar. Bake at 350 ° for about 40 minutes, or until apples are tender. Serves 6.

Spiced Baked Apples with Orange & Cinnamon

- 6 medium apples, peeled, cored and cut in half lengthwise
- 1 cup orange juice
- 3 tablespoons grated orange (1/2 medium orange)
- 4 tablespoons cinnamon sugar

- 1/4 cup chopped walnuts, (optional)

Place apples, cut side down, in a 9x13-inch baking dish. Pour orange juice on the top and sprinkle with grated orange and cinnamon sugar. Bake at 350° for 35 minutes, baste tops with the juices in the pan and sprinkle with the optional walnuts. Continue baking until apples are tender, not mushy, about 10 minutes. Serve warm or chilled. Serves 12.

Desserts

Cakes & Tortes

Cookies

Fruits & Cobblers

Ices

Pies & Tarts

Puddings

Soufflés

Strudels & Danish

Angel Cake with Fresh Strawberry Sauce

Angel cake is one of the low calorie desserts. It is light and satisfying. Serving it with non-fat frozen yogurt and fresh fruit sauce is truly fit for a king.

6	egg whites, at room temperature
1/4	cup sugar
3/4	teaspoon cream of tartar
1	teaspoon lemon juice
1	teaspoon grated lemon zest (yellow part of the peel)
1/2	cup flour
1/4	cup sugar

Beat egg whites until foamy. Continue beating, adding sugar, 1 tablespoon at a time, until whites are stiff. Beat in cream of tartar and flavorings. Stir together flour and sugar and fold it gently into the egg white mixture.

Spread batter evenly into an ungreased 10-inch tube pan with a removable bottom and bake at 375° for about 20 minutes, or until top is golden brown. Remove cake from oven, and invert until thoroughly cooled. To remove cake from pan, run a knife along the edge and around the center, invert and then run a knife along the bottom. Give the tube a quick turn and release it from the cake.

Serve with a tablespoonful of Fresh Strawberry Sauce on top. Frozen, non-fat strawberry yogurt is good, too. Try both, if it is a special occasion. Serves 10.

Fresh Strawberry Sauce:

1 1/2	cups fresh strawberries
2	teaspoons sugar
2	tablespoons orange juice
2	teaspoons lemon juice

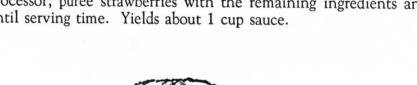

In a food processor, puree strawberries with the remaining ingredients and refrigerate until serving time. Yields about 1 cup sauce.

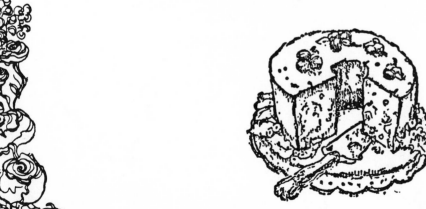

Chocolate Angel Cake with Frozen Chocolate Yogurt & Chocolate Sauce

For those who must have a little chocolate at the end of a meal, this great dessert is one to consider. Chocolate angel cake, a miser with calories, non-fat frozen chocolate yogurt and non-fat chocolate sauce...truly satisfying.

6	egg whites, at room temperature
1/4	cup sugar
3/4	teaspoon cream of tartar
1	teaspoon vanilla
3/8	cup flour
2	tablespoons sifted cocoa
1/4	cup sugar

Beat egg whites until foamy. Continue beating, adding sugar, 1 tablespoon at a time, until whites are stiff. Beat in cream of tartar and flavoring. Stir together flour, cocoa and sugar and fold it gently into the egg white mixture.

Spread batter evenly into an ungreased 10-inch tube pan with a removable bottom and bake at 375° for about 20 minutes, or until top is golden brown. Remove cake from oven, and invert until thoroughly cooled. To remove cake from pan, run a knife along the edge and around the center, invert the pan, and then run a knife along the bottom. Give the tube a quick turn and release it from the cake.

Serve with a scoop of frozen chocolate non-fat yogurt or chocolate ice milk and a spoonful of non-fat chocolate sauce.

Note: -There are many non-fat chocolate sauces to be found on the market, so purchase a good one.

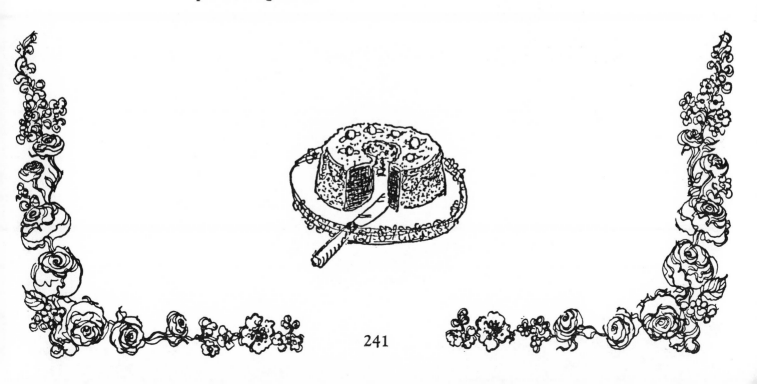

Cranberry & Orange Tea Cake with Vanilla Glaze

Frozen cranberries are available year round, so this delicious cake can be prepared at any time. This is a grand cake to serve at a tea, for it is especially colorful and attractive. Careful when stirring in the cranberries. They impart a lot of color. Don't overmix or your cake will be tinted.

1/2	cup butter, softened
1/2	cup sour cream
1	cup sugar
1/4	cup orange juice
3	tablespoons grated orange (1/2 medium orange, grated)
2	cups flour
1	teaspoon baking powder
1	teaspoon baking soda
1	cup cranberries, coarsely chopped
1/2	cup chopped walnuts

Beat together first 5 ingredients until blended. Beat in next 3 ingredients until blended. Very lightly, stir in the cranberries. Spread batter into a greased 10-inch tube pan and press walnuts gently on top. Bake in a 325° oven for about 45 minutes, or until a cake tester, inserted in center, comes out clean. When cool, drizzle Vanilla Glaze on top and let a little drip down the sides. Serves 12.

Vanilla Glaze:

1	tablespoon cream
1/2	cup sifted powdered sugar
1/4	teaspoon vanilla

Stir together all the ingredients until blended.

The Best Apricot & Walnut Coffee Cake

This is a great cake to serve. Even purists with great palates have raved about this cake before they knew it's simple beginnings. When I bring this cake for a pot luck or barbecue, I glaze the top. It dresses the cake for a party.

1	package (18 1/2 ounces) Duncan Hines yellow cake mix. (Use a cake mix with no pudding added.)
1	cup sour cream
3	eggs
1/4	cup water
1/3	cup oil
1/2	cup dried apricots, coarsely chopped in food processor
1/3	cup sugar
1	teaspoon cinnamon
1/2	chopped walnuts

In the large bowl of an electric mixer, beat together first 5 ingredients for 2 minutes or until batter is light. Beat in apricots until blended.

Spread 2/3 of the dough on the bottom of a greased 10-inch tube pan (with a removable bottom.) Stir together sugar and cinnamon and sprinkle on top of the batter. Spoon remaining batter over the cinnamon mixture and spread to even. Sprinkle top with chopped walnuts and press them gently into the batter to prevent them from burning.

Bake at 350° for 45 to 50 minutes, or until a cake tester, inserted in center, comes out clean. Allow to cool in pan. When cool, remove from pan. If you are preparing this for a special occasion, brush top with Apricot Glaze. Serves 12.

Apricot Glaze:
2	tablespoons finely chopped dried apricots
1	tablespoon orange juice
1/2	cup sifted powdered sugar

Stir together all the ingredients until blended.

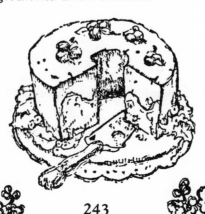

Fresh Apple Sour Cream Cake on Brown Sugar Walnut Crust

If you love fresh apple desserts, this one is a gem that you will treasure. A brown sugar cookie crust, topped with apples and sour cream and a hint of lemon is so joyously good, you will make it often.

1/4	cup flour
1/4	cup sugar
1/2	teaspoon baking soda
1/2	teaspoon cinnamon
1	egg
1	cup sour cream
1/4	cup apricot jam
2	tablespoons lemon juice
1	tablespoon butter
2	large apples, peeled, cored and very thinly sliced
1/2	cup yellow raisins

Beat together first 9 ingredients until blended, about 1 minute. Stir in the apples and raisins. Pour mixture evenly into Brown Sugar Walnut Crust and bake in a 350° oven for 40 minutes or until top is lightly browned. Allow to cool in pan.

Decorate with a faint sprinkling of powdered sugar and cut into wedges to serve. Serves 10.

Brown Sugar Walnut Crust:

1	cup flour
1	cup brown sugar
1/2	cup (1 stick) butter
1/2	cup chopped walnuts

In the large bowl of an electric mixer, beat together flour, sugar and butter until mixture resembles coarse meal. Stir in the walnuts. Pat mixture evenly on the bottom of a 10-inch springform pan and bake in 350° oven for 8 minutes. Allow to cool for 5 minutes before filling.

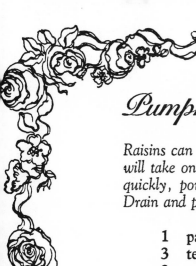

Pumpkin Orange Cake with Orange Glaze

Raisins can be substituted with 1/2 cup mini-semi-sweet chocolate chips. The cake will take on a totally different character but is equally delicious. To plump raisins quickly, pour boiling water over the raisins and allow to stand for 5 minutes. Drain and pat dry with paper towelling.

1	package (18-1/2 ounces) yellow cake mix (no pudding added)
3	teaspoons pumpkin pie spice
2	teaspoons baking soda
1 1/2	cups canned pumpkin puree
2	eggs
1/4	cup orange juice

3	tablespoons grated orange
1	cup chopped walnuts
1	cup golden raisins, plumped overnight in orange juice and drained

Beat together first 6 ingredients for 3 minutes. Beat in the remaining ingredients until blended. Pour batter into a greased and lightly floured 10-inch tube pan with a removable bottom.

Bake at 350° for 45 minutes or until a cake tester, inserted in center, comes out clean. Allow cake to cool in pan. When cool, remove from pan and drizzle top with Orange Glaze allowing a little to run down the sides. Serves 12.

Orange Glaze:

1 1/2	tablespoons orange juice
1	tablespoon grated orange peel
1/2	cup sifted powdered sugar
1/4	cup finely chopped walnuts

Combine orange juice and peel. Add only enough powdered sugar to make glaze a drizzling consistency. Stir in walnuts.

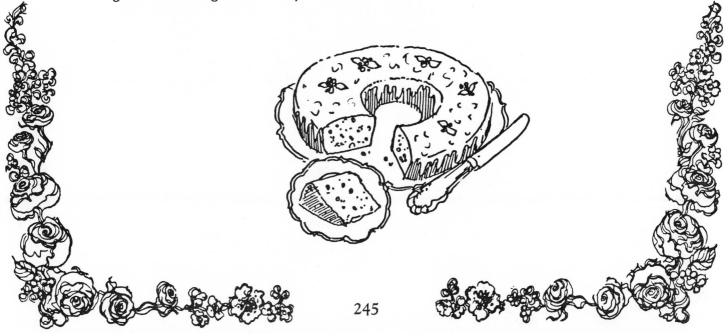

Walnut Cake with Raspberry & Lemon Glaze

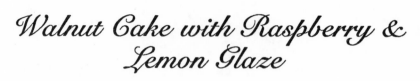

This is one of the most delicious nut cakes. It is a little larger than one I have given you before and it serves 12. Accented with raspberry jam and complemented with lemon, it is a beautiful balance of flavors. Best of all, it can be prepared in minutes in a food processor.

5	eggs
1	cup sugar
1 3/4	cups walnuts
1/2	cup flour
1	teaspoon baking powder
1	teaspoon vanilla
3/4	cup seedless red raspberry jam, heated

In the bowl of a food processor, blend together first 6 ingredients until the nuts are very finely ground, about 45 seconds to 1 minute. Pour the batter into a greased 10-inch springform pan, and bake at 350° for 30 minutes or until top is browned and a cake tester, inserted in center, comes out clean. Allow to cool in pan.

When cool, remove from pan and place on a lovely platter. Spread raspberry jam evenly over the top and then drizzle with Lemon Glaze in a decorative and lacy pattern. Cut into wedges to serve. Serves 12.

Lemon Glaze:
1	tablespoon lemon juice
1/2	cup sifted powdered sugar

Stir together lemon juice and powdered sugar until blended. Add a little more sugar or lemon juice to make glaze a drizzling consistency. This glaze should hold its shape and should not be too loose.

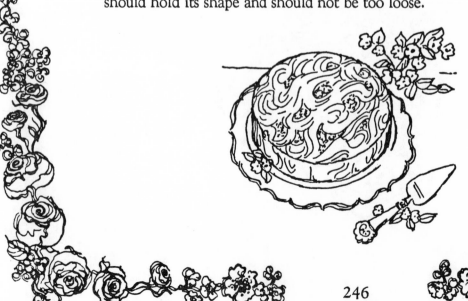

Banana Fudge Devil's Cake

This little treasure whips up in literally seconds and elevates a simple cake mix to gastronomical heights. Everybody loves this cake. It is moist, delicious and has a very fine texture.

1 package (18 1/2 ounces) Devil's Cake Mix (regular cake mix
    without pudding)
1/2 cup oil
1/2 cup water
1 cup sour cream
3 eggs

1 large banana, coarsely mashed, not pureed
1/3 cup chopped walnuts (for the top)

Beat together first 5 ingredients for about 4 minutes, or until batter is nicely blended and light. Stir in the bananas. Spread batter into a greased 10-inch tube pan and sprinkle walnuts on top. Press them gently into the batter (so that they do not burn.)

Bake at 350° for about 45 minutes or until a cake tester, inserted in center, comes out clean. Allow to cool in pan. When cool, remove from pan and place on a lovely platter. Sprinkle top lightly with sifted powdered sugar and serve 10 to 12.

Fresh Apple & Orange Pecan Torte with Orange Peel Glaze

Whenever I serve this moist and fruity cake, everyone asks for the recipe. I have given this recipe away so often. It is a great cake to have in your repertoire. It is simple to prepare and delicious to serve. The Orange Peel Glaze adds the perfect balance of tartness.

6	eggs
1	cup sugar
1 3/4	cups pecans
3/4	cup flour
1	teaspoon baking powder
1	teaspoon vanilla
1	apple, peeled, cored and cut into 8 pieces
1/2	medium thin-skinned orange, cut into 8 pieces

In the bowl of a food processor, blend together first 6 ingredients until the nuts are very finely chopped, about 45 seconds. Add the fruit and process for about 15 seconds more, or until the fruit is finely chopped, but not pureed. You should see little flecks of orange and apple.

Pour batter into a wax-paper-lined greased 10-inch springform pan and bake at 350° for about 40 to 45 minutes, or until top is browned and a cake tester, inserted in center comes out clean. Allow to cool in pan.

When cool, remove from pan and place on a lovely serving plate. Spread top with Orange Peel Glaze and let a little run down the sides. Beautiful and delicious. Serves 12.

Orange Peel Glaze:

1	tablespoon grated orange zest (orange part of the peel)
1	tablespoon orange juice
1/2	cup sifted powdered sugar

Stir together all the ingredients until blended.

Chocolate Fudge Torte
with Apricot & Chocolate Glaze

This is one of the easiest and best cakes that you can prepare. It is a moist and tender chocolate cake. Don't be misled by its simplicity. It is a fine torte, takes minutes to assemble, can be made ahead and, not the least of its virtues, it freezes beautifully.

5	eggs
1	cup sugar
1 1/3	cups walnuts
1	teaspoon vanilla
4	tablespoons flour
4	tablespoons cocoa
1	teaspoon baking powder

In a food processor, blend together all the ingredients for 1 minute, or until nuts are very finely ground. Pour batter into a wax-paper-lined 10-inch springform pan and bake at 350° for 25 to 30 minutes, or until a cake tester, inserted in center, comes out clean. Do not overbake. Remove from pan and place on a footed platter.

Spread top evenly with warmed apricot jam and with a teaspoon, swirl top with warm Chocolate Glaze, allowing some of the jam to show. Allow chocolate to set at room temperature, about 1 hour. Serves 12.

Topping:
    1/2   cup apricot jam, warmed

Chocolate Glaze:
    1/2   cup semi-sweet chocolate chips
    1/4   cup butter (1/2 stick), at room temperature
    1/2   teaspoon vanilla

In the top of a double boiler, over hot water, melt chocolate. Stir in butter until blended. Stir in vanilla until blended. Spoon over cake immediately while warm.

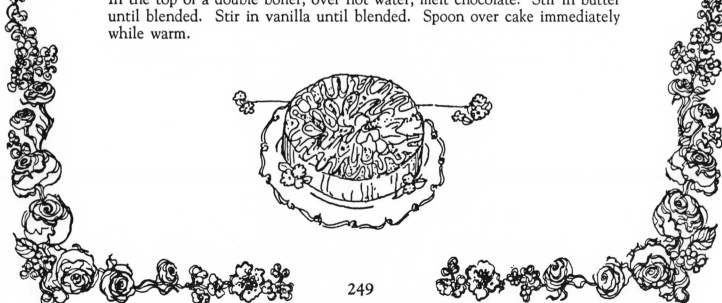

Chocolate Cheesecake with Chocolate Cookie Crust

If you are passionate about chocolate, as you know I am, I know you will enjoy this glorious chocolate cheesecake. Filling ingredients should be at room temperature to avoid lumps.

Chocolate Cookie Crust:
- 1 cup chocolate wafer crumbs
- 1/4 cup butter, melted
- 1/3 cup finely chopped walnuts

Combine crumbs, butter and walnuts and mix until blended. Press the mixture on the bottom of a parchment-lined 10-inch springform pan.

Chocolate Cheesecake Filling:
- 1/2 cup cream
- 8 ounces semi-sweet chocolate chips

- 3 packages (8 ounces, each) cream cheese, at room temperature
- 1 cup sugar
- 3 eggs, at room temperature
- 1 cup sour cream, at room temperature
- 2 teaspoons vanilla

In a small saucepan heat the cream. Add the chocolate chips and stir until chocolate is melted. Do this over low heat so that the chocolate does not scorch. Set aside.

Beat together the remaining ingredients until the mixture is thoroughly blended. Beat in the melted chocolate. Pour cheese mixture into the prepared pan and bake in a 350° oven for 50 minutes. Do not overbake. Allow to cool in pan and then refrigerate for about 4 to 6 hours. Overnight is good, too. Garnish top with chocolate curls or grated chocolate. Remove from refrigerator 20 minutes before serving. Serves 12.

To Make Chocolate Curls:
Take a vegetable peeler and run it down the sides of a chocolate bar that is at room temperature.

To Grate Chocolate:
Chocolate can be grated or very finely chopped in a food processor.

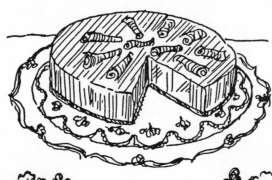

Fantasia Lemon Cheesecake with White Chocolate & Fresh Raspberries

This is one of the easiest cheesecakes to prepare as only the crust has to be baked. It serves beautifully with the fresh raspberries and white chocolate. If you are serving this outside of the summer months, then sprinkle the top with white chocolate and serve with a spoonful of frozen raspberries in syrup.

Lemon Cheese Filling:
- 2   packages (8 ounces, each) cream cheese, softened
- 1/2   cup low-fat sour cream
- 1 1/4   cups sifted powdered sugar
- 2   tablespoons lemon juice
- 2   teaspoons grated lemon zest (the yellow part of the peel)

Beat together all the ingredients until blended. Spread mixture evenly into prepared crust and refrigerate until firm. Place raspberries along the edge forming a 1-inch border and sprinkle grated white chocolate in the center. Serves 8.

Vanilla Lemon Cookie Crust:
- 1 1/2   cups vanilla wafer crumbs
- 1/4   cup finely chopped walnuts
- 2   teaspoons grated lemon zest (the yellow part of the peel)
- 3   tablespoons sugar
- 1/3   cup butter melted

Line a 10-inch springform pan with parchment paper and lightly grease the paper. In a bowl, stir together all the ingredients and press mixture on the bottom and 1-inch up the sides of the prepared pan. Bake at 350° for 8 minutes, or until top is just beginning to take on color. Set aside to cool.

Topping:
- 1   pint fresh raspberries
- 4   tablespoons grated white chocolate

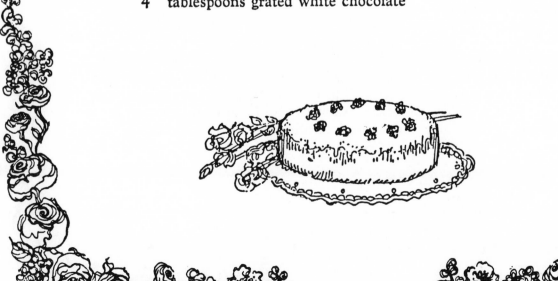

Lemon Butter Cookies

These are intensely lemon-flavored, so cut down on the lemon zest if you like it milder. If you do not own a zester, make certain the lemon zest is very finely grated on the smallest side of a 4-sided grater. These can be shaped into crescents or rings.

1/2	cup butter (1 stick), softened
1/4	cup sugar
1	teaspoon vanilla
1	cup flour
1	tablespoon finely grated lemon zest (yellow part of the peel)

Cream together butter, sugar and vanilla. Beat in flour until blended. Beat in lemon zest until blended. Shape 1 heaping teaspoon of dough into a ball and flatten to a 1-inch round. Place on a lightly greased cookie sheet and bake at 325° until dough is set and just beginning to take on color. Do not allow cookies to get brown. Allow to cool and sprinkle with sifted powdered sugar. Yields about 36 cookies.

Spicy Applesauce Bar Cookies with Orange Peel Glaze

2	eggs, beaten
2/3	cup sugar
1/3	cup oil
1/3	cup applesauce
3/4	cup flour
1	teaspoon baking powder
2	teaspoons pumpkin pie spice
	pinch of salt
2	tablespoons grated orange peel
1	cup chopped walnuts
1/2	cup dried currants (optional)

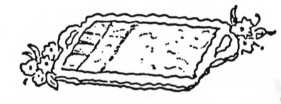

Beat together first 4 ingredients until blended. Beat in the remaining ingredients until blended. Spread batter evenly into a lightly greased 9x13-inch baking pan and bake at 350° for 15 minutes or until a cake tester, inserted in center, comes out clean. Allow to cool in pan. When cool, brush top with Orange Peel Glaze and cut into bars to serve. Yields 40 cookies.

Orange Peel Glaze:

1	tablespoon grated orange peel
1	tablespoon orange juice
1/2	cup sifted powdered sugar

Stir together all the ingredients until blended.

Lemon Cloud Cookies

This is an adaptation of my Mom's Lemon Cloud cookies. I have adjusted the original recipe to yield 48 cookies. It requires the same amount of work and any extra cookies can be frozen.

Butter Cookie Crust:

3/4	cup butter (1 1/2 sticks) cut into 8 pieces
1 1/2	cups flour
1/2	cup sifted powdered sugar
2	teaspoons grated lemon zest (the yellow part of the peel)

Lemon Cloud Filling:

3	eggs
1 1/2	cups sugar
3	tablespoons flour
1	teaspoon baking powder
2	teaspoons grated lemon zest (lemon part of the peel)
4	tablespoons lemon juice

In a food processor, beat together butter, flour, sugar and lemon zest until butter is the size of small peas. Pat mixture on the bottom of a greased 9x13-inch baking pan and bake at 350° for 20 minutes, or until crust is lightly browned. Meanwhile, beat together filling ingredients until blended. Pour filling into baked crust and continue baking for 30 minutes or until it is set. Allow to cool in pan. To serve, cut into squares or bars and sprinkle with sifted powdered sugar. Yields 48 cookies.

The Original Best Mandelbread

Throughout the years, I have given you many, many variations of this old family recipe. Orange, walnuts, cinnamon, pecans, yes, even chocolate. But on looking over my notes, I notice that I never gave you the original. So, here it is. Shaping and baking the loaves in a foil pan is not traditional, but it saves a lot of time. Also, preparation is easier and the cookies are more uniform.

1/2	cup butter (1 stick)
1	cup sugar
3	eggs
1	teaspoon almond extract
1	teaspoon vanilla
2	cups flour
1 1/2	teaspoons baking powder
1	cup chopped almonds
1/3	cup chopped maraschino cherries

More →

(Best Mandelbread, Cont.)

Beat butter and sugar until creamy. Beat in eggs, one at a time, beating well after each addition. Beat in almond and vanilla. Beat in flour and baking powder until blended. Stir in almonds and cherries.

Divide dough between 3 greased and floured 9x5-inch foil loaf pans, place pans on a cookie sheet and bake at 350° for about 30 minutes, or until tops are lightly browned and a cake tester, inserted in center, comes out clean.

Allow to cool in pan for 5 minutes, and then remove from pans and place on a cutting board. Cut into 3/4-inch slices with a serrated knife. Place slices on a cookie sheet, return to oven, and lightly toast on both sides, about 10 minutes.. Yields about 36 cookies.

Cookie Bracelets with Sesame Seeds
Roscas-Biscochos

This is an old Greek recipe for a very pleasant cookie. They are round, crisp, rather plain and not very sweet, but for some reason everybody loves them They are great for dunking, keep well in a cookie jar and freeze beautifully.

    3   eggs
    1/2 cup oil
    1/4 cup orange juice
    1   cup sugar
    1   teaspoon vanilla

    3   cups flour
    2   teaspoons baking powder

    1   egg, beaten, for brushing on tops
        sesame seeds for sprinkling on top

Beat together first 5 ingredients until blended. Beat in flour and baking powder until blended.

On a heavily floured pastry cloth, drop a 1 to 1 1/2-inch ball of dough. With floured hands, roll balls into 7-inch ropes. Press ends together forming a circle. Place onto a greased 12x16-inch pan and brush tops with beaten egg. Sprinkle generously with sesame seeds. Repeat with remaining dough. Bake at 350-degrees for about 12 to 15 minutes or until tops are lightly browned.

When all the Roscas are baked, collect them in one pan, turn the oven off, place pan in turned-off oven, and allow Roscas to crisp in oven, until oven cools. Yields 24 Roscas.

Fudge Brownies

This is a rich brownie, but as it only uses 1/2 the butter, it could be richer. Keep the portions small and enjoy on some special occasion.

    4   ounces unsweetened chocolate
    1/2 cup butter, (1 stick)

    2   cups sugar
    4   eggs

    3/4 cup flour
    1   tablespoon vanilla
    1   cup chopped walnuts (optional)
    1   cup semi-sweet chocolate chips (optional)

In the top of a double boiler, over hot water, melt chocolate with butter. Allow to cool slightly. Beat sugar with eggs for 2 minutes. Beat in chocolate mixture. Beat in remaining ingredients until blended. Spread mixture in a greased 9x13-inch baking pan and bake at 350° for 30 minutes or until top appears dry, and a cake tester, inserted in center, comes out with a few moist crumbs clinging to it. Allow to cool in pan. (Refrigerating makes it easier to cut.) When cool, cut into small squares. Yields 35 cookies.

Butterscotch & Chocolate Chip Blondies

These crisp and crunchy bars are great to serve with milk. Notice that they do not contain any eggs. A non-stick baker is important as these can stick to the pan.

    1   cup butter, softened
    2   cups brown sugar
    1/2 cup sour cream
    2   teaspoons vanilla

    2   cups flour
    1   teaspoon baking powder
    3/4 cup chopped walnuts
    1   cup butterscotch chips
    1/2 cup semi-sweet chocolate chips

In the large bowl of an electric mixer, beat together first 4 ingredients until blended. Mix together the remaining ingredients and stir into the butter mixture until blended. Do not overmix.

Spread batter evenly into a greased 10x15-inch non-stick baking pan and bake at 325° for about 30 minutes, or until top is browned. Allow to cool in pan. When cool, cut into 1 1/2-inch squares to serve. A sprinkling of sifted powdered sugar is nice if you want to dress them up a bit. Yields 60 cookies.

Pecan Cherry Bar Cookies

3/4 cup butter or margarine, softened (1 1/2 sticks)
1 egg yolk
3/4 cup sugar
1 3/4 cups flour, sifted
1 teaspoon vanilla

1 lightly beaten egg white
1 cup chopped pecans
3 tablespoons finely chopped Maraschino cherries

In a bowl combine butter, egg yolk, sugar, flour and vanilla. Beat mixture until just blended. Do not overbeat.

Pat dough evenly into a lightly greased 10x15-inch cookie pan. Brush top lightly with beaten egg white. Sprinkle top with chopped pecans and chopped cherries. Pat nuts and cherries gently into the dough. Bake in a 350° oven until top is lightly browned, about 25 minutes. Remove from the oven and cut into 1 1/2-inch squares or diamonds while still warm. Remove from cookie pan and cool on a brown paper bag. Yields about 60 cookies.

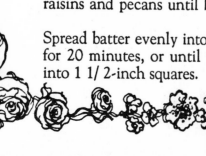

Praline Butterscotch Raisin Cookies

The brown sugar and pecans, give these cookies the flavor of Southern pralines. The raisins are a tart addition and balance the sweetness of the butterscotch.

1 cup butter, softened
2 cups brown sugar
2 eggs
2 teaspoons vanilla

2 1/4 cups flour
1/2 teaspoon baking powder
1/2 teaspoon baking soda

1/2 cup butterscotch morsels
1/2 cup yellow raisins
1 cup coarsely chopped pecans

Beat together first 4 ingredients until blended. Combine the next 3 ingredients and beat into butter mixture until blended. Stir in butterscotch, raisins and pecans until blended. (Batter will be thick.)

Spread batter evenly into a greased 10x15-inch jelly roll pan and bake at 375° for 20 minutes, or until top is golden brown. Allow to cool in pan and cut into 1 1/2-inch squares. Yields about 60 cookies.

Date Nut Bar Cookies

    3/4   cup flour
    1   cup sugar
    1/2   teaspoon baking powder
          pinch of salt

    2   eggs, beaten
    1/2   cup oil
    1   teaspoon vanilla

    1   cup chopped pitted dates
    1   cup chopped walnuts

Combine flour, sugar, baking powder and salt. Add eggs, oil, vanilla all at once and stir to mix thoroughly. Stir in dates and nuts. Spread mixture into a 9x13-inch lightly greased baking pan and bake at 350° for 25 minutes.

Remove pan from the oven and cut into squares while warm. Remove cookies from the pan immediately and cool on brown paper. When cool, store in an airtight container. Makes about 48 cookies.

Raspberry Bars on Butter Cookie Crust

    1 3/4   cups flour
    3/4   cup sugar
    3/4   cup ground almonds
    1/2   cup butter

    1   egg beaten
    1/2   lemon, grated, about 1 1/2 tablespoons fruit, juice and peel

    1   cup raspberry jam

In the large bowl of an electric mixer, beat together first 4 ingredients until mixture resembles coarse meal. Beat in the egg and lemon until just blended. Set aside 2/3 cup of dough, wrap and refrigerate. With floured hands, pat the remaining dough into a lightly buttered 9x9-inch baking pan. Dough is very soft. Bake at 350° for 15 minutes. Spread top of crust with raspberry jam.

Divide the reserved dough into 8 pieces and with floured hands, roll and pat dough out into 9-inch strips. Lay the strips over the jam lattice-fashioned. Bake at 350° for 30 to 35 minutes or until top is golden brown. Allow to cool and then cut into 3x1 1/2-inch bars. Yields 18 cookies.

Hungarian Walnut & Apricot Squares on Lemon Shortbread Cookie Crust

This is an adaptation of a delicious cookie my mother-in-law made often. She used apricot jam, but raspberry jam works very well, too. It is important to heat the jam as it will spread easily and will not tear the crust. The Lemon Glaze adds the perfect tart accent.

Lemon Shortbread Cookie Crust:

1	cup butter, cut into 8 pieces
1	cup sugar
2	cups flour
2	tablespoons grated lemon peel

3/4	cup apricot jam or raspberry jam, heated

In the large bowl of an electric mixer, beat together butter, sugar and flour until blended. Beat in lemon until blended. Do not overbeat. Dust dough lightly with flour and with floured fingers, pat dough on the bottom and 1/2-inch up the sides of a greased 9x13-inch baking pan. Bake at 350° for 15 minutes or until dough is just beginning to take on color.

Spread apricot jam on crust to 1/2-inch from edge. Spread Walnut Filling over the jam and spread evenly. Return pan to 350° oven and bake for another 30 minutes, or until a cake tester, inserted in center, comes out clean. All to cool in pan. Sprinkle top lightly with sifted powdered sugar or drizzle top with Lemon Glaze. Cut into small squares to serve. Yields 48 cookies.

Walnut Filling:

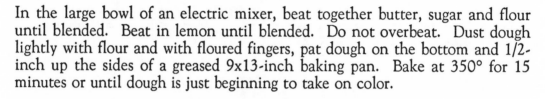

4	eggs, beaten
2	cups brown sugar
1/4	cup flour
1/4	teaspoon baking powder
2	teaspoons vanilla

2	cups walnuts, finely ground in a food processor with 1/4 cup sugar

Beat together first 5 ingredients until blended. Beat in walnuts until blended.

Lemon Glaze: Stir together 1 1/2 tablespoons lemon juice and 3/4 cup sifted powdered sugar until blended.

Raspberry Pecan Bar Cookies

If you love raspberry jam with pecans, make these cookies soon. They are a great blend of flavors and textures. All together...a butter cookie crust with a hint of lemon, a fruity raspberry layer, a crunchy nut topping, and a drizzle with a tart lemon glaze...delicious!

Lemon Cookie Crust:
- 1/2 cup butter or margarine
- 1/2 cup sugar
- 1 egg, beaten
- 2 tablespoons grated lemon peel

- 1 1/4 cups flour

- 1/2 cup raspberry jam, heated

Pecan Filling:
- 2 cups pecans, finely ground in a food processor with 1/4 cup sugar
- 2 eggs, beaten
- 1/2 cup sugar
- 1/4 cup flour
- 1/4 teaspoon baking powder
- 1 teaspoon vanilla

To Make Lemon Cookie Crust: In the large bowl of an electric mixer, beat together butter and sugar until blended. Beat in eggs until blended. Beat in lemon until blended. Beat in flour until blended and a soft dough forms. Do not overbeat. Dust dough lightly with flour and with floured fingers, pat dough on the bottom and 1/2-inch up the sides of a greased 9x13-inch baking pan. Bake at 350° for 20 minutes or until dough is just beginning to take on color. Spread raspberry jam on crust to 1/2-inch from edge.

To Make Pecan Filling: Beat together filling ingredients until blended and spread it evenly over the jam. Continue baking at 350° for 25 minutes or until filling is set and golden brown. Cut into squares or bars to serve. A faint sprinkle of sifted powdered sugar is a nice touch. Yields 48 cookies.

The Best Oatmeal Cookies with Chocolate Chips & Walnuts

These cookies are soft and chewy. They are delicious with chocolate chips and walnuts and also delicious with raisins and pecans.

1   cup butter
1   cup brown sugar
1   cup granulated sugar
2   eggs
1   teaspoon vanilla

1 1/2   cups quick oats
1 1/2   cups flour
1   teaspoon baking soda
1/2   teaspoon baking powder
1   cup chopped walnuts
1   package (6 ounces) chocolate chips, semi-sweet

In the large bowl of an electric mixer, beat together butter, sugars, eggs and vanilla until mixture is light, about 2 minutes. Stir in the remaining ingredients until blended.

Drop batter by the heaping tablespoonful, on a greased cookie sheet. Bake at 350° for about 15 minutes or until cookies are very lightly browned. (It is important not to overbake.) Yields about 48 giant cookies.

Oatmeal Cookies with Raisins & Pecans:
Delete walnuts and chocolate chips and substitute with 1 cup of chopped pecans and 1 cup of raisins.

Greek Butter-Pecan Cookies

These are very small, petite morsels of deliciousness that are nice to serve with frozen yogurt or ice cream. These can also be shaped into crescents or small rings.

1/2   cup butter (1 stick), softened
1/4   cup sifted powdered sugar
1/2   teaspoon vanilla
1   cup flour, sifted
1/3   cup very finely chopped walnuts or pecans

Cream together butter, sugar and vanilla. Beat in flour until blended. Beat in nuts until blended. Shape 1 heaping teaspoon of dough into a ball and flatten slightly. Place on a lightly greased cookie sheet and bake at 350° until dough is set and just beginning to take on color. Amount of time will vary as to the size of the cookie. Do not allow cookies to get brown. Allow to cool and sprinkle with sifted powdered sugar. Yields about 36 small cookies.

Baked Apples with Orange, Macaroon & Walnut Sauce

In this recipe, the orange juice and honey are baked until the juices become very concentrated and intense in flavor. Crumbs and walnuts may be omitted, but they are a nice addition.

- 1 cup orange juice
- 2 tablespoons honey
- 1/2 teaspoon cinnamon
- 1/4 teaspoon nutmeg
- 1/4 teaspoon ground cloves

- 6 apples, peeled, cored and sliced

- 6 tablespoons macaroon cookie crumbs
- 6 tablespoons finely chopped walnuts

Stir together first 5 ingredients until blended. Place apples in a 9x13-inch baking pan and place orange juice mixture over all. Bake in a 350-degree oven until apples are tender and most of the juice has evaporated, about 40 minutes. Sprinkle top with cookie crumbs and walnuts and bake an additional 10 minutes. Serve warm (not hot), at room temperature or slightly chilled. Serves 8.

Substituting Fruits:
To Bake 6 Pears: Bake at 350-degrees for 20 minutes.
To Bake 8 Peaches: Bake at 350-degrees for 30 minutes.
To Bake 8 Apricots: Bake at 350-degrees for 30 minutes.

Substituting Juice:
Apricot nectar or apple juice can be substituted for the orange juice.

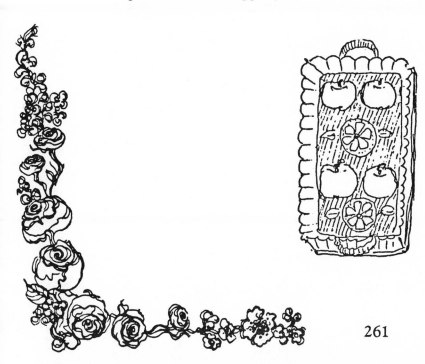

Wine-Poached Pears with Almonds & Apricot Glaze

This is a light dessert and remarkably easy to prepare. Pears, glazed with butter and apricot jam, and sprinkled with macaroons and almonds, are just heavenly. Can be prepared earlier in the day. If you are making this for company, then serve with a dollop of Creme Fraiche Vanilla. Serve warm or at room temperature.

    6   large Bartlett pears, peeled, cored and cut into halves

Apricot Glaze:
    1/4   cup apricot jam
    2   tablespoons melted butter
    2   tablespoons sugar
    1/2   cup dry white wine
    2   tablespoons lemon juice
    1/4   teaspoon cinnamon
    1/8   teaspoon nutmeg
    1/8   teaspoon powdered cloves

    1/4   cup almond macaroon cookie crumbs
    1/2   cup chopped almonds

Place pears in a 9x13-inch porcelain baker, cut side down. Stir together the next 8 ingredients until blended and drizzle mixture evenly over the pears. Bake in a 350° oven for 20 minutes, basting now and again.

Sprinkle crumbs and almonds over the pears and continue baking for 10 minutes or until pears are tender and almonds are toasted. Serves 6 or 12.

Creme Fraiche Vanilla:
    1/2   cup low-fat sour cream
    1/4   cup half and half
    1   tablespoon sugar
    1/2   teaspoon vanilla

In a jar, stir together all the ingredients until blended. Allow to stand at room temperature for 3 hours and then refrigerate until serving time. This can be prepared 2 days before serving.

Instant Low-Fat Vanilla Sauce:
Place 1 cup of frozen low-fat or non-fat vanilla yogurt in the refrigerator for 2 hours before serving. Yogurt will be partially melted. Give it a good stir and serve. Yields 16 tablespoons.

Baked Apples with Raisins, Apricots, Pecans & Vanilla Yogurt Sauce

This dessert brought cheers and cries of "Bravo" at a recent event in our home. Everyone enjoyed the rich and satisfying taste and loved the light, fresh feeling. It is an easy dessert, really, and using the frozen yogurt as a sauce, makes it feel extravagant.

6	apples, cored and peeled 1-inch from the top
1	cup orange juice
6	tablespoons yellow raisins
6	tablespoons finely chopped dried apricots
6	tablespoons finely chopped pecans
3	teaspoons cinnamon sugar

In a 9-inch round baking pan, place the apples and drizzle with the orange juice. Combine the next 3 ingredients and stuff mixture into each apple center. Any leftover raisin mixture can be sprinkled in the pan. Sprinkle tops of each apple with 1/2 teaspoon cinnamon sugar. Bake at 350° for 45 minutes, or until apples are tender, but not mushy. Can be served warm or at room temperature.

To serve, divide apples and juice in 6 shallow bowls and spoon Vanilla Yogurt Sauce over the top. Enjoy! Serves 6.

Vanilla Yogurt Sauce:
  1 cup frozen non-fat or low-fat vanilla yogurt

Place yogurt in a serving bowl and refrigerate for 2 hours. It will be partially melted. Give it a good stir, and serve. Yields 16 tablespoons sauce.

Note: -Non-fat vanilla yogurt can be substituted for the frozen yogurt.

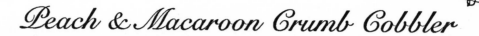

Peach & Macaroon Crumb Cobbler

Apples can be substituted for the peaches in this recipe. If you enjoy the fruit simply baked, then omit the cookie crumb topping.

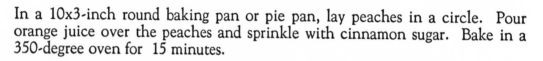

- 6 medium-sized peaches, peeled, pitted and thinly-sliced or
  1-pound bag frozen sliced unsweetened peaches, thawed
- 1/4 cup orange juice
- 2 teaspoons cinnamon sugar

- 1/2 cup macaroon cookie crumbs
- 2 tablespoons coarsely chopped walnuts
- 1/2 teaspoon ground cinnamon
  dash each of ground nutmeg and ground cloves

In a 10x3-inch round baking pan or pie pan, lay peaches in a circle. Pour orange juice over the peaches and sprinkle with cinnamon sugar. Bake in a 350-degree oven for 15 minutes.

Meanwhile toss together crumbs, walnuts and spices and sprinkle over the peaches. Return to oven and bake for an additional 15 minutes, or until crumbs are lightly browned and peaches are tender. Serves 6.

Winter Cobbler with Apples, & Cranberries

This is a lovely winter dessert, on the tart side, and very satisfying. It can easily be made into a most enjoyable summer dessert by substituting peaches for the apples. The Streusel Topping made with oats adds a nice texture.

- 6 large apples, peeled, cored and sliced
- 1 package (12 ounces) frozen cranberries
- 1/2 orange, grated (about 3 tablespoons)
- 1 tablespoon grated lemon
- 1/2 cup sugar

In a large bowl, toss together all the ingredients until blended. Place mixture into a 10x3-inch round baking pan. Sprinkle Streusel Topping on top and bake at 350° for about 1 hour or until topping is lightly browned. Serves 8.

Streusel Topping:
- 1 cup quick-cooking oats
- 1 cup flour
- 3/4 cup sugar
- 1/2 cup butter, softened

In a mixer, beat together all the ingredients until mixture is crumbly.

After-Dinner Cold Cappuccino

This is a great touch for dessert. It is delicious and refreshing to serve for a summer dessert or as a light ending to a meal. I made this up for a friend who would not consider a meal complete without a cup of cappuccino. Add a cookie and it is sheer perfection. Serve this in stemmed goblets with a pretty colored straw.

> 2   cups low-fat vanilla ice cream
> 1   tablespoon Amaretto liqueur
> 1   tablespoon Creme de Cacao liqueur
> 1/2 teaspoon instant espresso or instant coffee

In the large bowl of an electric mixer, beat together all the ingredients until blended. Divide mixture between 4 stemmed glasses. Sprinkle a little ground chocolate over the top and add a little liqueur to taste (optional). Serve with a straw but have a spoon close by. Serves 4.

Granita di Caffé

This is a refreshing granular ice, served in lovely stemmed glasses with a short decorative straw. It is a nice alternative to the Caffé Espresso.

> 1   cup water
> 1/4 cup sugar
> 4   cups strong espresso coffee

In a 2-quart jar, stir together water and sugar until sugar is melted. Stir in the coffee. Place mixture in ice cube trays and freeze, stirring from time to time, to form a granular ice. If it freezes solid, crush the coffee cubes in a blender before serving. Serve with a splash of Kahlua and a tablespoon of cream. Serves 6.

Caffé Espresso

Caffé Espresso is made with very finely ground Italian coffee, and is served in a demitasse or Espresso glass. In the absence of an Espresso coffee maker, you can purchase Instant Espresso in most markets. Traditionally served with a twist of lemon peel, I very much prefer the addition of a dash of Kahlua Liqueur and a dollop of whipped cream.

Old-Fashioned Mud Pies with Double Coffee Ice Cream & Hot Fudge Sauce

This is an updated version of an old classic. The combination of chocolate and coffee, sparkled with almonds is totally irresistible. The Hot Fudge Sauce is one of the easiest and a little "treasure" for last minute preparation.

Chocolate Cookie Crust:
- 1 1/2   cups chocolate cookie crumbs (use a good quality cookie)
- 3   ounces melted butter (3/4 stick)
- 1/4   cup chopped toasted almonds

Double Coffee Ice Cream:
- 1   quart light coffee ice cream, softened
- 2   teaspoons instant coffee

Instant Hot Fudge Sauce:
- 1   package (6 ounces) semi-sweet chocolate chips
- 2   tablespoons butter
- 3/4   cup cream
- 1/2   teaspoon vanilla

To make crust:
Combine crumbs, butter and almonds and stir until blended. Press mixture on the bottom of a 9-inch pie plate and bake in a 350° oven for 7 minutes. Allow to cool.

To make Double Coffee Ice Cream:
Stir together softened coffee ice cream with instant coffee until blended. Spread mixture on cooled cookie crust. Place in freezer until firm.

To make Hot Fudge Sauce:
When ready to serve, place chocolate chips and butter in blender container. Bring cream to a boil and pour into blender container. Blend for 1 minute or until chocolate is melted and mixture is smooth. Stir in vanilla.

To serve, cut pie into wedges and serve with a spoonful of Hot Fudge Sauce, a dollop of whipped cream and a sprinkling of chopped toasted almonds. Delicious! Serves 8.

Note: - This produces 1 1/2 cups sauce. Sauce can be prepared in advance and can be heated at serving time, in the top of a double boiler, over hot, not boiling water.

Frozen Strawberry Yogurt in Meringue Shells

This is one of the easiest desserts to prepare, as the shells and frozen yogurt can be purchased. It is, also, a beautiful choice for a formal or informal summer dinner. It looks spectacular with its white base, a mountain of frozen pink yogurt and red strawberries, sparkled with liqueur, on the top and sides. The meringue shells can be purchased in most bakeries. They can be filled with the yogurt earlier in the afternoon and stored in the freezer. Remove from the freezer 5 minutes before serving. Spoon the fresh strawberries on the top and sides just before serving. Recipe for Meringue Shells follow, if you choose to prepare your own.

8	meringue shells, about 4-inches in diameter
4	cups frozen non-fat strawberry yogurt
1 1/2	pints fresh strawberries, sliced (reserve 8 large strawberries for decorating the tops)
3	tablespoons Grand Marnier liqueur
4	teaspoons chopped toasted almonds (optional)

Pile yogurt into meringue shells in a high swirl, (4 ounces in each), cover with plastic wrap and freeze until serving time. Mix together sliced strawberries and Grand Marnier about 1 hour before serving and store in the refrigerator. To serve, spoon the strawberries over the yogurt and place one whole strawberry on top. A sprinkling of chopped toasted almonds is a nice addition, but optional. Serves 8.

Frozen Peach Yogurt & Raspberry Sauce in Meringue Shells:
-Substitute non-fat peach yogurt and top with defrosted raspberries in syrup.

Frozen Chocolate Yogurt & Chocolate Sauce in Meringue Shells:
-Substitute non-fat chocolate yogurt and top with a drizzle of chocolate syrup or chocolate sauce.

Meringue Shells

While these are available at most bakeries, the recipe is included in the event your bakery does not sell them. The shells are attractive filled with frozen strawberry yogurt and drizzled with sliced strawberries. Chocolate frozen yogurt, a drizzle of chocolate sauce and a sprinkle of toasted sliced almonds is also beautiful. Meringue shells are basically not baked but dried in the oven. Don't allow them to brown. Meringue kisses can be crushed and served as a base for the yogurt.

3	egg whites, at room temperature
3/4	cup sugar

More →

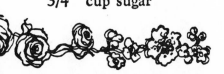

(Meringue Shells, Cont.)

In the large bowl of an electric mixer, at medium speed, beat whites until they are foamy. Start adding the sugar, a tablespoon at a time and increase speed to high. Keep beating while adding the sugar slowly, until meringue is stiff and shiny. Line a cookie sheet with parchment paper and drop meringue by the heaping tablespoon onto the paper. With the back of a spoon, indent the center and build up the sides. Bake at 225° for 1 hour, turn oven off and allow meringues to dry for several hours in the oven. Shells should not brown. This will yields 12 meringue shells.

To Make Meringue Kisses:
These are low-calorie, non-fat little kisses that you may want to serve with non-fat yogurt on another occasion. They can be crushed and served as a base or they can be served whole on the side. Follow instructions as above, but drop meringue by the heaping teaspoonful onto a parchment-lined pan. Yields about 48 small kisses.

Strawberry & Vanilla Bombe with Chocolate & Grand Marnier

1 1/2	quarts strawberry sherbet, softened
1 1/2	quarts vanilla ice cream, softened
3	tablespoons Grand Marnier liqueur
1	cup almond macaroons, rolled into crumbs
3/4	cup chopped semi-sweet chocolate
1/4	cup chopped toasted almonds

Line a 3-quart bombe mold or bowl with strawberry sherbet and freeze until firm. Beat the softened vanilla ice cream with the remaining ingredients until blended. Place vanilla ice cream mixture into the sherbet lined bowl and pack down to even. Cover the bowl and freeze until firm.

To unmold, place mold in hot water for a second or 2 and invert onto a platter that can be placed in the freezer. Decorate with large rosettes of whipped cream and sprinkle top and sides with shaved chocolate and finely chopped toasted almonds. Return to freezer and freeze until firm. Cover bombe with double thicknesses of plastic wrap and then foil.

To serve, remove wrappings and leave at room temperature for about 5 to 10 minutes. Serves 8.

Walnut Raspberry Tart on Cookie Crust

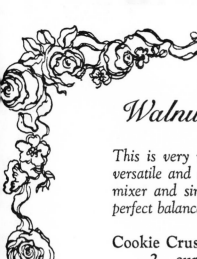

This is very much like a Linzer tart with a few variations The cookie crust is versatile and can be used for other pies and tarts. It can easily be prepared in a mixer and simply patted into the pan. The Walnut Raspberry Filling adds the perfect balance of flavors.

Cookie Crust:
- 2   cups flour
- 1/2 cup sugar
- 1   cup butter (2 sticks)

- 1   egg

In the large bowl of an electric mixer, beat together flour, sugar and butter until mixture resembles coarse meal. Add the egg and beat until mixture is blended and forms a dough, about 1 minute. Do not overbeat. Pat 2/3 of the dough on the bottom and 1/2-inch up the sides of a 10-inch springform pan. Bake at 350° for 15 minutes.

Spread Walnut Raspberry Filling over the dough. Pinch off pieces of the remaining dough, roll it into 1/4-inch ropes, flatten them slightly and lay them over the walnut filling, lattice-fashioned. Bake in a 325° oven for about 40 minutes or until top is golden brown. Allow to cool in pan. To serve, cut into wedges or squares and sprinkle with a faint hint of sifted powdered sugar.

Walnut Raspberry Filling:
- 1   cup grated walnuts
- 1/2 cup sugar
- 1/3 cup seedless raspberry jam
- 1   egg, beaten

In a bowl, combine all the ingredients and stir until thoroughly blended.

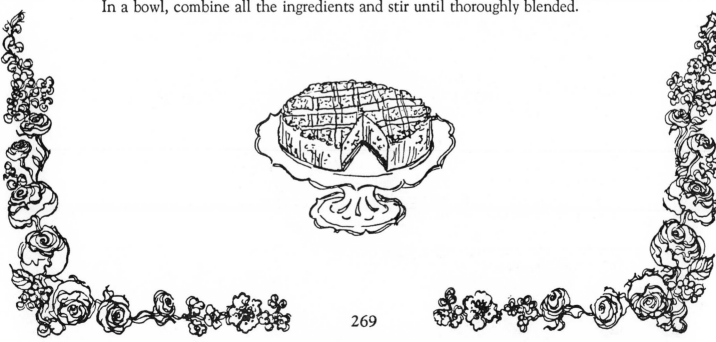

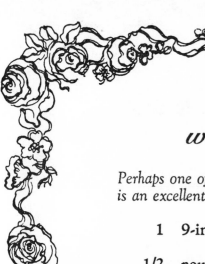

Cream Cheese Pie
with Strawberry Orange Sauce

Perhaps one of the simplest pies to prepare and really quite a good one. The sauce is an excellent accompaniment.

1	9-inch Graham Cracker Pie Shell

1/2	pound low-fat cream cheese
3/4	cup powdered sugar, sifted
1	tablespoon lemon juice
1	teaspoon lemon peel
1	cup whipping cream

Strawberry Orange Sauce

Cream together cream cheese, sugar, lemon juice and lemon peel until light. Whip cream until stiff and on the low setting, beat it into the cream cheese mixture. Pour into prepared pie shell and refrigerate until serving time. Serve with Strawberry Orange Sauce spooned over the top. Serves 8 to 10.

Graham Cracker Pie Shell:
1/4	cup butter, melted
1 1/4	cups graham cracker crumbs
1/2	cup coarsely chopped walnuts
3	tablespoons cinnamon sugar

In a 9-inch pie pan, combine all the ingredients and mix to thoroughly combine. Press crumbs evenly along the bottom and the sides of a 9-inch pie pan. Bake in a 350° oven for about 8 minutes or until just beginning to color. Cool before filling.

Strawberry Orange Sauce:
1	package (10 ounces) frozen sweetened sliced strawberries
3	ounces (1/2 package) frozen orange juice concentrate. Do not dilute.

In a bowl, stir together strawberries and orange juice concentrate. Cover bowl and refrigerate until ready to use. Spoon a little sauce over each serving.

Old-Fashioned Lemon Meringue Pie
on Lemon Cookie Crust

When we were growing up, this was one of our favorite pies. Visions of this tart and tangy pie on a delicious lemon cookie base, with mountains of meringue piled on top, will please the most discriminating pie lover.

Lemon Cookie Crust:
1/2	cup butter (1 stick)
4	ounces cream cheese
1	egg yolk
1/4	cup sugar
1	tablespoon grated lemon
1 1/4	cups flour

In the large bowl of an electric mixer, beat together first 5 ingredients until mixture is blended. Beat in the flour until blended. Place dough in floured wax paper, wrap securely and refrigerate for several hours. Roll dough out to measure a 12-inch circle. Place dough in a 10-inch pie pan and pierce bottom with the tines of a fork. Bake in a 350° oven for about 30 minutes or until crust is beginning to brown. Allow to cool in pan.

Fill crust with hot Lemon Filling. Swirl Meringue decoratively on top of hot lemon filling and cover every bit of crust. Bake in a 350° oven for 12 to 15 minutes or until top is lightly browned. Cool for 3 hours before serving. For easy cutting, use a wet knife. Serves 10.

Lemon Filling:
2	cups boiling water
2	tablespoons finely grated lemon peel
1/4	cup butter, softened
1/8	teaspoon salt
1/2	cup sugar
4	egg yolks
1	cup sugar
1/2	cup cornstarch
2/3	cup lemon juice

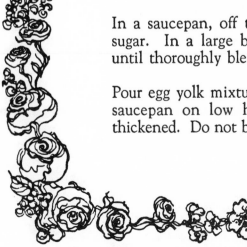

In a saucepan, off the heat, stir together hot water, peel, butter, salt and sugar. In a large bowl, beat the yolks, sugar, cornstarch and lemon juice until thoroughly blended.

Pour egg yolk mixture into hot water mixture and stir until blended. Place saucepan on low heat and cook and stir constantly until mixture has thickened. Do not boil or filling will curdle.

More →

(Lemon Meringue Pie, Cont.)

Meringue:
>   5   egg whites
>   pinch of salt and cream of tartar
> 2/3   cup sugar
>   1   teaspoon vanilla

Beat whites until foamy. Continue beating and add salt, cream of tartar, sugar (1 tablespoon at a time) and vanilla, until meringue is very stiff.

The Easiest & Best Lemon Tart

Lemon Cookie Crust:
>   1   cup flour
> 1/2   cup butter (1 stick)
> 1/4   cup sugar
>
>   1   egg, lightly beaten
>   2   tablespoons grated lemon peel

In a food processor, blend together first 3 ingredients, until mixture is the size of small peas. Add the beaten egg and lemon peel, and pulse 4 or 5 times or until dough clumps together. Place dough on floured wax paper and shape into a disc. Sprinkle top with a little flour.

With floured fingers, pat dough on the bottom and sides of a lightly greased 10-inch tart pan with a removable bottom. Bake at 375° for 20 minutes, or until crust is lightly browned. Allow to cool for 15 minutes.

Pour Tart Lemon Filling into prepared crust, place pan on a cookie sheet (to catch any drippings) and continue baking for 15 to 20 minutes, or until custard is set. Allow to cool. Decorate top with fresh berries. Serves 12.

Tart Lemon Filling:
> 2/3   cup lemon juice
> 1/2   cup sugar
>   2   tablespoons melted butter
>
>   4   eggs

Beat together first 3 ingredients until blended. Beat in eggs, one at a time, until thoroughly blended.

Almond Tart with Raspberry Jam on Lemon Cookie Crust

I never tire of making tarts with the combined flavors of almonds and raspberries. This is one of my favorites. It resembles the little tarts called Maids of Honor that we enjoyed when we visited the English countryside. Lovely to serve at tea.

Lemon Cookie Crust:
1 1/3	cups flour
1/4	cup sugar
1/2	cup butter (1 stick)
2	tablespoons grated lemon
1	egg, beaten
1	teaspoon vanilla
3/4	cup seedless raspberry jam

In the large bowl of an electric mixer, beat together first 4 ingredients until mixture resembles coarse meal. Beat in the egg and vanilla until a soft dough forms. Do not overbeat. Pat dough on the bottom and 1-inch up the sides of a greased 10-inch springform pan and bake at 350° for about 18 minutes, or until dough is set and just beginning to take on color. Spread the jam evenly over the warm crust.

Spread Almond Macaroon Topping over the jam and continue baking for 35 to 40 minutes, or until top is lightly browned. Remove rim and allow tart to cool. When cool, sprinkle lightly with sifted powdered sugar. Serves 8 to 10.

Almond Macaroon Topping:
7	ounces almond paste
3	eggs
1/3	cup sugar
1	teaspoon almond extract
1/2	cup flour
1/2	cup sliced almonds

Beat together first 5 ingredients until blended. Beat in almonds until blended.

Torta de Pascal

(Easter Lemon Ricotta Pie)

Butter Cookie Crust:
- 1 1/2   cups flour
- 3/4   cup butter (1 1/2 sticks)
- 3   tablespoons sugar

- 2   tablespoons grated lemon
- 1   egg yolk
- 2   tablespoons water

In a food processor, beat together flour, butter and sugar until mixture resembles coarse meal. Pulse in the grated lemon only until blended. Beat together egg yolk and water and add, all at once, pulsing only until blended and dough holds together. Add a few drops of water, if necessary, to make a soft dough.

Pat dough on the bottom and 1-inch up the sides of a greased and parchment paper-lined 10-inch springform pan. Bake at 350° for 20 minutes or until crust is just beginning to take on color.

Spread Ricotta Filling evenly over the crust, return pie to oven and continue baking for 35 to 40 minutes, or until filling is set and lightly browned. Allow to cool in pan. Using the parchment paper to help you, slide pie onto a serving platter and cut into wedges to serve. Serves 10.

Ricotta Filling:
- 1   pound Ricotta cheese
- 1   package (8 ounces) low-fat cream cheese, at room temperature
- 3/4   cup sugar
- 1   tablespoon vanilla

- 3   eggs, at room temperature

- 1/2   lemon grated. (Use fruit, juice and peel. Remove any large pieces of membrane.)

Beat together first 4 ingredients until blended. Beat in eggs, 1 at a time, until blended. Beat in lemon until blended.

Rustic Orange Cheese Tart with Raisins & Chocolate on Orange Cookie Crust

This unusual and very delicious raisin cheese pie is fresh and zesty and nicely accented with the flavors of orange and chocolate. It is a grand finale to an informal dinner in an Italian mood.

Orange Cookie Crust:
- 1 1/2 cups flour
- 1/3 cup sugar
- 1/2 cup butter
- 2 tablespoons grated orange peel

In the large bowl of an electric mixer, beat together all the ingredients until mixture resembles coarse meal. Pat mixture evenly on the bottom and 1-inch up the sides of a lightly greased 10-inch springform pan and bake at 350° for 15 minutes or just until crust is beginning to take on color.

Pour Cheese Cake Filling into prepared crust and continue baking for 35 to 40 minutes, or until filling is just set. Allow to cool in pan. Remove rim and serve with a faint sprinkling of sifted powdered sugar. Serves 8 to 10.

Cheese Cake Filling:
- 1 pound Ricotta cheese, at room temperature
- 1/2 cup sugar
- 2 eggs
- 1 tablespoon finely grated orange zest (the orange part of the peel)
- 1 teaspoon vanilla

- 1/2 cup raisins plumped in orange juice and drained
- 1/3 cup semi-sweet mini-chocolate chips

Beat together first 5 ingredients until blended. Beat in raisins and chocolate until blended.

The Best Apple & Rhubarb Pie in a Flaky Pastry Crust

Very fruity and tart, this delicious pie is beautiful with large rounds of flaky pastry allowing the apples and rhubarb to show through. As the dough is soft, it can be pressed into the pan, avoiding the need to refrigerate or roll the pastry. This can be made in a 10-inch tart pan with a removable bottom.

Flaky Pastry:
1	cup butter (2 sticks)
2	cups flour
1/4	cup sugar
1	egg
2	tablespoons water (plus a few drops, if necessary, to hold dough together)
1	teaspoon cinnamon sugar

In a food processor, blend butter, flour and sugar until butter particles are the size of small peas. (Do not overprocess or the flakiness will be lost.) Lightly beat together the egg and water until blended. Add to the butter mixture and pulsate 4 or 5 times, or just until dough clumps together (adding a few drops of water, if necessary.) Place dough on floured wax paper and shape into a disc.

Pat 2/3 of the dough onto the bottom and up the sides of a greased 10-inch heart-shaped pan with a removable bottom. Bake in a 375-degree oven for 20 minutes, or until crust is lightly browned. Place Apple & Rhubarb Filling evenly over the crust. Divide remaining dough into three parts. With floured hands, pat each part into a 5-inch circle and place on top of pie. Sprinkle top with 1 teaspoon cinnamon sugar. Continue baking for about 30 minutes, or until top is golden brown. Serves 10.

Apple & Rhubarb Filling:
1 1/2	cups frozen rhubarb
1/4	cup orange juice
1/4	cup sugar
1	tablespoon lemon juice
3	large apples, peeled, cored and thinly sliced
1/3	cup sugar
3	tablespoons flour

In a saucepan, simmer together first 4 ingredients for 5 minutes. Place mixture in a large bowl. Add the remaining ingredients to the bowl and toss and stir until all the ingredients are nicely mixed.

Flaky Pastry Peach & Cranberry Pie

Peaches and cranberries are paired in this ultra-delicious pie. Very fruity and tart, it also serves beautifully, with large petals of flaky pastry surrounded by peaches and cranberries. It is further simplified with the preparation of a softer dough that can be pressed into the pan, avoiding the need to refrigerate or roll the pastry.

Flaky Pastry:
1	cup butter (2 sticks)
2	cups flour
1/4	cup sugar
1	egg
1	tablespoon water
1	teaspoon cinnamon sugar

In a food processor, blend butter, flour and sugar until butter particles are the size of small peas. (Do not overprocess or the flakiness will be lost.) Lightly beat together the egg and water until blended. Add to the butter mixture and pulsate 4 or 5 times, or until dough clumps together. Place dough on floured wax paper and shape into a ball.

Pat 2/3 of the dough onto the bottom and up the sides of a greased 10-inch heart-shaped pan with a removable bottom. Bake in a 375-degree oven for 20 minutes, or until crust is lightly browned. Place Peach & Cranberry Filling evenly over the crust. Divide remaining dough into thirds, pat each into a 6-inch circle and place on top of pie. Sprinkle top with 1 teaspoon cinnamon sugar. Continue baking for about 30 minutes, or until top is golden brown. Serves 8.

Peach & Cranberry Filling:
4	large peaches, peeled, stoned and thinly sliced
1/2	pound frozen cranberries, picked over. Do not defrost.
1/2	cup sugar
2	tablespoons flour
1/2	small orange, grated (optional)

In a bowl, toss together all the ingredients until nicely mixed.

Fig & Walnut Tart on Butter Cookie Crust

If you like figs, you'll love this pie. It is truly delicious. Sometimes, it is a little hard to cut through the figs if they are not softened enough. But the round circles of figs are so pretty to serve. So, if you are in a rush, chop the figs coarsely and in this manner, cutting the pie will not be a problem.

Butter Cookie Crust:

1 1/2	cups flour
4	tablespoons sugar
1/2	cup butter (1 stick), cut into 8 pieces
1	egg beaten with 1 tablespoon water

In the bowl of a food processor, beat together flour, sugar and butter until mixture resembles coarse meal. Beat in egg mixture, only until dough clumps together. Do not overbeat. Remove dough from processor and, with floured hands, shape into a ball. Pat dough onto the bottom and 1-inch up the sides of a greased 10-inch springform pan. Bake at 375-degrees for about 20 minutes, or until shell is beginning to brown. Remove from oven and allow to cool.

Walnut Fig Filling:

15	dried figs with tough stems cut off and cut in halves, crosswise
3	tablespoons grated orange peel
1/2	cup orange juice
2	eggs
1/2	cup sugar
1/2	cup milk
2	tablespoons melted butter
2	teaspoons vanilla
1/2	cup flour
1/2	teaspoon baking powder
3/4	cup finely chopped walnuts
1	tablespoon cinnamon sugar

Simmer figs and peel in orange juice for 10 minutes or until figs are softened. Set aside. Beat together next 5 ingredients until blended. Mix together flour and baking powder and add to egg mixture, beating until blended. Stir in walnuts. Pour batter evenly into prepared crust. Press figs evenly on top in a decorative fashion and sprinkle top with cinnamon sugar. Bake at 375-degrees for about 35 minutes, or until a cake tester, inserted in center of cake (not the fig) comes out clean. Allow to cool in pan. Serves 10.

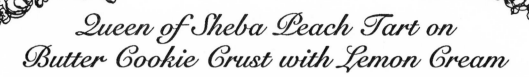

Queen of Sheba Peach Tart on Butter Cookie Crust with Lemon Cream

If you prepare this when peaches are out of season, frozen peaches can be used. If you use frozen peaches, they must be defrosted, thoroughly drained, and patted dry with paper towelling.

Butter Cookie Crust:
- 2 cups flour
- 1/4 cup sugar
- 1 cup butter (2 sticks), softened
- 1 egg
- 3 tablespoons cream

Beat together flour, sugar and butter until mixture resembles fine meal. Beat together egg and cream and add, beating until just blended. Do not overbeat. Pat dough on the bottom and 1-inch up the sides of a greased and parchment-lined 10-inch springform pan and bake at 350° for 20 minutes, or until top looks dry and is just beginning to take on color.

Lemon Cream Filling:
- 1 1/2 pounds fresh peaches, peeled, stoned and sliced (or 1 pound frozen peaches, thinly sliced and thoroughly drained)
- 1 cup low-fat sour cream
- 1 egg
- 6 tablespoons sugar
- 2 tablespoons grated lemon (use peel, fruit and juice)
- 1 teaspoon almond extract

Layer peaches into prepared crust, in a decorative manner. Beat together the remaining ingredients and pour evenly over the peaches. Bake at 350° for about 35 minutes, or until custard is set and just beginning to brown. Allow to cool in pan. When cool, remove from pan and cut into wedges to serve. Serves 8 to 10.

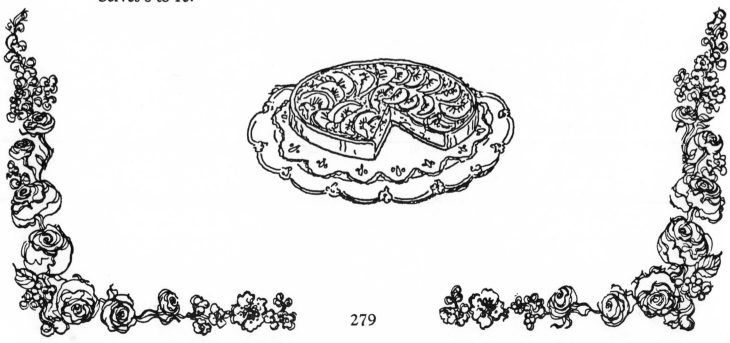

Winter Prune Tart with Apricots & Pine Nuts

Using dried fruits, this Italian-styled tart can be prepared at any time and with little notice. However, it is especially good in the winter when the fresh fruit of summer is not readily available.

- 1 cup butter
- 2 cups flour
- 1/3 cup sugar

- 1 egg
- 1 tablespoon water

- 1/2 cup apricot jam
- 1/2 cup pine nuts

- 1 teaspoon cinnamon sugar

In a food processor, blend butter, flour and sugar until butter particles are the size of small peas. (Do not overprocess or the flakiness will be lost.) Lightly beat together egg and water and add, all at once, to the food processor, pulsating 4 or 5 times, or until dough clumps together. Place dough on floured wax paper and shape into a ball. Cut off 1/3 of the dough, wrap it in wax paper and refrigerate.

Pat remaining 2/3 of the dough on the bottom and 1-inch up the sides of a greased 10-inch springform pan and bake at 350° for 20 minutes or until crust is lightly browned. Spread apricot jam on warm crust and sprinkle with pine nuts. Place Prune & Apricot Filling decoratively on the top. Divide remaining 1/3 dough into four pieces, pat each piece into a 4-inch oval and place evenly on top of pie to resemble petals. Sprinkle top with cinnamon sugar. Continue baking for 35 minutes, or until dough on top is golden brown. Serves 8.

Prune & Apricot Filling:
- 6 ounces soft pitted prunes, cut in half lengthwise
- 6 ounces dried apricots, cut into halves
- 1/2 cup orange juice
- 1/2 cup sugar

In a saucepan, simmer together all the ingredients for 10 minutes or until prunes and apricots are softened. Place mixture in a strainer, drain and reserve any juice for another use.

Holiday Spiced Pumpkin Pie with Praline & Cream

What a divine way to end a Thanksgiving feast. The Praline Pecan Topping adds a delightful touch.

1	deep dish frozen pie shell (9-inch) Prebake in a 350° oven for 8 minutes.

3	eggs, beaten
3/4	cup brown sugar
1/4	teaspoon salt
3	teaspoons pumpkin pie spice (or to taste)
1 1/2	cups half and half (can use 1/2 cream for a richer taste)
1	can (1 pound) pumpkin

Prepare pie shell. Combine the remaining ingredients and beat until blended. Pour mixture into prepared pie shell. Place pie on a cookie sheet and bake in a 350° oven for 40 minutes. Spread Praline Pecan Topping carefully on the top and continue baking for about 10 or 15 minutes, or until a knife, inserted in center, comes out clean. Serves 8.

Praline Pecan Topping:
Stir together 1/4 cup melted butter, 1/2 cup brown sugar and 3/4 cup chopped pecans.

Easiest & Best Southern Pecan Pie

This is an absolutely extravagant and rich pie. Using the frozen pie shells makes it available to you at a moment's notice. No need to decorate, but for a special occasion, a dollop of whipped cream is very nice.

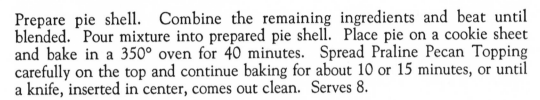

3	eggs
1	cup maple syrup
1	cup dark brown sugar
2	tablespoons flour
1/8	cup melted butter (1/4 stick)
1	teaspoon vanilla
1	9-inch shallow frozen pie shell. (Do not use the deep-dish shell.)
1 1/4	cups shelled pecans

Beat together first 6 ingredients until mixture is blended. Place pecans evenly into pie shell. Pour egg mixture into the crust. Place pie on a cookie sheet and bake it in a 350° oven for about 45 minutes or until pie is set and crust is browned. Serve at room temperature with an optional dollop of whipped cream. Serves 8 to 10.

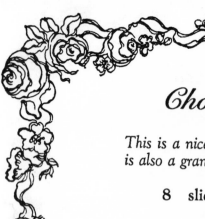

Chocolate & Walnut Bread Pudding

This is a nice economical dessert that is sparkled with rum and easily prepared. It is also a grand way to use some leftover bread that has become day-old.

- 8 slices egg bread, remove crusts and tear into pieces
- 1 cup half and half (milk is good, too)

- 1/4 cup butter, at room temperature
- 1 cup sugar
- 4 eggs
- 3 tablespoons sifted cocoa

- 1 cup chopped walnuts
- 1 tablespoon rum
- 1/2 teaspoon vanilla

In a bowl, soak bread in cream or milk. In the large bowl of an electric mixer, beat butter with sugar until blended. Beat in eggs and cocoa until nicely blended, about 1 minute. Beat in bread mixture, nuts and flavorings until blended.

Pour batter into a buttered 2-quart soufflé dish and bake in a 350° oven for 45 minutes, or until pudding is set. Spoon into dessert dishes and serve with a dollop of Creme Vanilla. Serves 6.

Note: - This is lovely served warm or at room temperature.
- These can be baked in individual soufflé dishes, which makes it a little more formal. Butter 6 individual soufflé dishes (ramekins) and divide batter. Bake in a 325° oven for about 25 minutes or until pudding is set.

Creme Vanilla:
- 1/2 cup cream, whipped
- 1/2 cup softened low-fat vanilla ice cream
- 1 teaspoon rum

Combine all the ingredients and stir until blended. Yields 1 cup sauce. This can be prepared 2 hours before serving.

Creamy Rice Pudding with Strawberry Sauce

Rice puddings have become a rage lately. Most restaurants seem to feature them... not the old-fashioned kind, but ones elevated with fruits, liqueurs, etc.

1/3	cup long-grain rice
3/4	cup water
2	cups milk (low-fat can be used)
1/2	cup sugar
2	tablespoons white rum
	pinch of salt
3	eggs
1	cup sour cream (low-fat can be used)

In a covered saucepan, cook together rice and water for 25 minutes, or until rice is very soft and liquid is absorbed. Stir in the next 4 ingredients and heat, stirring, until sugar is dissolved.

In a large bowl, whisk eggs with sour cream until blended. Whisk in rice mixture until blended. Pour mixture into a 10x2-inch round porcelain baker and bake at 300° for 1 hour and 10 minutes. Remove from oven and allow to cool. (A little lip will have formed around the edge and it will hold the Strawberry Sauce.) When cool, refrigerate until serving time. Before serving, spread Strawberry Sauce over the top, bring to the table and spoon into small dessert bowls. Serves 8.

Strawberry Sauce:
Stir together 1 package (10 ounces) frozen strawberries in syrup with 1 tablespoon frozen concentrated orange juice (undiluted). Place in a glass bowl and store in the refrigerator until serving time. Yields 1 1/4 cups sauce.

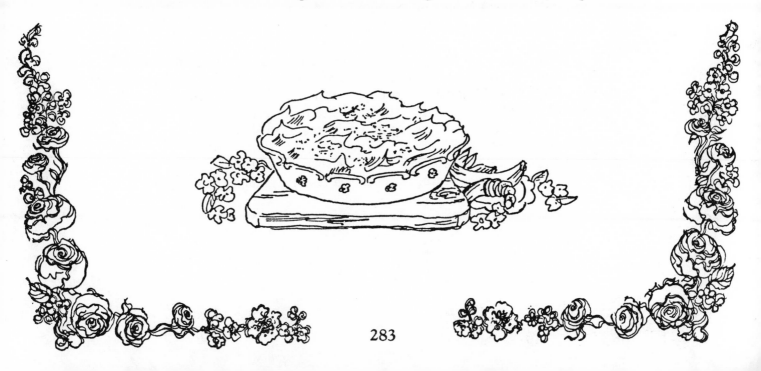

Creme de Kashmir with Papaya Sauce

There are few desserts you can prepare that are easier or more delicious than this one. Basically, it is creme fraiche sparkled with Cognac and set in a mold. If you own a 10x2-inch round or oval porcelain server, then, no need to unmold. Spread the sauce on top and spoon into dessert dishes at the table.

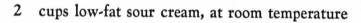

1/4	cup Cognac
1/4	cup water
2	envelopes unflavored gelatin

2	cups cream or half and half
1/2	cup sugar
2	teaspoons vanilla
	pinch of salt

2	cups low-fat sour cream, at room temperature

In a metal measuring cup, soften gelatin in Cognac and water. Place cup in a pan with simmering water and stir gelatin until it is dissolved.

In a saucepan, over low heat, heat together cream, sugar, vanilla and salt and stir until sugar is dissolved. Stir in gelatin. Place cream mixture in the large bowl of an electric mixer. Beat in the sour cream in 4 batches until the creme is completely smooth. Pour into a 10x2-inch round or oval glass or porcelain mold and refrigerate until firm. To serve, run a knife along the edge, set pan in warm water for a few seconds, and invert onto a larger rimmed platter. Surround with Papaya Sauce. Serves 8.

Papaya Sauce:

1/2	cup sugar
1/2	cup orange juice

3	tablespoons lemon juice
2	ripe papayas, peeled, seeded and thinly sliced, about 3 cups

In a saucepan, over low heat, cook together sugar and juice for 4 minutes, or until mixture is syrupy. Stir in the lemon juice and fruit and simmer mixture for 3 minutes. Allow to cool. When cool, puree fruit in a food processor until finely chopped. Allow a little texture to remain. Place in a glass bowl, cover with plastic wrap and refrigerate until serving time.

Note: -*Mangoes may be substituted for the papayas. Sliced fresh peaches is another lovely alternative. Fruit should be soft, so adjust cooking time.*

Royal Rice Pudding with Apricots & Raisins

Rice pudding is very popular lately...but, not the plain kind with a spot of cinnamon on top. This one is elevated with the added flavors of apricots and raisins.

3	eggs
1/2	cup sugar
3/4	cup low-fat sour cream
3	ounces dried apricots, chopped
1/4	cup yellow raisins
1/2	orange, grated. Use fruit, juice and peel, about 3 tablespoons.
3	cups cooked long grain rice
2	teaspoons cinnamon sugar

Beat together first 3 ingredients until blended. By hand, stir in the next 4 ingredients until blended. Place mixture into an oiled 9x9-inch baking pan and sprinkle top with cinnamon sugar. Bake at 350° for 45 minutes, or until pudding is set. This is a nice family dessert and with a spoonful of apricot sauce on top, it is a company dish. Serves 8.

Apricot Sauce:

1	cup dried apricots, chopped
1/2	cup orange juice
2	tablespoons sugar

In a saucepan, simmer together all the ingredients for 3 minutes or until sauce is slightly thickened. Serve sauce warm or chilled.

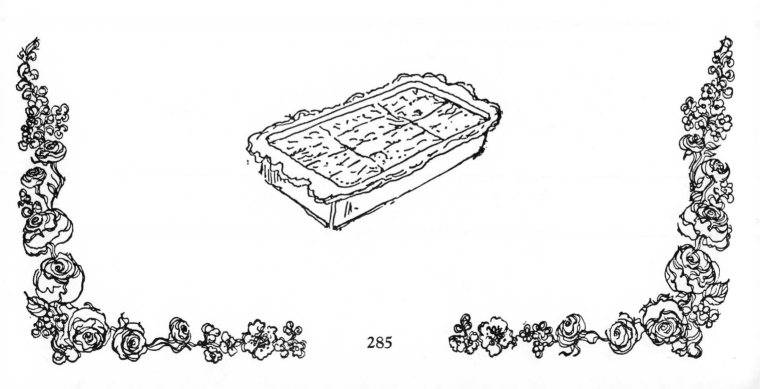

Chocolate Fudge Pudding Cake with Cocoa Cream

This simple little cake forms its own pudding sauce and can be assembled and baked AND served in the same dish.

1/2	cup milk
4	teaspoons butter, melted
1	teaspoon vanilla

1	cup flour
1/2	cup sugar
3	tablespoons cocoa, sifted
2	teaspoons baking powder
1/2	teaspoon salt

5	tablespoons cocoa, sifted
1/2	cup sugar
1 1/2	cups hot water

In a 2-quart oven-proof bowl or souffle dish, place milk, melted butter and vanilla. Stir in the flour, sugar, cocoa, baking powder and salt and stir until batter is blended and smooth. Spread batter evenly in bowl. Sprinkle cocoa and sugar evenly over the batter. Pour the hot water over all.

Place bowl in a 350° oven and bake for 40 minutes or until a cake tester, inserted in center, comes out clean. Cool. Frost with Cocoa Whipped Cream. When serving, spoon a little sauce that formed on the bottom, over the whipped cream. Serves 6.

Cocoa Whipped Cream:
3/4	cup cream
3	tablespoons sugar
4	teaspoons sifted cocoa
1/2	teaspoon vanilla

Combine all the ingredients and beat until cream is stiff. Spread over pudding cake. Refrigerate cake until ready to serve.

Note: -If you are planning to serve the pudding cake warm, then serve with a dollop of whipped cream. Do not frost.
- Cake is fudgy and very much like a brownie. Kids love it. However, it can be glamorized with the addition of 1 or 2 tablespoons of rum to the batter. Whipped cream can be enhanced with the addition of 1/2 tablespoon rum.

Danish Pastry Croissants with Lemon Cream Cheese Filling & Lemon Glaze

These wonderful melt-in your-mouth croissants are delightful for breakfast or brunch. The dough handles very easily and produces an exquisite pastry.

- 1/2 cup butter (1 stick), softened
- 1 cup small curd cottage cheese
- 1 cup flour

Lemon Cream Cheese Filling:
- 4 ounces cream cheese
- 1/4 cup sugar
- 1 tablespoon grated lemon peel

Lemon Glaze

In the large bowl of an electric mixer, beat together butter and cottage cheese until blended. Beat in the flour until blended. Shape dough into a 6-inch circle and wrap in floured wax paper. Refrigerate for 1 hour.

Beat cream cheese, sugar and lemon until blended.

Divide dough into thirds. Roll each third out on a floured pastry cloth until circle measures about 9-inches. Spread 1/3 of the Lemon Cream Cheese Filling over the dough and cut circle into 8 triangular wedges. Roll each triangle from the wide end toward the center and curve slightly into a crescent. Sprinkle with a generous shake of powdered sugar.

Place croissants on a lightly buttered cookie sheet and bake at 350° for about 30 minutes or until they are golden brown. Remove from pan and allow to cool on a rack or double thicknesses of paper towelling. When cool, sprinkle with sifted powdered sugar or brush with Lemon Glaze. Yields 24 croissants.

Lemon Glaze:
Stir together 1 tablespoon lemon juice with about 1/2 cup sifted powdered sugar until glaze is a drizzling consistency. Add a little lemon juice or powdered sugar if needed.

Old-Fashioned Apple Strudel

This is the best apple strudel, period. It is far easier to prepare than its original cousin, but this pastry is flakey and light and quite wonderful.

Quick Puff Pastry:
- 1 cup butter
- 2 cups flour
- 1 cup sour cream

To make the Pastry:
In the large bowl of an electric mixer, beat together butter and flour until mixture resembles coarse meal. Do not overbeat. Beat in sour cream for 30 seconds, until evenly spread. Place dough on floured wax paper, and sprinkle top with additional flour. Shape into a ball, wrap with the floured waxed paper, then foil, and refrigerate until ready to use. (Pastry can be prepared up to 3 days before using.)

Apple Strudel Filling:
- 3/4 cup apricot jam
- 2 apples peeled and grated
- 1 cup chopped walnuts and/or raisins
- 4 tablespoons cinnamon sugar

To Assemble:
Divide dough into 4 parts. Working one part at a time, roll it out on a floured pastry cloth to measure a 10x10-inches. Spread 1/4 of the apricot jam over each part of dough. Spread 1/4 of the apples over the jam. Sprinkle top with 1/4 of the walnuts and/or raisins and 1/4 of the cinnamon sugar. Roll dough up twice, jelly-roll fashion, ending with a roll that is 3x10-inches, and seam-side, down.

Place strudels on a lightly greased 12x16-inch baking pan, and bake the 4 strudels at one time. Bake at 350° for about 30 minutes, or until top is golden brown. When cool, brush with Vanilla Glaze or sprinkle with sifted Vanilla Sugar. Yields about 24 slices.

Vanilla Glaze:
- 1/2 cup sifted powdered sugar
- 1/2 teaspoon vanilla
- 1 tablespoon cream

Stir together all the ingredients until blended. Brush on pastry and allow glaze to dry.

Vanilla Sugar:
Place 1 pound of sifted powdered sugar into a cannister or jar with a tight-fitting lid. Snap 2 vanilla beans sharply into thirds and bury them in the sugar. Sift on pastries, cookies and wherever powdered sugar is called for. The vanilla beans will impart a gentle hint of vanilla to the sugar, which is just marvelous.

The Best Rugalahs
(Miniature Crescent Danish Pastries)

This tender, flaky pastry is one of the best. It has any number of uses. Sweetened, it can be used for pies, strudels, turnovers and more. Omitting the sugar, it is great with savory fillings...vegetables, cheese, to name a few. This Cream Cheese Pastry and my Quick Puff Pastry (see preceding recipe) can be used interchangeably. The Quick Puff Pastry is a little lighter and flakier.

Cream Cheese Pastry:
- 1 cup (2 sticks) sweet butter
- 1 package (8 ounces) cream cheese
- 1/3 cup sugar
- 2 cups flour

To make the pastry:
In the large bowl of an electric mixer, beat together butter and cream cheese until thoroughly blended. Beat in sugar until blended. Beat in the flour just until blended. Do not overbeat. Place dough on floured plastic wrap, shape into a ball, cover with the floured plastic wrap and refrigerate until ready to use. (Pastry can be prepared up to 3 days before using.)

To Assemble:
Divide dough into 4 parts. Working one part at a time, roll it out on a floured pastry cloth to measure a 12-inch circle. Sprinkle 1/4 of the filling over the dough and pat it down gently. With a sharp knife, cut the dough in half and then half, again. Cut it as you would a pie until you have 12 triangular wedges.

Roll each triangle from the wide side toward the center and shape into a crescent. Place them on a lightly buttered baking pan. Continue with remaining dough and filling. Bake at 350° for about 25 minutes, or until lightly browned. When cool, brush with Vanilla Glaze or sprinkle with sifted powdered sugar.

Raisin Walnut Filling (for four parts of dough):
- 12 tablespoons cinnamon sugar
- 1 cup yellow raisins, chopped
- 3/4 cup walnuts, finely chopped

In a jar, with a tight-fitting lid, shake together all the ingredients until blended.

Apricot & Walnut Filling (for four parts of dough):
- 1 cup apricot jam
- 1 cup chopped walnuts

In a bowl, stir together jam and nuts until blended.

More →

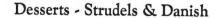

Rugalahs (cont.)

Chocolate Chip Filling (for four parts of dough):
- 12 tablespoons Nestle's Chocolate Quik (powder)
- 1 package (6 ounces) semi-sweet chocolate chips, coarsely chopped, (chocolate mini-morsels can be substituted)
- 3/4 cup finely chopped walnuts

In a jar, with a tight-fitting lid, shake together all the ingredients until blended.

Vanilla Glaze (for four parts of dough):
- 1/2 cup sifted powdered sugar
- 1/2 teaspoon vanilla
- 1 tablespoon cream

Stir together all the ingredients until blended. Brush on pastry and allow glaze to dry.

Easiest & Best Lemon Souffle with Strawberry Sauce

- 4 eggs
- 3 tablespoons lemon juice
- 6 tablespoons sugar
- 1 package (8 ounces) cream cheese, at room temperature

- 1 tablespoon finely grated lemon zest (yellow part of the peel)

- 1 cup sliced fresh sweetened strawberries or
  1 package (10 ounces) sweetened frozen strawberries

In a food processor, container, blend together first 4 ingredients for 3 minutes. Stir in the grated lemon zest.

Pour mixture into 6 small souffle dishes (ramekins) that have been buttered and coated with sugar. Bake ramekins in a 400° oven for 15 minutes. Centers should be a little soft. Serve with a spoonful of sweetened strawberries. Serves 6.

Note: -Souffles can be assembled several hours earlier and refrigerated. Add
        another 4 to 5 minutes baking time if you are baking them straight from
        the refrigerator.
      -This is not a large portion. If you want a lovely crown to form, then
        divide the lemon mixture into 4 ramekins and serve 4.

Soufflé Cakes with Chocolate Ganache

This is a great dessert...easy to prepare and easy to serve. Little soufflé cakes, set on a creamy chocolate sauce and topped with a little vanilla ice cream is simply lovely. An extra bonus...eggs do not have to be separated and best of all the soufflés can be prepared in advance. We had a very similar dessert at a restaurant recently, but they wouldn't share the recipe. This is an exact duplicate and probably a lot easier to prepare.

    3   eggs, at room temperature
    4   teaspoons sugar

    2/3 cup semi-sweet chocolate chips, melted

    1   teaspoon powdered (instant) espresso mixed with 1 tablespoon
        warm water
    1   tablespoon rum

Butter 4 8-ounce ramekins and sprinkle with sugar to coat. Preheat oven to 375°. In the large bowl of an electric mixer, beat eggs until foamy. Gradually beat in the sugar and continue beating, at high speed, until eggs have tripled in volume, about 5 minutes.

Meanwhile, in the top of a double boiler, over hot, not boiling water, melt the chocolate. Slowly beat the chocolate into the egg mixture, until nicely blended. Beat in the coffee and rum just until blended.

Divide mixture between the 4 ramekins, place ramekins on a cookie sheet and bake at 375° for 20 minutes. Allow to cool. Cakes will settle and firm up a little. Run a knife along the edge and remove cakes to a porcelain baker. To serve, warm them at 350° for 5 minutes.

Place 1 cake on each plate, drizzle a little Chocolate Ganache on the side and place 2 small scoops of ice cream on the Ganache. Serves 4.

Chocolate Ganache:
    3   tablespoons cream
    1/3 cup semi-sweet chocolate chips
    1   teaspoon rum

In a saucepan, heat cream. Add the chocolate and stir until melted. Stir in the rum. Serve sauce warm.

To Make Low-Calorie Ganache Sauce:
Soften 1 cup of frozen Chocolate Non-Fat or Low-Fat Yogurt in the refrigerator for 2 hours. Place in a sauceboat and spoon around souffle cakes.

The Index

292

Additional Copies of the Simply Delicious
RENNY DARLING COOKBOOKS
can be purchased at your local bookstore or ordered directly from:

ROYAL HOUSE PUBLISHING CO., INC.
433 N. Camden Drive, Ste. 400
P.O. Box 5027   Beverly Hills, CA 90210

Praise for Renny Darling's Cookbooks
Professional Reviews and Comments
♥ ♥ ♥

♥ (The Love of Eating) Combining a modern emphasis on quick-cooking techniques with an old fashioned design, this cookbook offers a trove of imaginative recipes. Darling establishes an intimate relationship with her readers, interpolating personal notes and helpful cooking tips. She successfully adds gourmet touches to easy-to-assemble dishes, offers such delights as Sour Cream Pumpkin Bread and novelties on the order of Cherry Herring Butter.   Publishers Weekly

♥ ♥ ♥

♥ (With Love from Darling's Kitchen) Darling's 7th cookbook, presents strong evidence that her imagination and flamboyant style have not let up in the least. Darling's inventive combinations of ingredients create recipes that are often easy to prepare, yet worthy of the most prestigious dinner guests. Darlings's love of desserts (and chocolate in particular) is obvious...such creations as chocolate torte royale with white chocolate and raspberry frosting...   Publishers Weekly

♥ ♥ ♥

♥ (Great Beginnings & Happy Endings)...Darling's assemblage of hors d'oeuvres includes not only one's meant for entertaining, but also plenty of breads, soups, vegetables...Exciting and appealing combinations of ingredients are used; Darling relies heavily on lemon, garlic and wine sauces.
   Publishers Weekly

♥ ♥ ♥

♥ ("The Joy of Eating French Food")...Renny Darling has compiled a collection of recipes for traditional French fare that is elegant, yet relatively simple to prepare. From hors d'oeuvres to desserts, her selection of recipes is broad and imaginative. A good cookbook to reach for when one is faced with unexpected dinner guests.   Publishers Weekly

♥ ♥ ♥

♥ (Easiest & Best Coffeecakes & Quick Breads) Darling's 8th book is so full of imaginative, easy-to-prepare recipes. The volume's range of recipes is enormous.   Publishers Weekly

♥ ♥ ♥

♥ (Entertaining Fast & Fancy) While the more than 350 recipes are exceedingly genteel, they are nevertheless versatile. All recipes are clearly written with tips for making and storing ahead, and serving directions to ensure a reliable and proper party.   Publishers Weekly

♥ ♥ ♥

♥ I have every reason to believe your book, "The Joy of Eating", will become a best seller as well as a classic and will take its place alongside the Settlement Cookbook as a must for every household..."
Ruth Ziony, KPFK

♥ ♥ ♥

♥ "If Renny Darling of Beverly Hills, author of "The Joy of Eating" served half the dishes appearing in her book to Harry, Joey, Jeffy and Debby" (her family, to whom the book is dedicated) then they have indeed, led a very joyous life. Lots of interesting recipes done with a flair and a direct understanding of family dining appeal." Rose Dosti, LA Times

♥ ♥ ♥

♥ Beautiful books. The recipes are a veritable symphony and so simple...save hours and hours of preparation. These cookbooks are extraordinary. They eliminate all the time-consuming, irritating steps...all the kinds of things you thought you couldn't do, Renny Darling has made possible to do efficiently. These are marvellous cookbooks.   Paul Wallach, KIEV

♥ ♥ ♥

♥ (Renny Darling's recipes were chosen to be transcribed in Braille.)
"We are delighted to feature your recipes and feel sure that The Joy will bring joy to all our blind cooks."   The Braille Mirror

♥ ♥ ♥

♥ "Your book is a delight to sell. Everyone is so impressed with the tempting recipes and the appealing format."
   Esther Baum, Banbury Book Shop, Woodland Hills

♥ ♥ ♥

♥ "We completely sold out. I'm delighted."   Fran C., United Book Distributors, CA

♥ ♥ ♥

♥ "About a year and a half ago, Ms Darling wrote THE JOY OF EATING and she labels her second venture "another simply delicious cookbook." That it is-- and every recipe fit for company. This is one of those softcover books that exudes with love. Introductions are written with tender loving care, and each recipe--whether it be Mushrooms Stuffed with Clams and Herbs or Carrot Cake with Chocolate Cream Cheese Frosting--says "try me." It's a true dilemma. Which one to cook next? A fun cookbook whose title tells it like it is." Mary Phillips, Sunday Mercury News

♥ ♥ ♥

♥ One of the joys in the way of cookbooks recently arrived on my desk. It's Beverly Hills resident, Renny Darling's THE JOY OF EATING. The book is based on Mrs. Darling's theory that it's possible to dine extravagantly without spending much time in the kitchen. Many of the recipes look very simple and delicious. Besides being attractively designed, the books should prove a boon to those who don't want to spend enormous amounts of time on kitchen chores, but want marvelous results. Natalie Haughton, Daily News

♥ ♥ ♥

♥ "We are delighted with the book sales." Liberty House, Oakland, CA

♥ ♥ ♥

♥ Ever since Renny Darling's first book, THE JOY OF EATING arrived on the cookbook scene, things have not been the same for California cooks. Imagine the joy of magnificent meals in a minimum of time, and assurance of success after success. That's Renny. Then came THE LOVE OF EATING and her new book, THE JOY OF ENTERTAINING more sensational recipes.
Director, Something More Cooking School, La Mesa, CA

♥ ♥ ♥

♥ Following in the wake of her two other marvelous cookbooks, comes a third no-panic , never- fail book filled with menus, recipes, planning pages, guest directories and more. With this one, Renny Darling makes entertaining easy, and yet certain to impress even the most discriminating guests. A host or hostess need no longer panic at the thought of cooking for company, and whether your choice be elegant or simple, formal or informal, you will be able to do it with ease. I always delve into Renny's books headfirst, knowing there are no failures ahead, therefore, I started by serving "An Italian Feast" on page 22.. sensational from start to finish. Once you've experienced cooking a la Renny Darling, you'll wonder how you ever got along without her. Cookbook Corner, San Diego

♥ ♥ ♥

♥ She mixes a dash of glamour with a touch of simplicity. Glamorous but simple...That is what the modern cook wants...THE JOY OF EATING, followed by THE LOVE OF EATING and THE JOY OF ENTERTAINING are so many years spent simplifying complicated recipes.
Opal Crandall, Food Editor San Diego Union

♥ ♥ ♥

♥ Healthy Cooking doesn't have to be boring. Pick up a copy of Renny Darling's "Moderation Diet" and you'll find a wealth of exciting, appealing and delicious light recipes for breads, muffins, casserole, small entrees, soups, salads,...It is not a diet book per se, but rather an eating lifestyle volume containing recipes low in calories, cholesterol, fat, sugar and sodium. Her philosopy is simple: A dish must taste delicious and be quick and easy to prepare--or it isn't worth the calories or time spent. "Combines the best of 2 worlds...eating for health and eating for pleasure."
Natalie Haughton, Food Editor, Daily News

♥ ♥ ♥

♥ Darling's book (Entertaining Fast & Fancy) made it on the best-seller list of home entertaining books in Beverly Hills without hard-cover or big beautiful pictures. The reason may have to do with her keen sense of her audience, who probably cook just the way Darling does. She offers recipes for calzones, bourekas, pumpkin soup, orzo, tartufo, lemon cheesecake, whole wheat orange pumpkin bread..interesting. Rose Dosti, LA Times

♥ ♥ ♥

♥ In response to the number of sales of national bestsellers, ("2" and "11") the answer to "Is anything selling better?"..."Oh, sure. The last 40 copies of Joy of Eating and Love of Eating went out like a shot. They're sensational cookbooks." Joan Ripley, American Bookseller

♥ ♥ ♥

♥ In response to "What is your favorite cookbook?" Renny Darling's, "The Love of Eating" was listed as one of the top ten. LA Times Poll

Samples of Praise from Renny Darling's Fans

♥ ♥ ♥

♥ Just a note of thanks for the many enjoyable hours in my kitchen with my "old friends"---your cookbooks! I discovered you in Pasadena several years ago. I bought my first Renny Darling cookbook there and it was "love at first sight..." I would be lost without my Renny Darling cookbooks. You have the talent and ability to reduce the chore of cooking to absolute simplicity and the recipes are delicious and never fail. I want to thank you for your love and warmth that has reached us here in Puerto Rico, and my husband joins me in sending our love back to you. You must know that you've made many people happy with your wonderful recipes. For me they have the special ingredient of caring and sharing. With love and best wishes. Sylvia K., San Juan, PR

♥ ♥ ♥

♥ HELP! I have lost my copy of "Entertaining Fast and Fancy". I have ALL of your cookbooks, of course. I have over 550 cookbooks but use yours as my "security blanket". My husband and everyone adores your "Crispy Chicken Oven-Fried. I have 4 daughters--so have to cook--but do not have the time (or want to, at this point!) to spend "fussing" in the kitchen....Thank you again for changing my life and in many ways, "saving" my life!   Henrietta S.

♥ ♥ ♥

♥ "If 'The Joy of Eating' by Renny Darling is still in print, I would like 3 copies. If this book is no longer available, please return my check and I'll slash my wrists." Linda W., Shandon, OH

♥ ♥ ♥

♥ "Dear Renny Darling, I want to explain to you how much you have done for me and my family by having written the most wonderful and exciting cookbooks I have ever used. Unfortunately, a few years ago, our only child contracted Hodgkins Disease. He had surgery, radiation and chemotherapy. Needless to say, his appetite disappeared. He just would not eat. I tried everything. Finally, my cousin went to L.A. for a visit and brought me back "The Love of Eating." Our son started to eat and enjoyed most of the recipes I tried. I have since acquired all your books. Our son is now attending Harvard, is President of the Student Body Gov't, on the debating team, soccer team. If I sound like a proud mother, I want you to know, you take a lot of the credit too."
     Shirlee S., Miami, FL.

♥ ♥ ♥

♥ "I am quite a cookbook fiend. I have all of your cookbooks--and are they ever super! When I want a recipe that really works and is an absolute knock-out, I don't look in Julia Child or Craig Claiborne or the Time-Life Series or in any of the other books I've got on the shelves. I just go straight to yours, and I'm never disappointed. I have such faith in all your recipes--you are quite a wizard. Again, a very warm thank you for all of your hard work and truly wonderful recipes!
     CeCe C., Long Beach, CA

♥ ♥ ♥

♥ "Dear Mr. President, I salute your editorial judgment! Recently I purchased 2 cookbooks that have become the treasures of my library, both written by Renny Darling. Please consider this high praise! I have never once felt compelled to offer praise where it is due. Having perused through countless books, I consider myself quite an authority on what works and what doesn't, in recipe presentation. Beyond simple praise, you deserve to know why your books excel. Hence:
     -First and foremost, you start with interesting recipes...these books offer a brilliant
       selection.
     -Secondly, the recipes are presented beautifully. The art...and borders are very
       tasteful and appropriate...It really can make the book fun to read (not just a sterile
       white page with black words...May I add, it's very refreshing to read "in color"...
     -Thirdly, and probably the most effective, is the journalistic flair that often
       introduces the chapters and precedes individual recipes. The text is clever,
       (sometimes emotional) and so enjoyable to stumble across. It adds a special human
       dimension to the pages...almost as if they were talking to me.
     -Finally, they're pretty books. I'm never ashamed when my guests see one of them
       on my counter...in fact, I'm rather proud.
I do hope the person or persons responsible for producing these books will know of my gratitude and appreciation. It is his/her flair that keeps the "JOY" books on my range when all my others are 2 rooms away. With my compliments... Lorelei A., Des Moines, IA

♥ "I have hundreds of cookbooks but I am cooking solely from yours."   J.D., Santee, CA

♥ ♥ ♥

♥ Thanks so much for the many great recipes. Every single one I have used has been a hit. From main meals to desserts, I could not get through Christmas without Easiest & Best Coffeecakes. Every year I try another recipe or two to give to friends and now they are requesting their favorites.
     Linda P., Bridgeport, CT

♥ ♥ ♥

♥ I have all of Renny Darling's books and love them very much.   M. G., Stamford, CT

♥ ♥ ♥

♥ Love your new cookbook, "Entertaining Fast & Fancy."   Barbara C., Portland, OR

♥ ♥ ♥

♥ The Renny Darling Cookbooks are FANTASTIC!!!!   Kathe K. M., Great Falls, MT

♥ ♥ ♥

♥ I have all your books and have given many to friends and really love all of them and use them often.   Nina H., Westlake Village, CA

♥ ♥ ♥

♥ The books are indeed beautiful and very inviting! I find them especially appealing because the recipes are so easy.   Michelle K., Encino, CA

♥ ♥ ♥

♥ I would very much like to obtain a copy of your wonderful recipe book (Joy of Eating) which a friend of mine bought in the U.S. some time ago.   Kay S., Sydney, Australia

♥ ♥ ♥

♥ She's Back! She's Back! Hooray! Hooray! (on hearing of new title ENTERTAINING FAST & FANCY)   Valerie E., Pasadena, CA

♥ ♥ ♥

♥ I own and love all your books.   Phyllis D., San Diego, CA

♥ ♥ ♥

♥ Where have you been all my life? Until last Saturday, I didn't think that a book existed which captured the essence of my favorite kind of baking. I love the whole layout, as well as innovative idea. What a treasure. Thank you...thank you. Alisa M., Pacific Palisades, CA

♥ ♥ ♥

♥ I just cannot cook without a Renny Darling cookbook. Please send me 3 copies.....
     Shirlee S. Miami, Fl

♥ ♥ ♥

♥ I have been reading your cookbook, EASIEST & BEST COFFEE CAKES & QUICK BREADS for the past several days. I must say I would like to begin at the beginning and "bake" my way through your book!! My appetite is whetted for more of your works.   Thelma C., Big Spring, TX

♥ ♥ ♥

♥ This is one (Joy of Eating French Food) of the finest cookbooks I have ever found, and my friends have so complimented my gourmet cooking that they want the book as well. Lois M., In. Wells, CA

♥ ♥ ♥

♥ I just love your books.   Barbara F., Oxnard, CA

♥ ♥ ♥

♥ I visited my son last weekend and saw your cookbook. The recipes are fabulous. D.W., Geneva, IL

♥ ♥ ♥

♥ Thank you for all the pleasure you have given me and my family and friends.
     Pat A., Woodland Hills, CA

♥ ♥ ♥

♥ A friend of mine has allowed me to borrow...The Joy, The Love, French Food..written by Renny Darling. I am thoroughly enjoying and using these books. I am anxious to have these in my cookbook collection. Please hurry!!!   Carole K., Plattsburgh, NY

♥ ♥ ♥

♥ Enclosed is my check for "The Moderation Diet".... What can I say except HURRY..I can't wait to receive it. I have Darling's cookbook The Love of Eating and it's become, out of my multi-collection of cookbooks, my all-time favorite. Thanks.   Liz M., Miami, FL

♥ ♥ ♥

♥ I am one of Renny Darling's biggest fans and I would appreciate any help you can give me in obtaining a copy of each of her cookbooks.   Ann R., Miami, FL

♥ ♥ ♥

♥ "Dear Ms. Darling, I collect cookbooks, and I live abroad, and so on a recent visit to the U.S., I bought one, then two of your cookbooks. I was so intrigued with the sound of your recipes that by the end our leave, I had bought all five. Now that I am at home in Bahrain, I am having a wonderful time preparing some of your grand food. You may be interested to know that several of your dishes were amongst those I served at a morning coffee that I gave in honor of Shaikha Hassa (Queen of Bahrain) last month. They were Banana Bread with Chocolate Chips, Orange Date Nut Bread, Cherry Almond Muffins, Carrot Cake and Apricot Bar Delice Cookies."
    Ruth T., Bahrain, Arabian Gulf

♥ ♥ ♥

♥ "Dear Ms. Darling, Thank you for opening the eyes to novice cooks--for making us feel that we can cook French food without the frustration and intimidation most recipes offer. It was a wonderful day when I paid my favorite bookseller for your copy of "The Joy of Eating French Food." Never have I labored so little, cooked with such fine ingredients, earned so many compliments from family and friends, and derived such true joy in cooking as I have with the advent of your book. Your other books are on order and I am looking forward to loving them as I am loving your French cookbook. The last batch of your Buttery French Croissants are ready to come out of the oven, so with that, I wish to thank you again and again for sparking my interest in cooking."
    Carol S., Skokie, IL

♥ ♥ ♥

♥ "Help! I can't live without THE JOY OF EATING FRENCH FOOD. If I keep the borrowed copy much longer, I'm in trouble."   Nancy D., Plymouth, MI

♥ ♥ ♥

♥ "I love you, Renny Darling! Heavens knows what (or if) I'd cook if I didn't have you to guide me. Yesterday I was down in the dumps (why is cooking dinner such a dread when you are down in the dumps?) when Federal Express arrived with ENTERTAINING FAST & FANCY. What poetry! What manner of good things! I don't know which I like better - your recipes or your delectable descriptions. There are so many goodies I can't wait to try that I invited company for dinner Friday and Saturday. My sweetheart and I thank you Renny, for lifting the summer doldrums and sparkling our social life. Stay well and happy and keep writing. A lot of us out here need you."
    Darlene S., Coral Gables, FL

♥ ♥ ♥

♥ "Fantastic Soufflé---$100.00 worth of music."   Lil P., Beverly Hills, CA
    (ED. Musicians at her party deducted $100.00 from their fee so that she would share with them Renny Darling's Chocolate Soufflé recipe.)

♥ ♥ ♥

♥ (Excerpted from a 6-page letter) "You've been in my life through your books for about 7 years. I have acquired many cookbooks, but yours have become my bible! I know that each and every time they will religiously make me a star. Your recipes have made eating at home as exciting as any fine restaurant. I'm very discreet revealing the source of my raves and compliments. Selfish I guess, not exactly good for you in the way of promoting book sales. It's a discovery very personal and dear to me. Thank you for helping me to discover the wonderful world of cooking and entertaining...for making food enjoyable to prepare and a banquet to eat. You have enriched my life and those who have the privilege to eat your glorious food."   Tracy S., San Mateo, CA

♥ ♥ ♥

♥ You are a joy to share the kitchen with! I have many cookbooks but I find I turn to yours most often because the recipes are easy, interesting and good (the bottom line.)
    Amy B., Lyndhurst, OH

♥ ♥ ♥

♥ This is certainly the most outstanding cookbook (Easiest & Best Coffee Cakes & Quick Breads) I've ever found.   Betty Sue B., Leaburg, OR

♥ ♥ ♥

♥ I am interested in purchasing a copy of Renny Darling's new cookbook, "Entertaining Fast & Fancy." Ms. Darling came to Mr. B's (New Orleans) for dinner one evening and left a copy of the cookbook with me. Since then, we've all been fighting over who would borrow it next.
    Monica G., Mr. B's Restaurant, New Orleans, LA

♥ ♥ ♥

♥ ♥ ♥

♥ I am truly one of your biggest fans. Everything I have ever made or baked has been a huge success. The recipes are easy to follow and a delight to make.   Corrinne R., LA, CA

♥ ♥ ♥

♥ I have been using your cookbooks from the Public Library for the last 2 years for Christmas and other occasions. Well, I've decided I would like to own my own copies. Mrs. O.D. P., Blanch, NC

♥ ♥ ♥

♥ Your books are great. I love them. Your recipes are great!   Julia F., Union, NY

♥ ♥ ♥

♥ After baking so very many of your wonderful recipes, I feel I am on a first-name basis with you. This note paper has probably picked up the delicious aroma of "Cinnamon Apple Cake with Raisins & Walnuts." This kitchen smells awfully good...I want to thank you for taking the time to publish your recipes. Each one seems better than the one before! I love your muffins using fresh oranges and apples. Thanks again Renny! "Easiest & Best Quick Breads" has become one of my most used cookbooks.   Martie R., San Bruno, CA

♥ ♥ ♥

♥ Through a friend, I have received a couple of your recipes and have served them many times with lots of compliments. Please help me...is there anyway I can purchase your recipes.   Signed "A White Chocolate Cheesecake Fan" Laurie T., London, England

♥ ♥ ♥

♥ Recently I purchased your cookbook by Renny Darling and love it! It is by far my favorite cookbook--every recipe that I tried is delicious, and I love how personal it is. Pamela P., Cary, NC

♥ ♥ ♥

♥ I recently was invited to a wonderful dinner at a friend's house. I had to have the recipe for the chicken dish, which she told me was from your cookbook. I live in Montreal and we do not have a lot of good cookbooks. I would love to buy your book.   Marla F., Montreal, Canada

♥ ♥ ♥

♥ I have Renny Darling's "Coffee Cakes" and it is the greatest! I wish to have more of her cookbooks.   Nadine D., Burlingame, KS

♥ ♥ ♥

♥ As a new wife, my mother-in-law lent me "The Joy of Eating French Food". Well, I've fallen in love with the many recipes, as has my husband. However, my mother-in-law wants the book back because she too enjoys cooking from it. Send me a copy as soon as possible. M. H., Middletown, CT

♥ ♥ ♥

♥ "I am going berserk over the cookbook. I've been using it every day." Mrs. D., Hawaii

♥ ♥ ♥

♥ "...fantastic...raved..went crazy...superb...Just a note to let you know how much I enjoyed seeing your demonstration." Mrs. Jody G. Santee, CA

♥ ♥ ♥

♥ "You're recipes are the kind I love, delicious and easy. Your cookbook is just great."
     Mrs. L.F., Baldwin, NY

♥ ♥ ♥

♥ "Luncheon Gourmet was at my house and the "Renny" menu was just beyond accolades. We had your Sweet Pea Soup with Toast Points, Cornish Game Hens with Brandy Butter Sauce (Oh what a wonderful stuffing!) Wild Rice with Raisins and Pine Nuts, Cranberry Tangerine Mold (still one of my favorites), and that super-sensational Praline Pumpkin Pie. I tell you, it was fit for a king."   Mrs. Larry G. Santos, CA

♥ ♥ ♥

♥ "The brothers of the Zeta House would like to thank you for saving our stomach's the other night. One of our brothers attempted to cook dinner.(the cook was out sick.) Trying to outdo himself, he attempted the "Easiest and Best Stroganoff." Don't know how easy it was, but it sure was best! So we just wanted to thank you for writing a cookbook simple enough to pass the acid test of forty self-proclaimed gourmets."   Brothers of Zeta Psi-Berkeley Univ.

♥ ♥ ♥

♥ I have been having a ball. To say I am enthused would be putting it mild. I love the recipes you sent. I won't rest until I have tried them all. Here is my Fig Newton recipes. Really this is just a great big THANK YOU for your recipes."   Gladys D., Seattle, WA

♥ ♥ ♥

302

♥ "My phone is always ringing from my friends wanting to share their latest wonderful "finds" in your cookbooks. My friends are effusive. One gave a dinner party, using your book, and had 4 converts on the strength of the Imperial Sauce Verte alone. She raved about the foolproof oven potatoes and said one guest was so thrilled because he hadn't that kind of potato since he was a little boy. You have opened up an entire new way of life for her and she can't wait to get in the kitchen now or to have friends over. What 'JOY' you have brought to all of us."   J. G., Santee, CA

♥ ♥ ♥

♥ "I love your recipes, especially the ones that are so delicious and look like you've spent the whole day in the kitchen. More than that, I love your spirit."   Mrs. Tamara C., Santa Clara, CA

♥ ♥ ♥

♥ "I own over 156 cookbooks and really love to cook. I don't need any more cookbooks. However, when I noticed your cookbook, I knew I had to have it. The ...recipes...turned out as well as I expected. Even my very picky children loved all three. This is my first fan letter of any kind. I am so pleased with your book that I had to let you know. Again, thank you for your lovely book."
Wendy P., Leucadia, CA

♥ ♥ ♥

♥ "I just returned home from a bridal shower.. my gift was one of your books and you should have seen the comments! As the gifts were being passed around for viewing, THE JOY OF EATING took the longest to make the circuit. Your recipes are just great. Your "Raw Apple Cake" has gained much fame for me. Everyone loves it."   Mrs. Glen G., LA, CA

♥ ♥ ♥

♥ Your cookbook has enabled me to do the entertaining I love with minimum time and pressure. My Mom was an excellent cook and entertaining was always a family tradition so I think I am a pretty good judge of food. Your recipes are delicious!   Mrs. E.N., Westlake, CA

♥ ♥ ♥

♥ We just keep happily and successfully "Renny Cooking" along. How neat to know you're never going to have a failure.   Mrs. Jill F. La Jolla, CA

♥ ♥ ♥

♥ Yesterday was breakfast at my husband's school and everyone had to take something. It was a sumptuous spread and everyone raved, raved, raved over my offering, with several saying it was the best they had ever had at the school and guess what it was? Renny Darling's Cheese Blintz Casserole.

♥ ♥ ♥

♥ One day last week, I came home after a difficult day at school and made your crescents. I brought them to the secretaries at school. They raved and raved...Thought I was terrific. You really deserve the kudos...The recipes are terrific. Thank you so much for helping me be a cook that gets raves.   Eve S., Woodland Hills, CA

♥ ♥ ♥

♥ I love cookbooks and collect them whenever I can. I just started to use your book because it looked good and time saving (I have a 13-month toddler). I can't tell you how much our family enjoys the delicious recipes.   Lorena F., San Francisco, CA

♥ ♥ ♥

♥ I've always been interested in cooking. But since I discovered your books my reputation as a good cook "especially desserts" has really increased. I've got to keep impressing my friends. Your books are my favorite gifts. Thank you so much for your great ideas.   Catherine Q., Mission Viejo, CA

♥ ♥ ♥

♥ To me you are Renny, Darling. I was an enthusiastic reader of JOY and would refer to you as Renny, Darling when something was exceptional. And now, with LOVE you have become Renny, my darling! JOY was very good, but LOVE is exceptional.
Dr. Morris E., Marina del Rey, CA

♥ ♥ ♥

♥ My daughter is a Home Ec teacher and if I don't get her a copy of each of your cookbooks, she'll take mine!   Mrs. Robert C., Columbus, KS

♥ ♥ ♥

♥ While browsing through a bookstore, I picked up one of your books and was very impressed by just its appearance. I have never seen it or heard about it, but bought it nevertheless because it caught my eye. After several recipes, I found it not only the best cookbook I have ever owned, but my husband and all of our friends are a captive audience every time I make any recipe from your book. I can honestly say I have made at least half of the recipes and plan on making all in time. We have been so happy with your book since the day we found it.   Mrs. Phyllis R. C., Brewster, NY

♥ ♥ ♥

♥ "I adore your recipes."   Bobbi L. San Francisco, CA

♥ ♥ ♥

♥ While traveling, I saw two of your cookbooks and promptly bought them for my daughter. But being a selfish mother I read them and KEPT them! Now, I want to tell you how inventive and truly easy your recipes are. Fantastic!! Your books are my favorite reading material. Love your recipes ...most enjoyable...PS. I bought my daughter the two books also! Nathalie O., Flushing, NY

♥ ♥ ♥

♥ Every time I take my son to the orthodontist, I enjoy reading your cookbook,. I would like to have my own copy as my son is almost finished at the dentist and as much as I like your book, I can't keep going back and copying the recipes.   Carol G., Vienna, VA

♥ ♥ ♥

♥ I love your books. I collect cookbooks, hundreds, and yours are my favorite. B. K., Hazleton, PA

♥ ♥ ♥

♥ To begin with, I love your cookbooks. Your velvet cheesecake with strawberry orange sauce has caused my friends to die of ecstasy. They think it is the best they have ever tasted. I agree.   Yvette L., Encinitas, CA

♥ ♥ ♥

♥ Just want to thank you for the wonderful recipes you've provided me over the last few years. Recipe reading and experimenting are my greatest joys and your books and monthly recipes have been a delight to have. Your recipes and comments are clever, creative and great fun. Thank you again for the pleasure you have brought to me.   Maggie G., Columbia, MD

♥ ♥ ♥

♥ Everything I try in any of the books (and I have them all) comes out good! Thank you.   Kathe M., Great Falls, MT

♥ ♥ ♥

♥ You're cookbooks are the very best I have ever seen. We have truly enjoyed all the recipes we have tried. The recipes are simple, unique and delicious. Thank you.   Nancy J. Woodland Hills, CA

♥ ♥ ♥

♥ I had to write and let you know how much I enjoy your recipes. I have used your recipes on many occasions and all I have gotten are compliments and "ooh's and aah's". If only they knew how easy it all was.   Mrs. Janice G. West Hollywood, CA

♥ ♥ ♥

♥ "Sure have been enjoying your recipes. My favorite recipes are the easy ones that make me look good...like I worked all day."   Davida R., Tarzana, CA

♥ ♥ ♥

♥ "I still rave to everyone about your cookbooks. Your recipes are simple, quick, elegant for our rushed existence."   Mrs. Sue Carol I., Montreal, Canada

♥ ♥ ♥

♥ You have great talent!   Earl W., Watertown, WI

♥ ♥ ♥

♥ " Your cookbook is more than a JOY. It is a LOVE. I love it."   Dr. H.S., Beverly Hills, CA

♥ ♥ ♥

♥ "Your cookbooks are fabulous. Thank you." Mrs. James B. Rancho Mirage, CA

♥ ♥ ♥

♥ "Your cookbooks are fantastic." Mrs. S.C.I., Montreal, Canada

♥ ♥ ♥

♥ "I love your cookbooks. They're great." Mrs. Fred B., Eugene, OR

♥ ♥ ♥

♥ "I love your recipes."   Mrs. Lee M.

♥ ♥ ♥

♥ In an interview with Carrol McCrumb (in the Fresno Bee). What are your favorite cookbooks? "I'm a recipe book collector. Any of Renny Darling's cookbooks are my favorite."

♥ ♥ ♥

♥ In an interview with Betty Brown, St. Charles, MO (in Bon Appetit)..."An inveterate cookbook collector, she especially enjoys reading Renny Darling."